THE WORLD

PEOPLE, POLITICS AND INTERNATIONAL RELATIONS

Jim Cannon

Principal Teacher of Modern Studies
Craigmount High School, Edinburgh

Bill Clark

Formerly Head Teacher
Galashiels Academy

George Smuga

Head Teacher
North Berwick High School

Oliver & Boyd

Acknowledgements

The authors and publishers wish to thank all those who gave their permission for the reproduction of copyright material in this book. Information regarding the sources of extracts is given in the text. Photographs and other pictorial material are acknowledged as follows:

p.8, TASS; p.9, Reuter/Popperfoto; p.10, Popperfoto; p.13 (top) Topham, (bottom) Rex Features Ltd; p.14, Barnaby's Picture Library; p.16, J Allan Cash Ltd; p.18, TASS; p.19, TASS; p.21, McDonald's Restaurants Ltd; p.25, Popperfoto; p.27, ZEFA Picture Library (UK) Ltd; p.32, UN photo 94 896 MB/PAS; p.33, Popperfoto; p.37 (top right) Popperfoto, (top left) Reuter/Popperfoto, (bottom) Popperfoto; p.38, Topham; p.40, ZEFA Picture Library (UK) Ltd; p.41, Popperfoto; p.42, Rex Features Ltd; p.49, Reuter/Popperfoto; p.52, Rex Features Ltd; p.54, Novosti Press Agency; p.57 (top) Topham, (bottom) © 1990 by Tribune Media Services, reprinted by permission of Editors Press Service, Inc.; p.58, Popperfoto; pp.62–3, from *The Gaia Peace Atlas*, ed. Frank Barnaby, Pan Books; p.65, Reuter/Popperfoto; p.66, Popperfoto; p.68, © 1990 by Universal Press Syndicate, reprinted by permission of Editors Press Service, Inc.; p.71, *New Statesman and Society*; p.72 (left) Novosti Press Agency, (right) *Soviet Weekly/New Statesman and Society*; p.73 (top) Sally and Richard Greenhill, (bottom) Rex Features Ltd; p.75, © 1989, Washington Post, reprinted with permission; p.81, Popperfoto; p.86, from *The Gaia Peace Atlas*, ed. Frank Barnaby, Pan Books; p.87, Rex Features Ltd; p.90, Rex Features Ltd; p.97, Northrop Corp. California, print MARS, Lincs.; p.98, Camera Press; p.99, British Aerospace Military Aircraft Division, Warton; p.101, The Scotsman Publications Ltd; p.103, David Mitchell/North Star Picture Agency; p.104, Hutchison Library; p.106, *New World*, UNA publication, June 1988; pp.114, 116, Robert Hunt; p.121, Mark Edwards/Still Pictures; p.123, Hutchison Library; p.124, Panos Pictures; p.129 (top) Popperfoto, (bottom) Martin Turner/New Internationalist, August 1989; p.130 (top) *Africa Events*, May 1989, (bottom) © Harry Horse, by permission of *Scotland on Sunday*; p.135, J Allan Cash Ltd.

Every effort has been made to trace copyright owners. The publishers would be pleased to hear from anyone who has not been mentioned.

Oliver & Boyd
Longman House
Burnt Mill
Harlow
Essex CM20 2JE
An imprint of Longman Group UK Ltd

ISBN 0 05 004484 2
First published 1992

Typeset on an Apple Macintosh SE30 in Times 11/13pt
Produced by Longman Singapore Publishers Pte Ltd
Printed in Singapore

CONTENTS

Introduction

INTRODUCTION

The World, like its companion volume, *Britain*, is written primarily for pupils studying Standard Grade Modern Studies. The book is structured in such a way as to allow teachers to follow a complete chapter or to select individual units as appropriate.

The authors have attempted to provide a wide range of different material and exercises, but the book requires a considerable amount of teacher input and should not be seen as a stand-alone source or a complete course. In particular, there will be a need for input regarding the rapidly-changing events in Eastern Europe, Asia and the Middle East which, although up-dated at the last possible moment in the production of this book, will inevitably have moved on and changed since publication. While a variety of questions (based directly on the resources provided) and activities (designed as extensions to the book) is provided, teachers will wish to adapt and develop some of the ideas in the book to suit their own classroom needs. It is hoped, however, that teachers will find the examples provide a useful starting point both in terms of content and skill-based activities.

The World is designed to provide a balance between a traditional text-book with links and continuity through the text, and a range of source material, written and visual, to suit the requirements of pupil-centred activities in Standard Grade. A range of exercises suitable for pupils of all abilities is provided, although a conscious decision has been made that these should not be designated 'credit', 'general', or 'foundation'. While many of the resources and exercises are suitable for 'foundation' level pupils, the majority are aimed at pupils studying for the 'general' and 'credit' levels.

Within each Unit, a list of the essential Keywords encountered in the Unit is given to ensure that all pupils are aware of the key ideas covered in the Unit. The range of activities throughout the book is designed to provide examples of good practice, e.g. in letter writing, questionnaire design, interviewing and role play. Through these activities, pupils will gain experience of the essential elements of evaluating, investigating and participating which are central to Standard Grade Modern Studies.

The 'Arrangements in Standard Grade Modern Studies' published by the Scottish Examination Board recognise that, 'the ultimate goal of the subject is for pupils to use, in a constructive way, acquired knowledge and skills and, therefore, emphasise attitudes and values which help prepare pupils for participation in the social and political situations which they will meet in their adult lives.' The authors of *The World* have attempted to provide a resource which, together with the necessary teacher input, will assist pupils to achieve this goal.

PART 1 IDEOLOGIES

1

DEFINING COMMUNISM AND CAPITALISM

INTRODUCTION

We all have our own ideas or beliefs about a whole range of problems and issues. Some of these beliefs are connected with what we believe to be right or wrong in our dealings with other people. For example, most people agree that stealing is wrong but not everyone agrees that taking drugs is wrong. These beliefs are connected with moral or religious problems. Other types of beliefs are connected with the way we think society and the economy should be run and organised. These are our political beliefs and they most often show themselves in our support for a political party which shares our beliefs. When we group our political beliefs together to give a full statement of our views and attitudes to government, to society and to the economy we call this our political **ideology**. A political party has its own ideology – the Conservative Party's ideology is known as Conservatism.

In the period since the Second World War two major ideologies have dominated the world – **Communism** and **Capitalism** – and these two ideologies have become associated with different countries and groups of countries.

The geography of Capitalism and Communism

The main areas of Capitalism in the world have been:
– North America; the USA and Canada.
– Western Europe.
– Australia and New Zealand.
– South Africa.
– Parts of Asia such as Japan, Taiwan, South Korea and Hong Kong.
– Most of Central and South America.

The main areas of Communism in the world have been:
– The Soviet Union.
– Eastern Europe.
– China.
– Parts of Asia such as Vietnam and North Korea.
– Cuba.

Other countries in the world share some of the features of Capitalism and/or Communism but do not think of themselves as belonging to either ideology.

A checklist of Capitalism

The main traditional features of Capitalism are:
–   Businesses, property, agriculture, banks, (all aspects of the economy) should be privately owned.
–   The Government should interfere as little as possible in the economy.
–   Open competition and the need to make a profit will allow the economy to prosper. Efficient companies which provide a good service at a good price will do well and inefficient companies fail.
–   Prices for goods and services should be set by those who buy and sell them – this is known as 'market forces' and the law of 'supply and demand'.
–   People should be paid according to their value and importance to the economy. This means that some people will be paid more than others.
–   People should have freedom of choice in buying goods and services. This should also apply to welfare services such as education and health.
–   The political system should be based upon **democracy**, with free elections offering a choice between different political parties.
–   Freedom is very important in Capitalism – freedom to choose, freedom to work hard and grow rich, freedom of speech and freedom to vote for an alternative Government.
–   Equality is also important, for everyone should have full equal political and legal rights. But economic freedom does not mean equality in people's style of life, wealth and possessions. There will be wide gaps between the very rich and the very poor.

Adam Smith – *'The Father of Capitalism'*

Adam Smith is often considered to be the founder of economics. He was amongst the first thinkers to develop the theory of Capitalism.

Eighteenth-century Scotland was one of the intellectual centres of Europe and Adam Smith, born in Kirkcaldy in 1723, was one of its leading thinkers. In 1776 he published *The Wealth of Nations* in which he set out his economic theories. He argued that everyone sells their goods or their working skills as expensively as possible and buys them as cheaply as possible. Goods and work are produced in response to demand. If demand is greater than supply it is profitable to produce more. The price of goods and work will adjust itself in the market until supply equals demand. If Government interferes in the workings of the 'market' they will only upset the system. The need to make greater profit leads to competition and greater efficiency. This increases the amount and quality of goods produced and the income of workers. This in turn increases demand and restarts the cycle of economic growth.

A checklist of Communism

The main traditional features of Communism are:
–   Businesses, property, agriculture, banks, factories, should be publicly owned by the State on behalf of the people.
–   The Government should plan and organise the economy.
–   There is no need for competition and profit since all aspects of the economy are working for the people and in the interests of the people. This is taken account of in the Government plans.
–   The law of supply and demand and the working of the market do not apply since the Government will control prices and the supply of goods and services.
–   Since the Government will control the economy it will make sure that there are no sudden closures of factories resulting in large-scale unemployment.

–   People should be paid according to their needs and according to their work. There should not be great differences between levels of pay because everyone has an important contribution to make.
–   Everyone should have the same right to the best welfare services which the state can provide – the right to work, to free education, to free medical treatment, to housing and to care in old age.
–   The political system should be based on democracy of the people. All power in the country belongs to the people as a whole. The Communist Party stands for the interests and needs of all the people. There are no rich and poor classes of people. The Communist Party therefore represents the people and there is no need for other political parties.
–   Equality is very important in Communism. There

should be full equality in all aspects of life, with no one group or class enjoying a privileged life at the expense of others.

– Freedom is also important but real freedom will come only when all people are equal.

Karl Marx – 'The Father of Communism'

Karl Marx, born in Germany in 1818, is regarded as the founder of Communism. In works such as *The Communist Manifesto* and *Das Kapital* he set out the ideas which formed the basis of the ideology of Communism. Marx believed that society changed because of the struggle of one class against another. He described the society in which he lived as being dominated by the struggle between those who owned the wealth and controlled the economy (the 'capitalists') and those who sold their working skills to produce the wealth (the 'working class'). Marx believed that the capitalists were interested only in profit and could achieve most profit by exploiting the workers. Eventually the workers would rise up in revolution, overthrow the capitalists and set up a workers' state in which the economy would be controlled by and for the people and in which no one class would exploit any other group. A Communist society would be set up and an ideal state would be achieved.

A CTIVITIES

1. Using a library find out more about Adam Smith and Karl Marx, their lives and ideas.

2. Listed below is a set of statements. Some of them relate to the ideas of Capitalism whilst others relate to the ideas of Communism. Write out each of the statements and beside each write either capitalism or Communism.

- Everyone should have freedom of choice.
- People should be left to get on with their own lives, free from Government interference.
- People should work together to help each other rather than compete for their own personal gain.
- Freedom can exist only where people are equal.
- Individuals have the right to own their own businesses and work for their own profit.
- People should have the right to choose between different political parties for Government.

- The economy should be run for the benefit of all.
- Competition is essential for an efficient economy.
- We need only one political party which acts as the voice of all the people.
- Each person should give to society according to their skills and ability and be rewarded according to their needs.
- Decent housing, education and medical care are basic rights that should be available to all.
- In our system there are no wide gaps between the rich and poor.
- The hard-working and the able must be allowed to do well and must be rewarded for their work and their skills.
- Trying to make everyone equal only results in a poor standard of living for all.
- It is human nature to cooperate and look after each other.
- It is human nature to compete to secure a good life for ourselves and our families.

3. Divide into four groups. Each group should take one of the statements listed below. Each group member should then write down arguments for and against their statement. Someone in each group should be appointed as chairperson and then the group should discuss the arguments for and against the chosen statement. At the end of the discussion each group should write a brief summary of the main points raised and the chairperson for each group should report back to the whole class for a general debate on this topic.

- It is impossible to have equality in society because we all want to do better than others.
- People will work hard only if they are rewarded and those who work hardest or have special skills should be most rewarded.
- Freedom to make a profit leads to a society where a small group take all the rewards and the rest of the people suffer in poverty.
- Decent housing, education and medical care are all basic human rights and should be equally available to all. There should not be a better set of services available only to those who can pay.

Mikhail Gorbachev

A new Communism

In 1985 Mikhail Gorbachev became leader of the Soviet Union. Gorbachev began to introduce a wide range of reforms designed to introduce a new form of Communism into the USSR.

These reforms have had a major impact upon the USSR and upon its Communist neighbours in Eastern Europe. This impact has been so great that Communism in these countries is either being reformed dramatically or else it is being replaced by a different political and economic system similar to that of Western Europe, i.e. democracy and Capitalism.

Gorbachev's reforms

Gorbachev has aimed his reforms at three areas of Soviet life:

1. *Perestroika* – means economic restructuring and reform. It is aimed at modernising the Soviet economy by developing more modern, high-technology industry, by making consumer goods of better quality and in greater quantity, by encouraging factories to become profitable and by allowing small-scale private businesses and private agriculture.
2. *Glasnost* – means openness. It is aimed at opening up Soviet public life by encouraging more open debate in the press, on television and in other areas of public life.
3. *Demokratizatsiya* – means **democratisation**. It is aimed at making politics more openly democratic.

Communism in decline – 1989 'The Year of Revolution'

Gorbachev's reforms in the USSR began to spread into Eastern Europe. Poland, Hungary, Czechoslovakia, East Germany, Romania and Bulgaria had all become Communist after the Second World War, when they had been occupied by the Soviet Army. Stalin, the Soviet leader, had linked these countries to the Soviet Union through a military alliance called the Warsaw Pact and through an economic union called COMECON.

The Soviet Union was prepared to use force to make sure of the continuation of Communism if any of these 'satellite' countries showed any sign of wanting to change their political system. In Hungary in 1956 and in Czechoslovakia in 1968 Soviet troops put down by force attempts to break away from Communism. And in 1981 the Soviet Union supported the Polish Army in opposing the free trade union Solidarity when it seemed to be threatening Polish Communism.

However, now that Gorbachev was encouraging reform in the Soviet union, what would happen if reform began to spread into Eastern Europe?

The year 1989 produced a dramatic answer to this question when a remarkable series of political changes and revolution spread across Eastern Europe, destroying Communism as it had existed. In some countries, such as  Bulgaria, the Communist Party tried to reform itself as Gorbachev was doing in the USSR. Elsewhere the Communist Party could stay in power only by sharing government with another political group. In other countries the Communist Party collapsed, opening up the way for free, multi-party elections – as in Hungary, Czechoslovakia and East Germany. The most violent change came in Romania where the Communist leader, Nicolae Ceaucescu, was overthrown and executed. In 1990 Lech Walesa, the former Solidarity leader, was elected President in Poland, and East and West Germany united to form one country.

These dramatic events have had an impact upon the Soviet Union. Some Soviet politicians have criticised Gorbachev for not going further in his reforms and others have warned that things have gone too far, in that Communism is now itself under threat in the USSR. In early 1990 the Soviet Communist Party agreed that it should stop being the only political party in the USSR and that other political parties could stand in elections.

The historic opening of the Berlin Wall in 1989

Eastern Europe – 1989

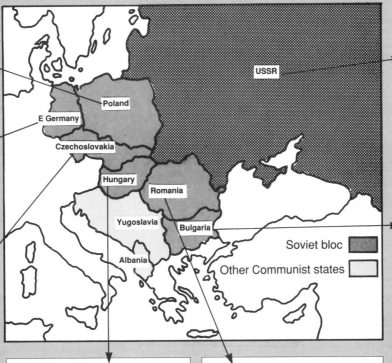

Poland
Open elections lead to Solidarity victory and a Government where power is shared between Solidarity and the Communist Party

East Germany
Communist Government forced to open borders including the Berlin Wall. Open multi-party election to be held. East and West Germany to re-unify

Czechoslovakia
Demonstrations lead to collapse of Communist Government. Dissident writer Vaclav Havel becomes President. Open multi-party elections to be held

USSR
USSR facing demands for independence from Estonia, Latvia and Lithuania in the Baltic as well as from Moldavia, Georgia and Armenia. Greater demands internally for economic and political reform

Bulgaria
Old-guard Communist leadership replaced by reformist Communist Government. Free elections to take place leading to an end to Communist Party control of Government

Hungary
Open multi-party elections to be held. Communist Party not guaranteed any seats or positions in Government

Romania
Demonstrations lead to overthrow of Communist Government, major conflict with security forces and execution of former Communist leader Nicolae Ceaucescu

Soviet bloc
Other Communist states

9

The symbol of the revolution in Romania in 1989 – the Romanian flag with the 'hammer and sickle' cut out

Revolution in Romania

'... For Romania, which had a communist party of less than 1,000 members, occupation by the Red Army at the end of the war meant the imposition of a completely alien communist leadership – something of a shock to this ancient monarchy.

By the early 1950s, the Romanians found themselves being led by the iron man of the communist bloc. Ceausescu liked to portray himself as a man who was prepared to stand up to the Russians...

While his people starved Ceausescu lived in the height of luxury. His wife is reported to have had a shoe collection of over 2,000 pairs... Many of the country's works of art were stolen from the Romanian National Gallery and replaced by fakes. Ceausescu entertained foreign guests with lavish banquets of roast meat whilst his subjects had a yearly meat ration of 20lbs per year.

Ceausescu would tolerate no opposition, and on the pretext of forging a new agricultural order he set about "systemisation" – a process where rural villages were razed or bulldozed to make way for vast agrarian complexes...

The Romanian population were prepared to die to rid themselves of the dreaded dictator

These were not the forces that were finally responsible for the final rebellion against Ceausescu – that was the result of deeper changes affecting the whole of eastern Europe – but they did produce a population that was prepared to die to rid itself of the dreaded dictator and his omnipresent *Securitate*. Ceausescu, for his part, was unrepentent to the end.'

(source: *The Indy*, 18 January 1990.)

Freedom to Party in Prague

THE POKER faces of the Czechoslovakians broke into broad smiles this New Year. Communism bowed to a new ideology and the citizens of Prague revelled in their new-found freedom.

Vaclav Havel, the dissident playwright, philosopher and leader of the main opposition group, Civic Forum, was inaugurated as President only the day before. The shackles of Communism had been thrown off and freedom was the order of the day.

On New Year's Eve thousands of former comrades, now proudly calling themselves citizens, gathered in Wenceslas Square. This was the celebration of Everyman, a mass demonstration of civic joy and happiness. It was the first time since the Second World War that the Czechs... had "freedom to party"....

The new Constitution, drafted by Civic Forum, includes the clause: "That which is not forbidden is permitted". To western ears the clause sounds ludicrously obvious, but for the Czech, long accustomed to the Communist government's arbitrary interpretation of the law, it heralds a new era.

Forty-five years of Communism has left an appalling legacy. The economy is virtually obsolete, the level of education ranks as 72nd in the world and Czechoslovakia has the most contaminated environment in Europe. But for a country that has endured totalitarianism and a diet of sauerkraut and dumplings for so many years, there is every hope that the harsh years ahead will be overcome.

(source: article by Daniel Renton, *The Indy*, 18 January 1990.)

Peaceful division of Czechoslovakia January 1993.

Hungary
Before and After 1989

The Hungarian Parliament

1988

Hungarian Communist Party	No. of seats	Percentage
	All	100.0

1990

HOW THE SEATS ARE DISTRIBUTED

	No. of seats	Percentage
Hungarian Democratic Forum	165	42.74
Alliance of Free Democrats	92	23.83
Independent Smallholders' Party	43	11.13
Hungarian Socialist Party	33	8.54
Federation of Young Democrats	21	5.44
Christian Democratic People's Party	21	5.44
Independents	6	1.55
Joint candidates	4	1.03
Agrarian Alliance	1	0.25
Totals	386	100.0

QUESTIONS

1. Explain the terms *perestroika* and *glasnost* and describe how they have affected Soviet life.

2. Name the countries of Eastern Europe.

3. Explain how these countries came to be Communist after the Second World War.

4. In what ways did the Soviet Union control the countries of Eastern Europe?

5. What importance did the reforms introduced by Gorbachev in the Soviet Union have for the countries of Eastern Europe?

6. '1989 – Year of Revolution'. List the countries of Eastern Europe and beside each write a brief note describing what happened to that country in 1989.

7. What change did the Soviet Communist Party introduce in 1990 which affected Soviet political life?

ACTIVITIES

1. Read the source extract on the Romanian Revolution and answer the following:

a) How did Romania become a Communist country at the end of the Second World War?

b) Who was the Communist leader of Romania from the early 1950s to 1989?

c) What evidence is there of the Romanian leader and his wife acting as corrupt and brutal dictators?

2. Read the source extract 'Freedom to Party in Prague' and answer the following:

a) Why were there celebrations in Czechoslovakia on New Year's Eve?

b) Who was made President of Czechoslovakia? What was his background and how do you think this made him different from previous Czech Presidents?

c) What problems had 'forty-five years of Communism' left for Czechoslovakia?

d) Do you think this article was written from a pro or anti-Communist viewpoint? Give reasons for your answer.

3. Monitor the foreign pages of a daily newspaper for the period of time you are studying this topic. Collect any information on recent events in Eastern Europe which show how those countries have moved from Communism. Collect and file these according to the different countries and compile a class reference folder.

KEYWORDS

The following Keywords are used in this Unit. Make sure you have understood what they mean.

ideology
Capitalism
Communism
democracy
perestroika
glasnost
democratisation

THE USA –
PEOPLE, POLITICS AND THE ECONOMY

- The USA is a country whose population is composed of people from a wide variety of different ethnic and cultural backgrounds. It has been described as 'a land of immigrants' since most of its population are either immigrants or are descendants of immigrants.
- The USA is a country with a strong democratic political system with a huge number of elected posts and with a many-layered pattern of political institutions.
- The USA is a very wealthy country with a powerful industrial economy. It is also a country with a wide range of rich and poor people.
  These aspects of the USA can be seen in the extracts/sources in this Unit, which give a glimpse of some US lifestyles and of the American ideology.

Speaking for my country

We have seen what the different ideologies are in theory. How do they show themselves in practice? Here are the views you might hear from a US Government

official in speaking about the values and lifestyle of the USA.

The 'American Way'

The United States of America is built upon the ideologies of democracy and Capitalism. These values are at the heart of the American way of life and have been since the USA declared its independence in 1776 with these famous words:

'We hold these truths to be self-evident, that all men are created equal, that they are endowed by their Creator with certain unalienable rights. Among these are Life, Liberty and the Pursuit of Happiness. To secure these rights Governments are instituted among Men, deriving their just powers from the consent of the governed.'
(Declaration of Independence)

Our political system is based on these ideas. It is 'government of the people, by the people, for the people.' Our democracy is framed by the US **Constitution** which guarantees an elected government serving for a limited term, one-person-one-vote, and a choice of political parties.

The Constitution guarantees our individual rights: the right to **free speech**, freedom of the press, freedom to protest, freedom to follow our own religion and freedom from arrest without charge.

Our system of Capitalism is also based upon freedom: freedom to own private property and freedom to compete openly to make a profit. It is open to

---

CTIVITY

Read the section 'Speaking for my country – The "American Way".' Here is a list of terms used in the passage and mixed up beside them is a list of definitions. Match the correct definition to each term:

a) ideologies

b) Capitalism

c) Constitution

d) elected Government

e) one-person-one-vote

f) individual rights

g) free speech

h) freedom of the press

i) freedom to protest

1) a set of rules and regulations which describe how a political system is organised

2) a group of leaders voted into power

3) the right to express your views

4) an economic system based upon the right to own property and make a profit

5) a system of elections where each individual has the right to vote

6) the right of newspapers, radio and television to express their views

7) the basic freedoms which each person enjoys

8) the right to demonstrate

9) the values and beliefs of a country

everyone to work hard, to create their own business and to make money. In this way everyone benefits. We also believe in the freedom of the individual to choose among various competing businesses. This also applies to welfare services such as hospitals, and colleges, many of which are privately owned. Competition for customers makes sure of the best services for all.

The USA is the wealthiest and most powerful country in the world. The Statue of Liberty has welcomed millions of immigrants from all over the world. They come to the USA to find political freedom and the chance to build a good life for themselves.

George Bush

Seal of the President of the USA

The Constitution

The political system of the United States is based upon a document written in 1787 called the Constitution. This short document lays down the framework of the American system of government. When the Constitution was first written the USA was a country of thirteen states which lay mainly on the Atlantic coast. Today the USA is a major power of fifty states which stretch from the Atlantic in the east to the Pacific in the west. And yet the same Constitution still applies despite the major changes affecting the USA since 1787. There have of course been changes and additions to the original document. These are known as Amendments, but there have been fewer than thirty of these and of these the first ten, which set out the basic individual rights of American citizens (known as the 'Bill of Rights'), were written by 1791.

Federal Government in the USA

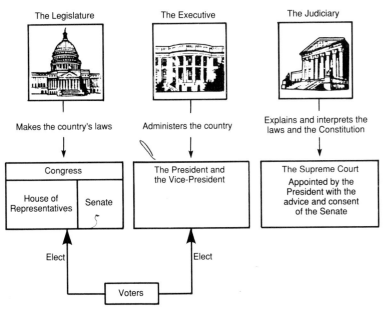

The Legislature — Makes the country's laws — Congress — House of Representatives — Senate — Elect

The Executive — Administers the country — The President and the Vice-President — Elect

The Judiciary — Explains and interprets the laws and the Constitution — The Supreme Court — Appointed by the President with the advice and consent of the Senate

Voters

Voters in an American election

QUESTIONS

1. Read the section headed 'The Constitution' and answer the following:
   - When was the US Constitution written?
   - How much has it changed since it was first written?
   - What does the Constitution describe?
   - What it the 'Bill of Rights'?
2. Study the diagram headed 'The Federal Government of the USA.' and answer the following:
   - What is the name of the body which makes the law in the USA? Name the two parts which make it up.
   - How are the members of this body chosen?
   - What is the name of the person who administers the USA?
   - How is this person chosen for this office?
   - What is the name of the Court which explains and interprets the law in the USA?
   - How are the members of this Court chosen?

1.   Here is a list of some recent American Presidents:

–   Ronald Reagan   –   Richard Nixon

–   Jimmy Carter   –   John F. Kennedy

   Use your class or school library to find out about these leaders and write a short note on each.

2.   Find out the names of the two main political parties in the USA.

3.   Use your class or school library to read about a recent Presidential election. Make a list setting out the similarities and differences between a US Presidential election and a UK General Election.

The US economy

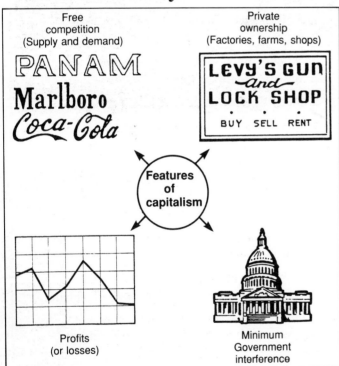

The features of US Capitalism

A CTIVITIES

1.   Copy out the diagram headed 'The features of US Capitalism'.

2.   Make a list of some leading American manufacturing companies whose products are sold (and even made) in the UK. Use the following categories: food; cars; aeroplanes; clothes; oil/petrol.

US society

Rich and Poor in New York City

'... The homeless sleeping in Grand Central Station (where someone recently died of malnutrition) or begging on fashionable Fifth Avenue. Pockets of slum housing scattered everywhere from upper Manhattan to the Bronx and Brooklyn. A huge 'underground economy' with street vendors selling anything from umbrellas to old magazines to scrape together a few dollars. The rich hiding in their limos or retreating to their penthouses high above the sights, sounds and smells of poverty.

   The widening gap between rich and poor, so familiar to those who know the streets of Bangkok or Bogota, is there for all to see in New York. Manhattan is surrounded by a hinterland of boroughs that contain some of the poorest slums in the US. Each morning subway trains filled with the workers (mostly black, Asian or Hispanic women) leave the boroughs and empty out in Midtown or Wall Street. These are the workers who keep New York's financial empires going or try and survive with $8000-a-year jobs in the 'rag trade' (garment industry)...'

(source: 'Life in the Shadows' by Richard Swift, in *New Internationalist*, December 1987.)

America Meets the World

I get off the subway train and buy tickets for tomorrow from the Jamaican teller. The stairs lead up to the street by the Greek restaurant. I saunter past a bar with an Irish name and another American style (whatever that means) restaurant run by Greeks. I resist the pizza cooked by the Italian because I had pizza cooked by a Puerto Rican for lunch and besides we'll probably have Sechuan or Hunan or Cantonese delivered tonight, if we don't jump in a taxi driven by a Haitian and go over to the Ukrainian part of the Lower East Side to eat Indian food.

   I pick up a *Village Voice* from the Pakistani newsstand. And we need bananas for breakfast so I stop in at the Korean deli. Rounding the corner, I catch our building's Dominican maintenance man and complain about a broken lock on the front door which he blames on the Spaniard who lives across the hall from us. Three blocks, five flights of stairs, and several cultures later and I'm home in New York City.

   Nearly 20 per cent of the foreign-born population of the United States lives in the immediate New York area. One out of four of the nearly eight million residents of New York City are foreign born...'

   (source: 'America meets the world' by John Beam, in *New Internationalist*, December 1987.)

Life In The USA

A USA TODAY poll of whites found agreement on some issues with a recent similar poll on blacks, but disagreement on some crucial questions.

Have opportunities for blacks improved in the last 10 years?

	White	Black
Improved	72%	45%
The same	20%	32%
Worse	4%	21%
Don't know	5%	2%

What portion of whites is prejudiced against blacks?

	White	Black
All	5%	5%
Most	25%	21%
Some	56%	56%
Few	10%	15%
Don't know	0%	4%

L'ANSE FOURMI ESTATE: For $1.5 million, this 220-acre resort in the Caribbean is yours.

For sale: Piece of paradise

BENSONHURST CASE: Yusuf Hawkins, the black youth killed in a New York racial incident, will be memorialized with a city youth employment program named for him. Hawkins had urged a program to give needy youngsters jobs while they attend school. Major Ed Koch, at a City Council "Day of Reconciliation" ceremony, said government, religious groups, society must fight racism, but "the key institution clearly is the family."

(source: *USA TODAY*, 22 September 1989.)

15

The chart uses Eastern Daylight Time. (CC) Closed-captioned (special decoder needed). (V) Movies available on videocassette. (r) Repeat.
* Listed is the national PBS schedule. Times may vary in some cities.

Movie ratings: ****=excellent, ***=good, **=fair,*=poor

	8:00	8:30	9:00	9:30	10:00	10:30	11:00	11:30	12:00
ABC	Full House: (Season premiere) The family is stranded.	Family Matters. (Premiere) (CC)	Perfect Strangers. (Season premiere) (CC)	Free Spirit: (Premiere) A housekeeper is a witch. (CC)	20/20: Efforts to prevent the crash of an airliner that lost part of its fuselage; Rolling Stones; motion sickness. (CC)		Local news.	ABC News Nightline: With Ted Koppel. (CC)	Local programming.
CBS	Snoops: (Premiere) A criminology professor and his diplomat wife investigate crime for fun and relaxation. (CC)		Dallas: (Season premier) Sue Ellen's blackmailing enrages J.R.; Cliff continues his quest for Afton; April gets an unwelcome visitor; Bobby and J.R. try to buy Weststar's leases. (CC)				Local news.	The Pat Sajak Show: Joanna Kerns; singer Stephanie Mills; Don Herbert (Mr. Wizard); video jockey Bobby Rivers; Tip O'Neil.	
NBC	Baywatch: (Season Premiere) Mitch and Craig suspect a reckless jet-skier caused a windsurfer's drowning. (CC)		Nasty Boys. The mayor and police chief form a secret team of vice agents to fight Las Vegas crime. With Jeff Kaake, Benjamin Bratt, Don Franklin. (1989) (NR) (CC)				Local news.	The Tonight Show: Guest host: Jay Leno. Guests: Timothy Busfield; Paul Reiser; actor Mykel T. Williamson	
PBS*	Washington Week in Review: Moderator: Paul Duke.	Wall Street Week: With Louis Rukeyser.(CC)	Moyers: Power of the Word: Living Language. Poets James Autry and Quincy Troupe bring poetry into the community. (CC)		Jessica Mitford: Portrait of a Muckraker. Mitford publishes controversial books on the funeral industry and prison system. (CC)		Local programming.		
ESPN	Distant Replay: A reunion of the 1966 Green Bay Packers who won the first Super Bowl.		Great American Events: At the State Fair. In Arkansas and Texas.		America's Wilderness.		Horse Racing: Pegasus Stakes. (Live)	Sports Center: Scores and highlights	Horse Racing: 1989 Breeders Crown Series.
HBO	Phantasm II. * Psychically linked teens (James Le Gros, Paula Irvine) cannot escape from the grave-robbing Tall Man of their nightmares. (1 hr., 36 mins.) (1988) (R: Profanity, nudity, violence.) (V)				American Gothic. * Ma (Yvonne De Carlo), Pa (Rod Steiger) and their backwoods brood kill stranded teens. (1 hr., 30 mins.) (1987) (R) (V)		One-Night Stand: Kevin Meany. (CC)	Kids in the Hall: Satire. (CC)	
CINE-MAX	Vibes. ** Psychics Nick (Jeff Goldblum) and Sylvia (Cyndi Lauper) are tricked into flying to Ecuador to find a fabled city of gold. With Julian Sands. (1 hr., 40 mins.) (1988) (PG: Profanity, violence.) (CC) (V)				The Blob. ** A teen rebel (Kevin Dillon) and a cheerleader (Shawnee Smith) fight formless slime oozing through town. (1 hr., 35 mins.) (1988) (R) (V)		The French Woman. (Starts 11.35: 1 hr., 37 mins.) (1977) (R: Profanity, nudity, violence.) (V)		
MOVIE CHAN	The Pick-Up Artist. * (From 7:30; 1 hr., 22 mins.) (1987) PG-13: Profanity.) (V)		Bulletproof. * The CIA sends Bulletproof (Gary Busey) to Mexico, where his old girlfriend (Darianne Fluegel) and a new tank are property of a Libyan colonel (Henry Silva). (1 hr., 32 mins.) (1988) (R) (V)				Hero and the Terror. * A policeman (Chuck Norris) searches an old theater for a killer called the Terror (Jack O'Halloran). (1 hr., 36 mins.) (1988) (R) (V)		
SHOW-TIME	Can't Buy Me Love. ** A teenager (Patrick Dempsey) buys a girlfriend (Amanda Peterson). (1 hr., 34 mins.) (1987) (PG-13: Profanity.) (CC) (V)		Comedy Club Network. (Starts 9:45)	Super Dave. (CC)	It's Garry Shaddling's Show. (CC)		Robocop. *** Scientists turn a dead Detroit policeman (Peter Weller) into a cyborg crime-fighter. With Nancy Allen. (1 hr., 43 mins.) (1987) (R) (CC) (V)		
DISNEY	The Light in the Forest. *** With Fess Parker. (From 7:00; 1 hr., 33 mins.) (1958) (NR) (V)		The Electric Horseman. ** A newswoman (Jane Fonda) and a rodeo star (Robert Redford) flee to Utah with a $12 million horse freed from a Las Vegas promotion. (2 hrs., 2 mins.) (1979) (PG) (V)				Ozzie & Harriet Ozzie promises to go hiking.	What's Up, Doc? *** With Ryan O'Neal, Madeline Kahn. (1 hr., 34 mins.) (1972) (G) (V)	
USA	Murder, She Wrote: Jessica suspects a murderous cover-up in a firm run by volatile siblings.		Alfred Hitchcock Presents.	Ray Bradbury Theater.	The Hitchhiker: Bum finds evil white powder.	Werewolf: A gang invades a diner	Miami Vice: Crockett and Tubbs fly to Columbia where they hunt someone robbing drug smugglers.		It's Alive. ** (1974) (PG) (V)
TBS	Baseball: Cincinnati Reds at Atlanta Braves. Eric Davis and Barry Larkin are the top hitters for Cincinnati. Darrell Evans and Jeff Treadway lead Atlanta. (From 7:30) (Live)				NWA Wrestling Power Hour: Top bouts from the National Wrestling Alliance. (Starts 10:20)		Night Tracks: Power Hits: Extreme, Motley Crue, Kix, Great White, Pat Benatar. (Starts 11:20)		The Ice Pirates. (Starts 12:20) (1984) (PG)
LIFE-TIME	Haunted by Her Past. ** A lawyer (John James) takes his wife (Susan Lucci) to a Colonial inn, where she reflects a fatal temptress (Finola Hughes) from another century. (1987) (NR)				Days & Nights of Molly Dodd. (CC)	Days & Nights of Molly Dodd. (CC)	Spenser: For Hire: Gunfire greets an author and self-proclaimed vigilante in a Boston bookstore.		What's Up, Dr. Ruth?: Peter DeLuise. (CC)

Neighbourhood graffiti, New York City

QUESTIONS

1. Read the two source extracts on New York City and answer the following:

   – In what ways does New York City show the gap between rich and poor?

   – How many inhabitants of New York are foreign-born?

   – Make a list of the various nationalities which are mentioned by the writer between getting off the subway and arriving home.

2. What does the advertisement 'The Perfect Third Car' tell us about the standard of living in the USA?

KEYWORDS

The following Keywords are used in this Unit. Make sure you have understood what they mean.

Constitution　　　　free speech

THE USSR – PEOPLE, POLITICS AND THE ECONOMY

- The Union of Soviet Socialist Republics is a land of great variety in terms of its population. Its fifteen Republics contain many different ethnic groups with a wide variety of customs, traditions and language. It is a country which has prided itself in being an equal society with no great class divisions. There have, however, been wide differences among various groups in Soviet society and this has shown itself in differing standards of living.

- The USSR is a country born from a Communist revolution in 1917. Since that time the Communist Party has played the leading role in developing the country. Recently there have been major reforms which may bring about widespread change in the way in which the country has been traditionally governed. The USSR is one of the world superpowers with an economy which has been run on Communist ideas. The recent reforms may also bring about widespread change in the country's traditional economic system. These political and economic changes are having an important effect on people's lifestyle and on the values and ideals of the country.

The extracts/sources in this Unit illustrate some aspects of the changing Soviet lifestyle and ideology.

Speaking for my country

We have seen what the different ideologies are in theory. How do they show themselves in practice? Here are the views you might hear from a Soviet Government official speaking about the values and lifestyles of the USSR.

The 'Soviet Way'

The USSR, or Union of Soviet Socialist Republics, is a country founded upon the ideas of socialism and Communism. Our political and economic systems have been based upon the ideas of Marxism and Leninism. Karl Marx was the founder of Communism and Lenin in 1917 led, through revolution, the Communist or Bolshevik Party to power, marking a new era in world history by making the Soviet Union the world's first Communist state.

Under Communism there are no clear class divisions caused by the unequal sharing of the country's wealth. All the major businesses, factories, all the large farms and so on are owned by the state on behalf of the people. All citizens are guaranteed the right to work, to free education and medical treatment and to be cared for in times of illness, disability and old age. We create real freedom for people because there can be no freedom without real equality.

All power in the Soviet Union belongs to the people and they can show this power through the **Soviets**, the councils which are freely elected by the people of the USSR. The supreme Soviet is the major political body in the USSR. The major political party in the Soviet Union is the Communist Party.

We have had only one political party because the Communist Party represents the interests of the workers, the peasants and the intellectuals. It has been the leading force in our society and has united the people. We have, however, recently recognised the importance of allowing other political parties to compete in open election in a multi-party democracy.

We recognise the need for the Soviet Union to change, to modernise itself to take account of changing times and to correct mistakes made in the past. Under our present leader, Mikhail Gorbachev, we have set out on a road which through *glasnost* will make our society more open and which through *perestroika* will make our economy more modern, more efficient and better able to meet the needs of the Soviet people. We are also working to make our society more democratic. This does not mean that Communism has failed. Rather the changes will strengthen our political and economic systems and allow the Soviet Union to advance further along its successful road.

A CTIVITIES

Read the section 'Speaking for my country – "The Soviet Way".'

On page 18 is a list of terms used in the passage and

following them is a list of definitions. Match the correct definition to each term.

a) ideologies b) Communism c) class divisions d) right to free education and medical treatment e) Soviets f) glasnost g) perestroika

1) a political system founded on the ideas of Karl Marx

2) political councils elected by the people of the USSR

3) a policy aimed at making Soviet life more open

4) the values and beliefs of a country

5) the splits in a society caused by wealth and power

6) the guarantee that everyone should be taught and given treatment when ill without having to pay

7) a policy aimed at improving the economy in the USSR

Use your class or school library to find out about the lives of some past leaders of the Soviet Union. Write a short note on each: Joseph Stalin, Nikita Khrishchev, Leonid Brezhnez.

The Communist Party of the Soviet Union (CPSU)

The Soviet Political System

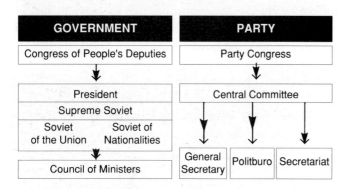

'The leading and guiding force of Soviet Society... is the Communist Party of the Soviet Union.'
– (*Article 6 of the Constitution*)

Key: Article 6

Soviet leader Mikhail Gorbachev wants the Soviet Constitution's Article Six – the Communist Party's key to power – repealed to allow multiparty government. Here's part of what the article says:

"The leading and guiding force of Soviet society and nucleus of its political system, of state organizations and public organizations, is the Communist Party of the Soviet Union.

"The Communist Party, armed with Marxism-Leninism, determines... the course of the home and foreign policy of the U.S.S.R., directs the great constructive work of the Soviet people, and imparts a planned, systematic and theoretically substantiated character to their struggle for the victory of communism.

"All party organizations shall function within the constitution framework."
(source: *USA TODAY*, 8 February 1990.)

For more than seventy years the Soviet Union has had only one political party – the Communist Party. This has meant that the Communist Party has become very powerful. Members of the Party occupy the most important government posts and have great influence throughout the political system. The **Politburo** (the leading group of Party leaders) has in effect been the real government of the USSR. There are approximately 18 million members of the Communist Party and 40 million Young Communist League members (aged between 14 and 28 years). The Young Pioneers organisation caters for 25 million younger children aged between 10 and 15 years.

Mikhail Gorbachev

To be accepted as a member of the Party has been a great honour and members are expected to play a leading role in Soviet society. Members of the Party have also enjoyed considerable privileges, including better housing, better education and generally a better lifestyle with access to special shops and better jobs.

Moscow rolls back the red tide

'THE Soviet Communist Party, which swore for decades that its red tide would cover the globe, bowed to a very different revolution yesterday and agreed to allow alternative political parties to compete for control in the Soviet Union.

The party central committee voted after an extended three-day session to ask parliament to end the party's monopoly on power... Svyatoslav Fyodorov, one of the participants, said in an interview on Red Square during a break in the closed-door meeting. *(cont.)*

QUESTIONS

Read the passage on the Communist Party of the Soviet Union (CPSU) and the source extract headed, 'Moscow Rolls Back the Red Tide' and answer the following:

1. What has been the importance of the Communist Party in Soviet politics?

2. What are the Young Communist League and the Young Pioneers Organisation?

3. In what ways has it been an honour and a privilege to be a member of the Communist Party?

4. What important change took place in the USSR in early 1990, regarding the position of the Communist Party in Soviet politics? Explain the reference to 'Article 6' in the source extract.

Soviet elections

The Soviet Union's national law-making body has been composed of elected representatives nominated by the Communist Party. Until recently the candidates for election stood unopposed. All citizens over the age of eighteen have the right to vote and vote is by secret ballot. Voters are asked to cross out the names of all candidates except the name of the person for whom the voter wishes to vote and then to drop the ballot paper into the ballot box. In practice, however, since there were few occasions when candidates were challenged, then all the voter had to do was collect a ballot paper and drop it into the ballot box unmarked. There was no need to make any mark on the ballot paper and voters who did would draw attention to themselves.

In 1989, as part of Gorbachev's *glasnost* reforms, elections were held for the Soviet Parliament. In this election most seats were contested by several candidates and Soviet voters had for the first time a genuine choice. Here are two source extracts which describe the importance of this change in Soviet elections.

Voters in a Soviet election

The way they voted, it could have been polling day anywhere

MOSCOW – If you disregarded the lady dressed in what was obviously her smartest suit, self-consciously excited as she showed voters into the yellow-curtained booths, you might have thought the Russians had been taking part in multi-candidate general elections all their lives.

Election station 115/1627 of the Taganka district on Marxistskaya Street is opposite the Moscow's largest supermarket, above which is the office of *The Independent*. Normally it is an administrative supply centre for the Moscow municipality. Yesterday it took like a duck to water to the role of polling station, one of 3,393 for Moscow's 6.7 million eligible voters. In this precinct, 1,498 people are on the electoral roll.

For years, Russians have stayed away from elections, knowing that with or without their participation, the Communist Party would claim a near 100 per cent victory. How many people exercised their new democratic right, to the bizarre accompaniment of light music issuing from a couple of loudspeakers, is still unknown. But if the steady flow during the 30 minutes I spent there was anything to go by, turnout was high.

Upon entering, the voter presented his or her internal passport to a girl sitting behind one of six tables, above which a neon sign showed the initial letter of the surname. Quickly she checked the name on the thick typed register in front of her. In return, the voter received an explanatory leaflet and two ballot papers.

The pale blue one, for the single regional vote covering all of Moscow, carried the names of Boris Yeltsin, the ousted Politburo radical, and Yevgeny Brakov, the director of the Zil car factory. On the other, ordinary white, were the names Alexander Samsonov and Valery Nosov, the two solid factory bosses who are candidates in the infinitely less compelling contest for our local seat. "Frankly I can't tell the difference between them," one woman said.

Rarely did they have to spend more than 30 seconds before casting their vote. If they did, the lady in the suit was equal to the problem, explaining the procedure. Inside, apart from the music and a giant portrait of Lenin flanked by red banners and with scarlet carnations underneath, it could have been polling day anywhere, in Baltimore, Bologna or Birmingham...

Rupert Cornwell

(source: *The Independent*, 27 March 1990.)

Soviet Elections – 1989

'Mr Gorbachev has kept his word. The first Congress of People's Deputies, supreme body of the state, was elected by universal suffrage. unlike the feeble Supreme Soviet which it replaced, most seats were contested by several candidates. Voting was genuinely secret.

In its turn the congress elected Mr Gorbachev as head of state, president of a Supreme Soviet slimmed to 542 members, the first full-time, professional parliament in the history of the country...'

(source: '1989: The Year of Revolution USSR' by Rupert Cornwall, in *The Independent*, 28 December 1989.)

QUESTIONS

1. Describe how Soviet elections were held before Gorbachev became leader – refer to the number of candidates and what voters were asked to do.
2. In what way did the 1989 election differ?
3. Make a list of words or terms used in the source extract '1989: The Year of Revolution USSR' which show the author believes these elections and the Parliament elected to be different from previous elections and Parliaments.

The Soviet economy

State planning in the USSR

GOSPLAN
(Central Planning Commission)

Industry   Agriculture   Trade

Sets prices of products — Allocates money for investment — Sets production targets

Assigns workers

Controls supplies of raw materials

Sends advisers to give technical and scientific help

Markets and distributes products

Controls exports and imports (quantities and prices)

RUSSIAN ROULETTE

...The best western guess is that the Soviet economy is about half the size of America's. It can match America's military might only by spending about 15% of its GNP on defence, compared with America's 7%. It is reckoned to be between seven and 12 years behind America in advanced computer-related technologies.

True, Russia has excelled in space, and it is a world-beater at churning out simple commodities in bulk. It produces more oil than Saudi Arabia, more gas than America, more steel than Japan. But the old obsession with quantity has too often led to the neglect of quality and efficiency, which matter more and more as customers become richer and choosier. Russian goods are notoriously shoddy... And the Russian-in-the-queue may well wonder why a country that can send cosmonauts on record-breaking space trips is incapable of providing enough toothpaste or tights.

However wide the "technology gap" between Russia and the West, the "consumer gap" is greater. A vast amount of time is wasted in queues: a housewife in Omsk probably has to spend at least six hours longer doing her shopping each week than a housewife in Omaha. Private telephones and decent meat are still luxuries in Russia. Personal computers are almost unheard of.

Cars are a good example of the size of the consumer gap. An American is 12 times as likely to own one as a Russian.

Last year a western study found that a person on an average salary needs to work for five months to afford a small car in Washington, for eight months in Paris or London – but for nearly four years in Moscow. Even if he has the money, the Muscovite will have to wait, because the queue for cars is eight years long. The car he eventually buys will break down more often than the one he would have bought in the West, and when it does it will be no fun trying to find spare parts...

(source: 'Special Survey of the Soviet Economy' by Daniel Franklin, in *The Economist*, 9 April 1988.)

The industrial revolution

The economic system has worked against technological dynamism. Research institutes have mostly stayed separate from factories. More important, factories have mostly remained detached from their customers: their bonuses have come from pleasing their bosses in the ministries by making enough tonnes of this or enough pairs of that. Competition has been non-existent, the threat of bankruptcy nil. In shortage-ridden Russia, everything sells. *(cont.)*

Shoddiness had become Russia's trademark. Before *glasnost*, the most exciting thing about watching Soviet television was that the set was liable to catch fire. Factories had become rusty... They had also become increasingly polluting, as efforts to satisfy the all-powerful plan took precedence over any concern for the environment...

Mr Gorbachev's plan for halting and, he hopes, reversing Russia's relative industrial decline has two main arms. An intense programme of investment in new technology is meant to provide the hardware necessary for a dynamic, modern economy. His reform of the management system is meant to ensure that the new equipment is well made and put to proper use...

Factories, so the theory of *perestroika* goes, will decide for themselves what investments are the most profitable...

At the base of the industrial hierarchy, the Law on the State Enterprise and its accompanying legislation give factories the right to deal directly with one another instead of simply following instructions from above. This, it is hoped, will make factories start producing what their customers want...

(source: 'Special Survey of the Soviet Economy' by Daniel Franklin, in *The Economist*, 9 April 1988.)

Soviet society

McDonald's comes to Moscow

Shopping in The USSR

IN RIZHSKY Market, on Moscow's Prospect Mira, they sell the sort of hotdogs and tea McDonald's could make very unfashionable. You can wait here, in the biting wind, for half an hour, only to get to the top of the queue and be told they have just run out. Meanwhile, in Pushkin Square on the other side of town, McDonald's is serving each of its customers within two minutes.

McDonald's, which opened last week with purpose-built processing plant and guaranteed supplies, is an object lesson in how to run a business in the Soviet Union. It has even imported the seed to grow its own special brand of potato, the Russet Burbank. "It's a specially long potato, which suits our friers," says Corinne Reed, McDonald's public relations manager. We eat the same variety in the UK.

At the Rizhsky Market, however, it is the Soviet economic system that is in operation, with all its flaws and contradictions.

The co-operative system is new to Russia. It is not the central plank of President Gorbachev's economic reforms, (the main aim is to make the state sector of the economy more responsive to the market) but it is one of the most visible examples of the changes taking place. Co-ops were introduced as part of a move to decentralise the economy, and they represent a fledging private sector.

Most visitors to Moscow begin their shopping not at the co-ops or markets, however, but in the GUM (Gosudarstvenny Universalny Magazin). This is the capital's most famous department store, the Harrods of its day, built in the 1890s to house more than 100 shops and merchant's offices. Even if GUM were not so big – and it is huge – it would attract attention by its position alone. It runs the whole length of Red Square, sitting glumly opposite Lenin's tomb and the Kremlin, a witness to all the drama of the square.

GUM, however, confirms all your worst expectations of Soviet shops. Long queues – mainly for soap, toiletries and perfume, – snake down the corridors and if two of you peer over something at the same time, a queue springs up immediately at your back.

Even on a good day, GUM is a dreary place, and Muscovites shudder at its mention. "I would never go there, never, never, never," says Sonya Berkovskaya. "GUM is only used by people who come to Moscow from outside. If you go day after day, you can find something, but the queues go on for kilometres. Muscovites never go into this shop."

Several things are common to all these shops: the big old fashioned abacuses that sit on all the counters and are used as speedily as calculators; the inevitable empty shelves; and the throngs of people.

(source: 'Moscow: Buying Time' by Sally Kinnes, in *Scotland on Sunday*, 4 February 1990.)

A TASTE OF THE LUXE LIFE

When the silver-plated telephone rings in Marina Osadchuk's clothing and beauty boutique, it chirps like a canary. These days it sounds as if a cageful of canaries has been let loose in Osadchuk's store in Moscow. People call constantly to inquire about the handmade suits and dresses, priced at 200 to 700 rubles ($320 to $1,120), or to make appointments to get their hair done for 15 rubles ($24). With 50 customers a day, Osadchuk has more business than she can handle.

Osadchuk's eager clientele largely represents a new class of Soviet consumer: the nouveau riche, of which she is a proud member. Better yet, call them yuccies—young upwardly mobile Communists. Osadchuk pays herself a monthly salary of 700 rubles, or $1,120, about three times the average Soviet salary and enough for her family to live very comfortably. Says she: "We buy anything we want." Thanks to the co-op movement, employee profit sharing and other budding forms of entrepreneurship, many Soviets are suddenly earning enough money to do more than just scrape by. They are enjoying a taste of the good life, and some are even becoming wealthy, at least by Soviet standards.

Yet the fling with materialism is problematic in a country that has officially scorned materialism and has trouble producing enough basic goods, much less luxury items. Even such Western staples as cars, refrigerators and washing machines are in chronically short supply. As a result, well-off Soviets often have much more money than they need for smaller indulgences, including restaurant meals, videos and stereo gear. "Money slips through our fingers," says Vladimir Ivlev, chairman of a Moscow clothing cooperative that pays him a monthly salary of 2,000 rubles ($3,200).

Ivlev, who often wears imported jeans and Adidas sneakers, has richly furnished the three-room apartment he shares with his wife Tanya and son Sergei. A sleek, ebony-colored bookcase holds a Korean color TV and matching video system. Ivlev says he paid 1,000 rubles ($1,600) for a Panasonic tape deck. "And we have better food because we shop at the open market, where prices are higher," he points out. Is their bank account growing? "It's not our

Ivlev is riding high

"We buy anything we want," says boutique proprietor Osadchuk

aim to save money," says Tanya. "We want to spend as much as we can."

Vladimir Yakovlev, 30, a former journalist, has cashed in on the co-op movement by starting a company to collect and sell information about such ventures. Yakovlev launched the firm, called Fakt, two years ago and already has more than 30 offices in the Soviet Union. Yakovlev, who last fall visited the U.S. for the first time to learn more about foreign trade, pays himself 1,500 rubles a month ($2,400), five times as much as he made as a journalist. His most enviable perk is a company car and driver. "I spend a lot of money every month on clothes and fancy restaurants," he says. "I have no bank account. No savings." Consumers have little incentive to save because such major expenses as housing and education are subsidized and bank accounts pay interest of only 2% to 4%.

Even if luxury goods are scarce, having extra income means being able to procure a better grade of necessity. For example, a pound of beef costs 1.4 rubles ($2.24) when it can be found in a state store, but is usually filled with lard and bone. Better-quality beef is readily available at co-op markets, but costs about 4.6 rubles ($7.36) a pound. The same is true of services. Well-off consumers seeking to avoid Moscow's public dentists flock to Joseph Bochkovsky, whose private office has such modern equipment as high-tech drills from Czechoslovakia and Japanese-made disposable needles for injecting anesthetics. Prices at his office are four times as high as those at state-operated polyclinics, where dentists use more rudimentary tools. But the 600 patients on his waiting list consider Bochkovsky's humane dentistry a welcome addition to the good life.

— **By Ann Blackman/Moscow**

(source: *TIME Magazine*, 10 April 1989.)

KEYWORDS

The following Keywords are used in this Unit. Make sure you have understood what they mean.

Soviets   *perestroika*
glasnost   **Politburo**

22

1. Read the source extract headed 'Shopping In The USSR' and answer the following:

 – How does the Moscow 'McDonald's' differ from typical Soviet restaurants?

 – What is GUM?

 – Why is GUM described as 'confirming all your worst expectations of Soviet shops'?

 – What three things are 'common' to all Soviet shops?

2. Read the source extract headed 'A Taste of the Luxe Life' and answer the following:

 – What does the article mean by the term 'yuccies'?

 – Why are some Soviet citizens 'earning enough money to do more than just scrape by'?

 – What problem do these 'new rich' face in spending their money?

 – How are the 'new rich' benefitting in terms of food and services?

 – Why might you find the features of Soviet society described in this article surprising in a Communist country?

EXIT FROM THE LAND OF FADING HOPES

No one needs reminding how incredible have been my four years as the first Moscow correspondent of *The Independent*. January 1987, when I arrived, was almost the dawn. Tiny demonstrations of Jewish refuseniks were still being broken up by KGB thugs in leather jackets. But Andrei Sakharov had just been released from Gorky.

Thereafter, at breakneck pace, the Soviet Union rejoined the world: political prisoners were freed, arms agreements signed, and Eastern Europe liberated. The West was courted, praised, and copied. The Communist Party lost its monopoly of power, new democratic movements flourished in every corner of the land.

But exhilaration turned to anarchy.

I am writing on the last day of a depressing 1990, with a frightening 1991 in prospect. The wheel has not yet turned full circle, but it is moving in that direction. Eduard Shevardnadze has resigned in protest at an "advancing dictatorship". The economy and the very structure of power are disintegrating. To stop the rot, Mikhail Gorbachev is reaching back to the party, the KGB, ultimately the army. He says he wants to save reform, not bury it; but the distinction scarcely matters. He no longer fashions events, he reacts to them.

Sometime in the summer of 1989, I was accused of belonging to the "catastrophist" school of perestroika observers. At the very least it seemed clear then that 1990 would be make-or-break. For the old perestroika, it has been break. What comes next, I fear to think. I am sad, but relieved to be leaving. The best prospect is of continuing muddle, out of which a completely new equilibrium might peacefully emerge; but I cannot believe the conservatives will permit the necessary shake-out.

As for Mr Gorbachev, he is a figure of transition. He has destroyed one system, but will not preside over the new one. Sooner rather than later, perhaps, he will be brought down by his own contradictions. Maybe the army and the KGB, maybe Boris Yeltsin, maybe someone we have never heard of, will replace him. Of course, as has happened often in the last four years, the ever-baffling Russians may prove me wrong.

(source: *The Independent*, 5 January 1991.)

Read the source headed 'Exit from The Land of Fading Hopes'. The article was written by the Moscow correspondent for *The Independent* newspaper. In the article the author gives his views on the major changes he has seen in his four years in Moscow.

1. Make a list of the major changes affecting the Soviet Union referred to in the second paragraph of the extract.

2. What problems facing the Soviet Union in 1991 are referred to in the third paragraph of the extract and how does the author think Gorbachev is trying to tackle these problems?

3. Why does the title of the article use the term 'the land of fading hopes' in describing the Soviet Union?

*A*CTIVITIES

1. Use your class or school library to find out about the following people mentioned in the extract:
   Andrei Sakharov
   Eduard Shevardnadze
   Boris Yeltsin

2. Read the foreign pages of a daily newspaper for the period of time you are studying this topic. Collect any information on recent events in the Soviet Union which show the fate of reform in that country.

CHINA – PEOPLE, POLITICS AND THE ECONOMY

China is a land with a huge population – over 1000 million people, approximately one quarter of the world's people. It is a country where about 85 per cent of the people are agricultural workers and have a standard of living which is poor in comparison to our own. It is a country which has made major progress in improving the basic life of its population in terms of education, health and food supplies.

Modern China is a country born from a Communist revolution in 1949. Since then the Communist Party has played the leading role in directing the country and China's Communist leaders have resisted strongly any attempts to change the way the country is governed.

The Chinese economy has been run on Communist lines with a strong emphasis on agriculture. Recent leaders have brought in major reforms which have been aimed at making China a modern industrialised country.

These aspects of China can be seen in the following extracts/sources which give a glimpse of the Chinese lifestyle and ideology.

Speaking for my country

We have seen what the different ideologies are in theory. How do they show themselves in practice? Here are the views you might hear from a Chinese Government official in speaking about the values and lifestyle of China.

The 'Chinese Way'

The People's Republic of China is a Communist country. Our values and ideals, our political and economic systems are based upon the ideas of Karl Marx and Lenin, the leader of the Russian Revolution in 1917. We should not, however, be seen as merely a copy of the Soviet Union. The Communist Party came to power in China in 1949 led by Mao Zedong, our first great revolutionary leader and thinker.

China was – and to a large extent still is – an agricultural country. Communism had to develop among the peasants in the countryside as much as among the workers in the towns. Because of this Chinese Communism became a model for all Third World countries. Under Communism China has made major advances in giving all its people the basics of life. No other agricultural country has developed as quickly as China, whilst creating at the same time a more equal society.

Since the death of Mao in 1976, our leaders have recognised that China must adapt and revise its previous economic policies. With such programmes as the **Four Modernisations**, China has set off on a road towards economic modernisation and reform which will transform the Chinese economy and make China a true world superpower.

In all these changes the 'leading and guiding' role of the Communist Party has been of crucial importance. There have been those who have sought to weaken and destroy the leading role of the Communist Party but they have not been successful and China does not intend to follow the present path of the Soviet Union in allowing other political parties to challenge the Communist Party.

Communism has been a success in China. We have only to remember life before the Revolution in 1949 when China was occupied and fought over by foreign powers and ruled by a privileged minority who grew rich by exploiting the Chinese workers and peasants. Since then we have made great steps towards creating a just and equal society and towards making China one of the world's superpowers.

A CTIVITY

Read the section 'Speaking for my country – "The Chinese Way"'. Here is a list of terms used in the passage and following them is a list of definitions. Match the correct definition to each term:

a) ideologies b) Communist country c) agricultural country d) equal society e) Four Modernisations f) leading role of the Communist Party g) privileged minority

1) a country whose political system is based on the ideas of Karl Marx

2) a policy aimed at reforming the Chinese economy

3) a description of the dominant part played by one political party

4) a small group of people who hold a very wealthy and powerful position

5) a country which depends on farming rather than industry

6) a system where no one group of people dominates or enjoys a better life-style

The Chinese Communist Party

Deng Xiaoping

The most important feature about the political system in China is that there exists only one political party – the Chinese Communist Party. It is the Communist Party which controls all aspects of government at all levels from the national level to the committees which run the factories and farms.

The CCP is not open to anyone to join. Membership is a great honour and involves hard work and much responsibility. Only about 2 per cent of the population are members – about 26 million. Young Chinese under 15 can join the Young Pioneers and those of 15–25 years can join the Young Communist Youth League.

At the head of the CCP is the Central Committee whose leading members form the **Politburo**. The leader of the Party is the Chairperson. From the foundation of the Communist state of China in 1949 until his death in 1976, the Chairman of the CCP was Mao Zedong. Since his death the most important leader in China has been Deng Xiaoping, although he has only held the post of Vice–Chairman. At national level the activities of the leaders in the Politburo decide the policies and direction of China. Below the national scene, at local level in the factories, on the farms and in the villages, the local Party officials are the key figures in explaining Government policy and in encouraging people to follow this policy.

Political challenge

In 1989 the Chinese Communist Party faced a serious challenge to its dominant role in Chinese political life when thousands of students occupied Tiananmen Square in the centre of Beijing. The students' demands were for greater democracy and for political reform similar to the reforms of *glasnost* and *perestroika* introduced by Mikhail Gorbachev into the USSR. Eventually, in June 1989, after several months of demonstrations, the Chinese leadership decided that 'enough was enough' and sent the army to clear the students from Tiananmen Square. This was done with great bloodshed and showed that China would not follow Eastern Europe or the Soviet Union on the road to democratic change. The Chinese Communist Party now see themselves as the real defenders of Communism and believe that the USSR under Gorbachev has betrayed 'true Marxism'.

Q UESTIONS

1. What is the importance of the Communist Party in Chinese politics?
2. What is the Politburo and what part does it play in Chinese politics?
3. Describe what happened in Tiananmen Square in 1989.
4. What did this show about the Chinese leadership's attitudes to political reform?

A CTIVITY

Use your class or school library to find out more about the lives of these two Chinese leaders: Mao Zedong; Deng Xiaoping.

The Chinese economy

Agriculture

Increases in grain production
Great improvements in mechanisation
Improved drainage and irrigation

Industry

Increased steel production
Introduction of modern technology
Greater efficiency, productivity and profits

Science & Technology

Rehabilitation of scientists
Re-establishment of research institutes and academies
Research into the 'Five Golden Blossoms' atomic science, semi-conductors, computers, lasers and automation

Defence

Modernisation of tanks, aircraft, ships and submarines
Increase and improvement of nuclear missiles
New links with Japan, Western Europe and the USA

The Four Modernisations

Following the death of Mao Zedong in 1976, China began a major programme of economic reform and modernisation. This reform programme was called The Four Modernisations and was aimed at reforming the following areas of Chinese life: agriculture, industry, science and technology, and defence.

The Chinese also opened up their country to trade and investment from capitalist countries such as Japan, the USA and Western Europe. This became known as the 'Great Leap Outwards'. These two reform programmes have changed many traditional features of the Chinese Communist economy. Small-scale private companies have been allowed. People have been encouraged to make profits and workers have been encouraged to work harder by higher wages. More consumer goods, including foreign goods, have been introduced into the shops. The Party introduced the slogan 'Getting rich is glorious' as an encouragement to Chinese workers to follow the new reforms. A favourite saying of the Chinese leader Deng Xiaoping has been that 'it does not matter whether a cat is black or white as long as it catches mice'. This has been taken to mean that it does not matter whether his new reforms were in the spirit of Communism or not, as long as they worked.

Farming

Before the new economic reforms were introduced, all the land was owned by the state and worked by a system called **communes** in which the farmers grew what the state ordered. The farmers were paid according

Features of the new Chinese economic system

HAVING

A TV set and refrigerator are two of the "three bigs" a Chinese family dreams of buying. The third: a washing machine

ENTERPRISE

Let profits bloom.

TECHNOLOGY

The classic image of peasants tilling the good earth with oxen and wooden ploughs remains a part of China's present. But the reality of life today also includes white-suited workers running the gauge-filled control room of a giant power station

CHOICE

Though the Chinese are still limited in their freedom to pick a job or place to live, they now enjoy the luxury of selecting what to put on the dinner table.

to the work done and all the food produced was handed over to the state. The new reforms abolished the communes and, although the state still owns the land, it 'rents' out plots to individual families. Once the families have met the rent for the land, they can grow whatever they wish and sell it at whatever price they can get in the markets. Farmers are allowed to build privately owned houses on their state owned land.

Private enterprise

Under the new reforms, individuals are allowed to set up small **'sideline' businesses** and keep any profits. The first businesses were connected with farming – peasants would set up road-side stalls to sell their crops. This has now spread to a wide variety of businesses including restaurants, tailor shops and small-scale manufacturing. These small companies can even hire workers privately.

Industry

The new reforms changed the emphasis of China's industry from heavy industry such as steel-making towards consumer goods such as refrigerators and TV sets.

In addition, although there are still central plans for factory managers to meet, there is more freedom given for managers to buy supplies, produce goods and fix prices.

Foreign companies have been encouraged to set up in China and companies such as Coca-Cola have introduced Western tastes to the Chinese people.

*Q*UESTIONS

1. What was the aim of the 'Four Modernisations' and which four areas of Chinese life did it affect?

2. What was the 'Great Leap Outwards' and how did this affect Chinese life?

3. Describe how farming has changed as a result of the new reforms.

4. Describe how industry has changed as a result of the new reforms.

5. With reference to farming, industry and private enterprise in China today, give your views on whether the new reforms are typical of a Communist economy.

Living standards

Before the economic reforms a Chinese consumer would dream of owning the 'three bigs' – a bicycle, a watch and a sewing machine. Now Chinese people want to own a refrigerator, a washing machine and a TV set.

Member of The
Leading Hotels of the World

Address: SHAMIAN ISLANDS, GUANGZHOU, CHINA
Tel: 886968 Ext 12
Telex: 44688 WSH CN Cable: 8888
BEIJING RESERVATION CENTRE
Tel: 557496
SHANGHAI OFFICE
Tel: 582582 Ext 3337
HONG KONG OFFICE
Tel: 5-240192, 5-240193
Telex: 75050 WINGS HX

(source: *Observer Magazine* Survey, 'China: The New Lifestyle', 29 September 1985.)

China opens up to mass tourism

'OF RICE AND RICHES'

RECENTLY returned to MaGaoqiao village for the third time. This community of 2,000 people is on the western Sichuan plain about 70 kilometers north-west of Chengdu. It is not open to foreigners and a special travel permit has to be obtained from the Public Security Office.

As one approaches MaGaoqiao on foot from the distance of the railway embankment, the scene has a steady, ancient rhythm. Children cut grass for pig fodder, slow-moving buffaloes graze by the roadside, women wash clothes in a spring-fed stream, a blue-clad peasant with a wide straw hat is repairing an irrigation ditch and a village tractor driver hauls in a load of coal. Scattered clusters of farmhouses, the village office, school and clinic, all shaded by bamboo groves and stands of eucalyptus, appear to float in the surrounding paddy fields, small islands in a mirage of light green during the early summer season.

But remarkable changes have taken place since my first stay here in 1981. At that time the village was known as Number Eight Brigade of Lianglukou People's Commune; the people worked in collective groups called production teams and were proud of the co-operative medical clinic, the school, the electrified grain-processing mill, the big tractors, the methane-gas pits and other achievements created by the collective.

By the time I went back in 1983 there had been a startling reversal. The signboard of the commune had been taken down while the brigade had reverted to the name it had before the land reform of 1952: MaGaoqiao village. People no longer worked in collective groups for work points – instead family households contracted land from the production team. Under this system each family works the land, fulfills its obligations to the State and to the collective and then keeps the rest.

The tractors and buffaloes had been sold off to individuals; even the co-operative medical clinic had been abandoned and was contracted to the barefoot doctor who ran it as a business operation. People were encouraged to take up sideline commercial activities, start taxi or bus services, or raise poultry, pigs and rabbits for the markets. Now the subject on everyone's lips was the 'ten thousand yuan' households, the families who had found a lucrative speciality and were reportedly making themselves rich.

There were signs of new prosperity. A large chart running the length of a room in the village headquarters listed the names of 50 newly prosperous families along with their incomes for the previous year. About 20 per cent of families had built new brick-and-tile houses, there were more bicycles and even some television sets...

When I returned to MaGaoqiao in 1986 I found the short-term results of the reforms dramatic. The village continues to prosper... The per-capita annual income has doubled since the reforms were instituted and almost half the families have built new homes. It is hard to argue with success like this.

But along with the dismantling of the People's Communes and a weakening of collective responsibility has come some polarization[*] between the stronger and the weaker households – and the re-emergence of exploitation as the more successful individuals hire the labour of their neighbours. It has even been agreed, after much debate in the Communist Party's central committee, that party members may hire others to work for them provided the number is not too great...

Stephen Endicott

[*]   *polarization – division into two groups.*

(source: *New Internationalist*, April 1987.)

A CTIVITY

Read the source extract headed 'Of Rice and Riches' and answer the following:

1.   Describe what the village was like when the author first visited it in 1981.

2.   In what ways had the village changed when the author returned in 1983. Refer to the village name, how the land was farmed, who owned the equipment and animals, 'sideline activities' and the prosperity of the village.

3.   Explain how these changes showed a move away from traditional Chinese Communism.

4.   How had the village further changed by the time the author returned in 1986?

5.   Use the last paragraph to discuss the view that these changes are leading to a richer but more unequal society in China.

Chinese society

PEOPLE

China's 1,059 million people make it by far the world's most populous country. The vast majority of these belong to the dominant ethnic group, the Han (those we conventionally think of as 'Chinese') but China contains 56 nationalities.

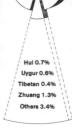

Han 93.3%

Hui 0.7%
Uygur 0.6%
Tibetan 0.4%
Zhuang 1.3%
Others 3.4%

Han ...

... Tibetan

(sources (pp. 28-29): *New Internationalist*, April 1987.)

消费 CONSUMPTION

Consumer durables per hundred households		
Urban households	1981	1984
Sewing machines	70	77
Watches	241	283
Bicycles	136	163
Radios	100	103
Televisions	58	87
Rural households	1981	1984
Sewing machines	20	43
Watches	27	109
Bicycles	31	74
Radios	17	61
Televisions	0	7

Television was made available in the countryside only a decade ago but by 1986 TV sets were found in 30 million rural homes – 11 per cent of rural households. 3,000 villages are called 'TV villages' where every family has at least one TV.

Cultural boom[2]	1949	1978	1984
Books produced (millions of copies)	105	3,770	6,248
Newspapers (millions of copies)	410	10,950	18,080
Public libraries (actual number)	55	1,256	2,217
Film projection units (thousands)	1	116	178
Television sales (millions)	0	1	11
Cameras produced (thousands)	17	179	1,262

One-child families

China has the strictest family planning policy in the world. Each couple is only allowed one child and great pressure is put on women to abort a second pregnancy.

Population changes	1950	1965	1976	1985
Total population (millions)	552	725	933	1059
Birth rate (per thousand people)	37	38	20	19
Death rare (per thousand people)	18	10	7	7
Natural rate of increase	19	28	13	12

A golden future – a poster in Xiamen urges on women the virtues of the one-child family.

Child mortality

The decline in the death rate of Chinese children under five – from 202 per thousand in 1960 to 50 per thousand in 1985 – is the eleventh sharpest fall in the world over that period.

生活的品质 QUALITY OF LIFE

There is certainly more money around in the new China – and a consumer boom is resulting, with sales of televisions and washing machines rocketing. But any new prosperity is founded on the dramatic improvements in health, education and nutrition brought about by the 1949 Revolution.

Life expectancy

1948 – 1949	36
1960	47
1973 – 1975	62–65
1985	69

Food

Calories available daily to each person as a percentage of their requirements stood at 111 in 1985, similar to that in Japan (113) and Australia (115).

Wealth

Between 1965 and 1984 the gross national product per head rose by an average of 4.5 per cent a year – the twelfth highest rise in the world over that period.
Between 1978 and 1985 the average farmer's annual income increased by 14.8 per cent after allowing for inflation.
But the Chinese Government admits that 60 million rural people still live in poverty, especially in arid western China (which includes Tibet).

Q UESTIONS

Study the source extracts on Chinese society and answer the following:

1. What is the population of China and how many nationalities make up its population?

2. In what way has life expectancy changed in China between 1948 and 1985?

3. What evidence is there that the Chinese have managed to overcome problems of food shortages?

4. What are 'TV villages'?

5. Explain China's family planning policy. Why do you think the Chinese Government have adopted a strict family planning policy?

KEYWORDS

The following Keywords are used in this Unit. Make sure you have understood what they mean.

Four Modernisations	communes
Poliburo	'sideline' businesses

2

HUMAN RIGHTS

OUR RIGHTS

What are our rights?

shelter
food
clothing

Everyone expects to have a roof over his or her head. We take it for granted that we will have enough to eat to keep us alive and reasonably healthy. We would be very disappointed if we did not have reasonable clothes to wear. These are very basic **human rights** which every one of us would expect to have.

We may not have as big a house as we would like, or as much food as we could sometimes eat, or as many expensive clothes as we would like to be fashionable, but we are all provided for to a standard where we can reasonably survive. These are the human rights to which we probably do not give a second thought. We all know, however, that there are people in some parts of the world who do not have even these basic rights. Ethiopia, Armenia, Brazil and many other places have been in the news in recent years because, for one reason or another, the people there have not enjoyed these rights.

Other human rights include the right to have medical treatment if we become ill, to be protected from cruelty and neglect, and to be educated. Many people also expect the right to free speech, the right to choose their own representatives to govern them and the right to be free to travel to other countries if they wish to do so. These basic freedoms are things we expect because we are human beings – that is why they are called human rights.

Some of these rights are protected by laws, but many others are not. Depending on where we live in the world we may enjoy all of these rights, some of them, or none. We have already seen that not everyone in the world receives all the human rights they might expect.

In this Unit we will find out more about our rights, about some of the organisations which try to make sure our rights are protected, and about human rights in three important countries, the United States of America, the USSR and China.

Human rights

> **HUMAN RIGHTS are:**
> - **rights which are basic, fundamental and essential**
> - **rights of everyone, everywhere**
> - **rights which include moral as well as legal rights**
> - **rights which governments and states have no power to deny to individuals and groups**
> - **rights limited only in that they do not interfere with the rights of other people**

While there is no worldwide agreement on what human rights include, an attempt to list them was made in 1948. When the United Nations Organisation (UNO) was set up after the Second World War, one of its most important aims was to encourage all countries to cooperate,

> *... in promoting and encouraging respect for human rights and for fundamental freedoms for all, without distinction as to race, sex, language or religion.'*

On 10 December 1948 all the member countries in the UN General Assembly signed a document called the *Universal Declaration of Human Rights*. This document was drawn up by the UN as a result of the horrors of the Second World War and the many examples of ill-treatment of people during the war. It aims to set out the standard which all nations and people should aim to achieve, without exception.

The Declaration is a long document setting out rights and freedoms. Here are some of the most important things it says:

THE HELSINKI PROCESS

Since 1945 there has also been concern for human rights outside the UNO. In 1973 and 1975 representatives of 35 governments met in Helsinki, the capital of Finland, to try to produce a definition of peace and stability between the countries of the East and the West. This had been impossible during the period known as the Cold War in the 1960s and early 1970s.

The Soviet Union wanted the western countries to recognise the frontiers it had established in Eastern Europe at the end of World War 2. In return, the western countries pressed for concessions on human rights and freedom of movement and information between East and West. In spite of the hopes of the western countries, the Helsinki Agreements were not seen as legally binding – there was no way of enforcing them. Most countries saw them only as recommendations or moral commitments.

Nevertheless, the human rights statements have been widely accepted as setting the international standard to be aimed at for human rights. The Helsinki Agreements created, like the *Universal Declaration of Human Rights*, widespread expectations about proper human rights behaviour, and have helped in the monitoring of human rights policies of countries.

Children have rights

Children, because of their vulnerability, need special care and protection. The United Nations Convention on the Rights of the Child, drawn up in 1990, sets out the basic rights which all children are entitled to enjoy. These rights exist on the understanding that parents or whoever is legally responsible for the child also have rights, responsibilities and duties in giving appropriate direction and guidance as the child develops, and these rights exist only if they do not affect the rights of others.

THE UN CONVENTION ON THE RIGHTS OF THE CHILD (1990)

All children, regardless of race, colour, religion, sex or nationality, have the right to –
1. **LIFE**
2. **EQUALITY**
3. **A NAME** and a **NATIONALITY**
4. **FREEDOM** to hold and express an **OPINION**
5. **FREEDOM** of **THOUGHT**, **CONSCIENCE** and **RELIGION** (including the right to enjoy their own culture and practise their own religion and language if a member of a minority community)
6. **EDUCATION** aimed at developing his/her personality and talents; preparation for adult life; fostering respect for basic human rights; and developing respect for cultural and national values
7. **PROTECTION** from – interference with privacy, family, home and correspondence; libel & slander; kidnapping; physical/mental violence, injury or abuse, neglect or exploitation; work which is a threat to health, education or development; drug abuse; sexual exploitation; sale, trafficking or abduction; torture, cruel treatment, capital punishment, life imprisonment, unlawful arrest or imprisonment; the effects of armed conflict; harmful materials in the media
8. **SPECIAL CARE** and **PROTECTION** if they are handicapped, refugees or victims of neglect, maltreatment, exploitation or torture
9. The **BENEFITS** of–an adequate standard of living; social security; health and medical services; leisure and play; respect for their human rights if accused or guilty of committing an offence
10. **BE SUPPORTED** in their upbringing and development by both parents, and only be adopted if it is in their best interests

QUESTIONS

1. Write your own definition of 'Human Rights'.
2. What would you list as your top four human rights? Write a sentence about each one, explaining why it is important.
3. Why are the Helsinki Agreements important for human rights?

ACTIVITY

In groups of four, discuss the ways in which the rights of children, set out in the *UN Convention on the Rights of the Child (1990)*, are different from those for adults described in the *Universal Declaration of Human Rights*. Prepare a summary of the special rights which apply to children.

The United Nations Organisation and human rights

The Charter of the United Nations (1945) begins by reaffirming a, 'faith in fundamental human rights, in the dignity and worth of the human person, in the equal rights of men and women and of nations large and small.'

Its aims include, 'promoting and encouraging respect for human rights and for fundamental freedoms for all without distinction as to race, sex, language or religion.'

It is equally true, however, that the UN cannot interfere in matters which are the responsibility of an individual country's Government. This means that the UN finds it very difficult to protect human rights in many parts of the world. The UN has continually since 1945 investigated, discussed and tried to assess a large number of human rights problems. It has made recommendations and has suggested what action should be taken to improve matters.

UN Resolutions are decisions taken by the member countries which are policies which all members are expected to follow, e.g. after the invasion of Kuwait by Iraq in 1990, the UN Security Council adopted Resolutions which said that Iraq must withdraw its forces, UN member countries should stop trading with Iraq and the Iraqi Government should free foreign hostages.

UN Headquarters, New York City

THE UNITED NATIONS IS INTERESTED IN HUMAN RIGHTS FOR –

* CHILDREN
* REFUGEES
* STATELESS PERSONS
* WOMEN (EQUAL RIGHTS)
* VICTIMS OF WAR (MILITARY and CIVILIANS)
* VICTIMS OF RACIAL DISCRIMINATION
* VICTIMS OF APARTHEID
* PEOPLE IN SLAVERY
* FORCED LABOUR
* MIGRANT WORKERS
* VICTIMS OF DISCRIMINATION IN EMPLOYMENT

The parts of the UN responsible for human rights suffer from the difficulties which affect the whole of the UN because it does not have power over individual Governments. Any action the UN takes, therefore, is often slow and not completely effective.

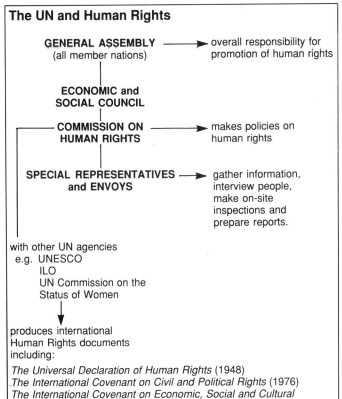

The UN and Human Rights

GENERAL ASSEMBLY ——→ overall responsibility for
(all member nations)   promotion of human rights

ECONOMIC and
SOCIAL COUNCIL

COMMISSION ON ——→ makes policies on
HUMAN RIGHTS   human rights

SPECIAL REPRESENTATIVES ——→ gather information,
and ENVOYS   interview people,
         make on-site
         inspections and
         prepare reports.

with other UN agencies
 e.g. UNESCO
    ILO
    UN Commission on the
    Status of Women

produces international
Human Rights documents
including:
The Universal Declaration of Human Rights (1948)
The International Covenant on Civil and Political Rights (1976)
The International Covenant on Economic, Social and Cultural Rights (1976)
The Convention on the Rights of the Child (1990)

The UN and Iraq

August 1990
… Iraqi troops invade Kuwait

Threat to human rights
… Kuwait now part of Iraq against the wishes of the Kuwaiti people
… Foreign workers taken as hostages to be used as a 'human shield' at airbases, military bases, oil refineries and industrial centres

UN response
… Resolutions that Iraq withdraw from Kuwait, foreign hostages to be released and no UN member to trade with Iraq
… UN Secretary General visits Jordan to meet Iraqi foreign minister to demand release of hostages

Superpower response
… Forces sent to Gulf area by USA and other countries to defend Saudi Arabia against possible invasion by Iraq
… Meeting between President Bush and Mr Gorbachev in Helsinki to agree to cooperate against Iraq within the framework of the UN Resolutions.

In this human rights crisis the UN was effective in organising world opinion against Iraq and was influential in getting women and children hostages set free.

Convention on child rights wins approval

AFTER ten years of negotiations and controversy, the United Nations General Assembly yesterday unanimously adopted the first Convention on the Rights of the Child, thereby creating the most comprehensive treaty in history for the protection of children.

The convention draws together in a single document the key provisions of existing international declarations affecting children. It breaks new ground on adoption, survival, protection from sexual exploitation and drug abuse.

A special signing ceremony will be held in January for states to ratify the convention, which then makes the provisions of the treaty binding on the signatories and requires them to report back to a UN monitoring group. Twenty states have to ratify the convention before it becomes international law.

The 54-article document is a compromise that leaves enough room for difference on religion, adoption and other issues. – Reuter

(source: *The Scotsman*, 21 November 1989.)

Refugees from Kuwait board a Soviet transport plane. They were seated on mattresses and held on to ropes for take-off and landing

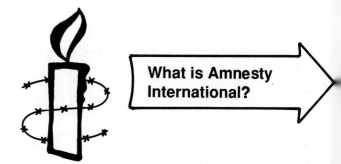

What is Amnesty International?

The work of Amnesty International

Many voluntary and charitable organisations all over the world fight for human rights. Probably the most important of these is Amnesty International (AI). It was set up in 1961 when a British lawyer, Peter Benenson, wrote a newspaper article calling on people in all walks of life to begin working peacefully for the release of prisoners. These 'prisoners of conscience' were the thousands of men and women imprisoned throughout the world for their political and religious beliefs. AI is now the world's largest international voluntary organisation dealing with human rights. It has over 500 000 members and has supporters in more than 150 countries.

How Does It Work?

When the news of an arrest reaches Amnesty, the facts are examined to establish if the victim is a prisoner of conscience. The case is then 'adopted' by one of the worldwide network of Amnesty groups. Letters are sent to governments, embassies, leading newspapers and the prisoner's family and friends. In addition, members organise public meetings and arrange special publicity events, such as vigils at embassies. They collect signatures for international petitions and raise money to send relief, such as medicine, food, and clothing, to the prisoners and their families. In the case of prisoners facing torture or the death penalty, Amnesty International uses an Urgent Action Scheme which generates a flood of telegrams and express letters to the appropriate government authorities.

How Does Amnesty International Get Its Information?

Amnesty International attaches great importance to impartial and accurate reporting of facts. Its activities depend on meticulous research into allegations of human rights violations. The International Secretariat in London (with a staff of nearly 300, comprising some 35 nationalities) has a Research Department which collects and analyses information from a wide variety of sources...

Amnesty International also sends fact-finding missions for on-the-spot investigations and to observe trials, meet prisoners and interview government officials.

What is Amnesty International?

...a worldwide movement which is independent of any government, political faction, ideology, economic interest, or religious creed. Its activities focus strictly on prisoners:

–it seeks the **release** of prisoners of conscience. These are men and women detained anywhere for their beliefs, colour, sex, ethnic origin, language or religion who have neither used nor advocated violence.

–it advocates **fair and early trials** for **all political prisoners** and works on behalf of such people detained without charge or without trial.

–it opposes the **death penalty** and **torture** or other cruel, inhuman or degrading treatment or punishment of **all prisoners** without reservation.

AMNESTY INTERNATIONAL is a volunteer organisation and is financed entirely by subscriptions and donations...
AMNESTY INTERNATIONAL was awarded the Nobel Peace Prize in 1977 for its 'activity for the defence of human worth against degrading treatment, violence and torture.' This was followed in 1978 by the United Nations Human Rights Prize.

Where Do The Prisoners Come From?

Amnesty has evidence of prisoners of conscience being held in nearly half the countries of the world, and at the present time Amnesty has adopted prisoners in more than 60 countries. In over 50 countries citizens can be detained without charge or trial, and in 134 nations the death penalty is in force – in many for politically related offences. Prisoners are being tortured in one out of every three countries.

KEYWORDS

The following Keywords are used in this Unit. Make sure you have understood what they mean.

human rights   **Amnesty International**
Universal Declaration of Human Rights

How You Can Help

Many people feel strongly that political imprisonment, torture and executions are wrong but believe that there is little they can do. Amnesty International has shown that this is not so. These are the ways in which you can actively work for the release of prisoners of conscience:

Become A Member

Affiliate
Ask your club, trade union branch, society, school or church to become an affiliated member.

Join the Urgent Action Scheme
Some prisoners need immediate aid, perhaps because they might be tortured or executed.

Write A Letter
Take part in Amnesty's Letter Writing Campaign – each edition of our magazine 'Amnesty' carries details of prisoners in need of help. They may be facing execution, be ill or have been detained for a prolonged period in severe conditions. Send special letters or cards on behalf of these prisoners to government authorities as proof of the mounting weight of public opinion.

Join A Group

Send A Donation

Amnesty International
will only be satisfied when it is redundant. Only when the use of torture and the death penalty become as unthinkable as slavery, only when political imprisonment is recognised as a degrading answer to the challenge of ideas, will the work of Amnesty International become unnecessary.
The world is a long way from that point.

(Reprinted with the permission of Amnesty International, British Section.)

A CTIVITIES

1. Imagine you are a member of AI. Write a letter to a government or a newspaper protesting at the illegal imprisonment of a prisoner.

2. You have been invited to a public meeting to outline the aims and activities of AI. Write a speech, to last about five minutes, which you would make.

3. Find out more about AI by writing to them for information. Your teacher will give you guidance about your letter.

HUMAN RIGHTS IN THE USA

'We hold these truths to be self-evident, that all men are created equal, that they are endowed by their Creator with certain unalienable rights. Among these are Life, Liberty and the Pursuit of Happiness. ...Whenever any form of government becomes destructive of these ends, it is the Right of the People to alter or abolish it...'
(President Thomas Jefferson, 1776)

'Give me your tired, your poor, Your huddled masses yearning to breathe free. The wretched refuse of your teeming shore. Send these, the homeless, tempest-tost to me. I lift my lamp beside the golden door.'
(Inscription on the Statue of Liberty, New York)

Human rights – USA

The USA is a democratic country (see Chapter 1) which prides itself in allowing individual people a great amount of freedom in their daily lives without interference by the Government. It is sometimes referred to as 'the land of the free'. The very first British settlers who went to America in the seventeenth century went because of the opportunities and freedom which were offered – to own land, to become rich if they worked hard, and to follow their own religion. At the time America won its independence from Britain in 1776, this emphasis on freedom and the rights of the individual was recognised by the new American Government.

Jefferson was really talking about political freedom, but the US Constitution of 1787 stated that Americans had individual rights to life, liberty and the protection of their property, which were their 'birthright' – they couldn't be taken away by anyone. The idea that all Americans are created equal and are free to follow their own chosen way of life and take advantage of the wealth and opportunities in the USA is still important today. The 'American Dream' is that anyone can be successful and wealthy if they work hard enough.

The inscription on the Statue of Liberty at the entrance to New York harbour suggests that everyone is welcome in the USA. In fact, many people have found that the 'American Dream' does not exist for them. Later in this Unit we will look at the problems of the American Indians, black people and Hispanic people in the USA, and the problem of violence and crime for all Americans as a result of the freedom to carry guns.

In its relations with other countries, particularly the Soviet Union, the USA has put forward the idea of being the defender of the 'free world' and the protector of human rights. While there is some truth in this, we will see that the USA does not always uphold the human rights of its own people or of people in other countries. Presidents of the USA have often criticised other countries for restricting the human rights of their people, while doing little to improve the human rights of some groups of people in the USA.

Melting Pot or Salad Bowl?

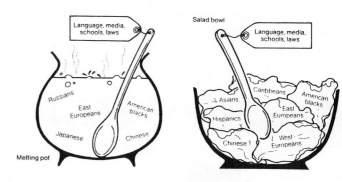

The American people

The population of the United States of America is made up of people from many different backgrounds. Along with the original inhabitants of America, the American Indians, there are many millions of people who have come, or whose ancestors came from, Europe, Central America, the Caribbean and Asia.

The mixture of these different groups has been described as the 'melting pot', in which they all became American citizens because they lived under the same laws, went to the same schools, were influenced by the same TV programmes and newspapers and spoke the same language – English. More recently this situation has been described as the 'salad bowl', in which the different groups live in the same country, but keep their own identities, customs and beliefs.

Whichever description is the more accurate for the USA in the 1990s, all these groups of people are supposed to enjoy equal human rights in the USA today. Unfortunately, many examples of differences still exist.

QUESTIONS

1. Why is the USA sometimes called 'the land of the free'?
2. What is the 'American Dream'?
3. Why has the USA been a popular destination for immigrants?
4. Which groups do not share in the 'American Dream'?

Jesse Jackson

Martin Luther King Jr.

Blacks in the USA

Black people in the USA have always been different from other groups of immigrants because they were originally taken to America as slaves to work on tobacco and cotton plantations. As slaves they had no human rights at all, and were bought and sold like cattle.

After the American Civil War in the nineteenth century, slavery was abolished but life for black people did not improve in spite of their freedom. In the 'Deep South' where most of the black population lived, they were kept apart from the whites by laws, by prejudice and by not being able to vote in elections. During the twentieth century many black people have moved to the large cities in the northern USA and to California in search of jobs and prosperity. They have frequently met with little success, having to live in the poorer parts of the cities. Areas such as Harlem in New York and Watts in Los Angeles became black ghettoes, where the blacks suffered from widespread poverty and discrimination.

In the 1950s, the Civil Rights Movement was an attempt by black people to achieve equal rights by peaceful means. This non-violent protest movement had some major successes. In 1954 the US Supreme Court ruled that all schools were to be mixed. In 1964 the Civil Rights Act prohibited racial discrimination and in 1965 the Voting Rights Act made it illegal to prevent blacks from voting. In spite of these successes, however, black people still suffered from poverty and social inequality. Few had good jobs or decent houses, and hardly any were elected to important positions. A new type of black protest movement known as 'Black Power' developed, and it used more violent methods to fight for the rights of black people. Demonstrations and violent riots in US cities dominated newspaper headlines and television screens. Race relations became one of the biggest problems facing the US Government.

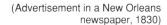

NEGROES FOR SALE – A negro woman, 24 years of age, and her two children, one eight and the other three years old. Said negroes will be sold SEPARATELY or together, as desired. The woman is a good seamstress. She will be sold low for cash or exchanged for groceries. For terms apply to Matthew Bliss & Co.

(Advertisement in a New Orleans newspaper, 1830)

Malcolm X, Black Muslim leader

Even by the late 1960s, the Kerner Commission which was set up to investigate the causes of the problem reported that:

'Our Nation is moving towards two societies, one black, one white – separate and unequal... White racism is essentially responsible for the explosive mixture which has been accumulating in our cities... The events of the summer of 1967 are in large part the culmination of 300 years of racial prejudice.'

(Kerner Commission)

Since the 1960s, race relations have gone through a much calmer period. In the 1970s blacks began to register as voters and to use their political power. Many more blacks were elected as State Representatives, and blacks became mayors in large cities such as Los Angeles, Detroit and Washington D.C. These successes did not mean that blacks had reached a position of equality with white people however. Today, black people still hold only one per cent of all elected posts in the USA, although they make up 12 per cent of the population.

Blacks in the 1980s and 1990s

Black people continued to make political progress during the 1980s. Many more black people turned out to vote at elections and more blacks were elected to positions of power. The Reverend Jesse Jackson became the first black man to try to gain Presidential nomination in the 1984 Presidential election. He wanted to bring together blacks and other minority groups, including the poor, in a movement called 'The Rainbow Coalition'. He failed in his bid to become the Democratic Presidential candidate, but he was able to get a great deal of publicity for the problems of minority groups. In the 1988 election he came even closer to becoming the Democratic candidate.

The problems Jesse Jackson highlighted continue to be problems for black people today. The black 'underclass' is at the very bottom of American society. Living most often in the ghetto areas of American cities, the main features of this 'underclass' are poor housing, poverty, ill-health, crime and drugs. It is in this sense that black people in the USA continue to be denied their basic human rights. They are trapped in the inner-city areas as the wealthier whites move out to the suburbs, where there is a better quality of life which few blacks can afford. Forty per cent of black families are headed by a single female parent, life expectancy for blacks is lower than for whites and crime rates are much higher. Inner-city schools have a much lower standard of education, with the result that their black students get only the poorest jobs if they find a job at all.

In spite of the success of many blacks who became part of the middle class during the 1970s and 1980s, the picture for the vast majority of black people is one of inequality, discrimination and prejudice.

Fire-gutted buildings in New York's Bronx district

US POPULATION in millions (1987)	
TOTAL	242.8
WHITE	205.5 (84.6%)
BLACK	29.6 (12.2%)
OTHER	7.7 (3.2%)

US % UNEMPLOYMENT RATES (1987)		
TOTAL UNEMPLOYED	6.2%	
WHITES UNEMPLOYED (TOTAL)		5.3%
(age 16–19)		14.4%
(age 20–24)		8.0%
BLACKS UNEMPLOYED (TOTAL)		13.0%
(age 16–19)		34.7%
(age 20–24)		21.8%
HISPANICS UNEMPLOYED (TOTAL)		8.8%

AVERAGE WEEKLY EARNINGS IN US$ (1987)	WHITE	BLACK	HISPANIC
Total Families with Earners	592	412	425
Married Couple Families	647	529	473
Families with one Earner	416	289	292
Families maintained by Women	329	284	285

YEARS OF SCHOOL COMPLETED (1987)	ALL PERSONS	BLACK PERSONS
% WITH LESS THAN 5 YEARS SCHOOLING	2.4	5.0
% WITH 4 YEARS AT HIGH SCHOOL OR MORE	75.6	63.4
% NOT HIGH SCHOOL GRADUATES	24.4	36.6

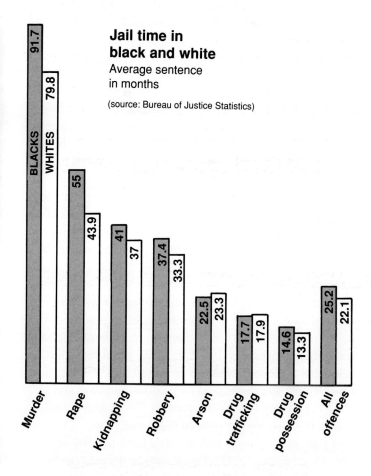

Jail time in black and white
Average sentence in months

(source: Bureau of Justice Statistics)

BLACKS / WHITES

Offence	Blacks	Whites
Murder	91.7	79.8
Rape	55	43.9
Kidnapping	41	37
Robbery	37.4	33.3
Arson	22.5	23.3
Drug trafficking	17.7	17.9
Drug possession	14.6	13.3
All offences	25.2	22.1

*Q*UESTIONS

1. Describe the difference between the 'melting pot' and the 'salad bowl'.
2. How do black people differ from other groups or immigrants?
3. Describe how life has improved for black people in the USA during the 1960s and 1970s.
4. Describe the problems faced by black people in the 1980s and 1990s.

*A*CTIVITY

In groups of four, look carefully at the tables and charts of unemployment, earnings and income, poverty, education, health and crime. The Factfile on page 40 also contains some useful information. Your group has to present a petition to the US President, *either* supporting the view that black people are denied human rights in the USA, *or* arguing that they are not really discriminated against. Use the evidence to prepare a protest document of not more than 200 words, arguing your group's case to the President.

%POPULATION BELOW THE OFFICIAL POVERTY LEVEL (1987)

	PERSONS	FAMILIES
TOTAL	13.5%	10.8%
WHITE	10.5%	8.2%
BLACK	33.1%	29.9%
HISPANIC	28.2%	25.8%

OF POPULATION COVERED BY HEALTH INSURANCE (1985)

	WHITE	BLACK	HISPANIC
...vered by private health insurance	79.6	55.7	55.2
...vered by MEDICAID	5.0	21.6	15.9
...t covered by any health insurance	12.4	19.3	27.0

HOMICIDE VICTIMS: RATE PER 100 000 POPULATION (1986)

Total		9.0
White	Male	8.6
	Female	3.0
Black	Male	55.0
	Female	12.1

PRISONERS IN THE USA (1987)

	WHITE	BLACK	OTHER RACES
% of Inmates	54.2	42.0	3.6
Number of prisoners under sentence of death (actual no.)	1138	— 846 —	
Number of prisoners executed	13	12	NIL

(source of all Tables: US Bureau of the Census, Statistical Abstract of the United States: 1989 (109th edition), Washington, DC, 1989.)

Equal before the law?

'It seems as if there's justice for Whites only in this society.'

(Will Smith, Black minister of religion, Texas, 1988)

'There is a view in this country that if you're poor or Black or Hispanic or Native American, you won't get a fair deal...
And the basic contentions that there are biases at every level of the system are well-founded.'
(James B. Eaglin, Chairman, National Association of Blacks in Criminal Justice)

In July 1988 a jury in the town of Hemphill, Texas, (pop. 1350) found three white police officers not guilty of violating the civil rights of Loyal Garner. He was a black truck driver who had been arrested for drunk driving and who died, allegedly after being beaten in jail. Of the 200 blacks in Hemphill, only one was on the jury. Lee Handy, a 45-year-old cleaner, believed the policemen were guilty, but she voted for them to be acquitted because, "I was just one black against all those white people." There are many more recent examples of cases in which there is some doubt about whether black people receive fair treatment in courts in the USA.

The American Indians

As well as black people, there are other minority groups which suffer from racial discrimination and social and economic problems in the USA today.

The American Indians have long been the forgotten people of the USA, limited to living on 'Reservations'. These original people of America have had little opportunity to become part of the 'melting pot' or the 'salad bowl'. Many find it difficult to make a living. They rely on craft industries and selling souvenirs to tourists. The American film industry for many years showed the Indians as wild, uneducated savages who had to be destroyed so that the white people could bring progress to America. This image, created by Hollywood, is far from the truth. The American Indians, robbed of their land and their food supply, were exploited and cheated as the white settlers pushed 'civilisation' westwards.

In spite of the fact that public opinion is changing, and now many white Americans such as Burt Reynolds and Marlon Brando have openly admitted and been proud of their Indian ancestry, the vast majority of American Indians continue to be disadvantaged, and many live in real poverty.

A Navajo woman weaving, Utah, USA

Wife of jailed American Indian in Moscow

THE HISTORY of American Indians is a history of their struggle for their rights, and Leonard Peltier is a symbol of that struggle, Stephanie Peltier, wife of jailed activist Leonard Peltier, told a press conference on her arrival at Moscow's Sheremietevo airport last week.

Stephanie Peltier was part of an American delegation from the committee in defence of Leonard Peltier, in the USSR at the invitation of the Soviet Peace Committee.

Human rights are constantly violated in the United States and what is important is international support for the just struggle of the American Indians, because the US government has to reckon with world opinion, Mrs Peltier stressed.

"We are confident that if we achieve a retrial Leonard Peltier will be released. Not only are we spiritually and morally right, we are also legally right," she pointed out.

Stephanie Peltier also visited the offices of the Soviet newspaper **Komsomolskaya Pravda** which has been conducting a campaign in defence of Leonard Peltier. Over 13 million signatures have been collected demanding that the White House release than man fighting for the rights of the American Indians.

"We hope that the campaign of solidarity with my husband launched in the Soviet Union will be an example which the public of other countries will follow," Stephanie Peltier said.

Letters from young people, from the USSR, Holland, Canada, Poland and all over the world have boosted confidence in the just nature of the cause and have inspired all American Indians with the hope that truth will ultimately triumph and Leonard Peltier will again be free.

The policy of the US administration towards the indigenous population of America has always been based on colonialism and neo-colonialism and the suppression and physical elimination of Indians, said Billy Joe Wahpepah, of the International Council for Observance of the Indian Treaties at the UN.

According to Wahpepah the US authorities have been stepping up suppression of the Indians' movement.

In the Soviet Union the past two years had seen the publication in the mass editions of three books on American Indian history and culture.

(source: *Soviet Weekly*, 18 January 1986.)

ACTIVITIES

1. Describe the problems of the American Indians today.

2. Read the newspaper article, 'Wife of jailed American Indian in Moscow'. Describe how the Soviet Union has tried to help Leonard Peltier. Why might this article be said to contain biased views about human rights in the USA?

The Hispanics

The largest minority group after the blacks are the Hispanics. There are believed to be around 12 million Spanish-speaking people in the USA, 3.5 million Puerto Ricans and possibly as many as seven million illegal immigrants, mainly from Mexico. About one-fifth of the populations of California and Texas are Hispanics. The Hispanics suffer similar problems to the blacks; more than 20 per cent live below the poverty line and their level of unemployment is almost double that of white Americans.

The Hispanics are not one united group of people with a common background and interests. Cubans have tended to prosper in the USA, and as a result have become the enemies of those blacks who see the Cubans as having leap-frogged over them to take jobs and incomes while the blacks remain in poverty. On the other hand, the extreme racist group, the Ku Klux Klan,

QUESTIONS

1. Who are the Hispanics?
2. 'The Hispanics are not one united group.' Explain this statement.
3. What problems do the Hispanics have in the USA today?

ACTIVITY

Refer to the tables and charts. Write a speech of no more than 100 words which a Hispanic spokesperson might make to the press, putting forward the view that her or his group are the poorest people in the USA today.

has threatened Cubans as well as blacks. Most of the Mexican Americans who have come to the USA to find jobs still find themselves near the bottom of the pile.

Violent America

One result of the emphasis on individual rights and freedoms in the USA is that gun laws are much less strict than in most other countries. Everyone has seen films in which the settlers protect their families and land against the enemy with their rifles or pistols. Cowboy films in which the Colt 45 is used to shoot down the bandits were Hollywood's biggest attractions for many years, featuring stars such as John Wayne and Clint Eastwood. More recently, gangster films and films about 'heroes' such as Rambo have been shown in cinemas throughout the USA and other countries.

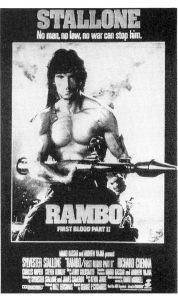

Sylvester Stallone as Rambo

The one thing which all of these films have in common is their emphasis on violence. In many cases these films may be seen as a reflection of North American society. The carrying of guns is seen by many US citizens as something they have a moral and constitutional right to do. It is part of their history. The National Rifle Association is a powerful organisation which has over three million members and persuades the US Government to continue to allow people to own and use guns. The problem is that many people's rights are destroyed because they are victims of shootings and other crimes. The USA's gun laws could be seen as a threat to the human rights of many American people.

Why violence?

There are many reasons for the high level of violence in some areas of the USA. In the ghetto areas of the cities, violence is often the result of poverty and frustration. Unemployment is another reason, especially among some of the minority groups. Violence can also erupt when there are large sudden inflows of immigrants, such as the Cubans into Florida. Drugs are increasingly a cause of violence – either directly or because of the need for money to buy them.

The most important reason, however, is that guns of all types are easily available. It was estimated in 1989 that between 50 and 60 million US households owned at least one gun – that is one in every two households in the country.

> 'A well-regulated militia, being necessary to the security of a free State, the right of the people to keep and bear arms shall not be infringed.'
>
> (US Constitution)

Although some states have laws against the illegal possession of guns, and others have licensing laws, guns are easily available from pawnshops and gunshops in most states. Many shops advertise openly and guns are available through mail order catalogues.

John Lennon shot dead

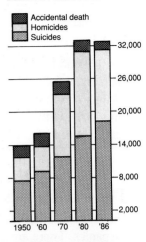

DEATH BY FIREARMS

- Accidental death
- Homicides
- Suicides

32,000 — 26,000 — 20,000 — 14,000 — 8,000 — 2,000

1950 '60 '70 '80 '86

John Lennon (40) one of the founders of the Liverpool pop group The Beatles, was shot dead as he was returning to his Manhattan apartment with his wife Yoko Ono on Monday night. A 25-year-old man from Hawaii has been charged with his murder. He had apparently had his copy of Lennon's new record autographed earlier in the day but accosted the singer as he got out of his car. There was an argument and Lennon was shot five times.

(source: *Guardian Weekly*, 14 December 1980)

SENSELESS SHOOTINGS – WHOSE RIGHTS?

April 1987 – William Bryan Cruse (59) shot 16 people, 6 fatally, at a shopping mall in Palm Bay, Florida. He apparently became angry when a teenager walked on his lawn.

weapon used: .223-cal. rifle

February 1988 – Richard Wade Farley (39) allegedly shot to death 7 employees of a Sunnyvale, California, computer company after being dismissed from his job with the company.

weapon used: 12-gauge shotgun

May 1988 – Laurie Wasserman Dann (30) killed 1 student and wounded 5 others at an elementary (primary) school in Winnetka, Illinois.

weapons used: .357 Magnum pistol, .22-cal. pistol, .32-cal. pistol

January 1989 – Patrick Purdy (26) killed 5 Asian-American children and wounded 30 other people in the playground of an elementary school in Stockton, California, before fatally shooting himself.

weapons used: AK-47-style rifle, 9-mm pistol

February 1989 – A gunman opened fire on 200 students leaving Woodrow Wilson High School in Washington D.C., wounding 4, after an earlier argument in the school. Police arrested an 18 year old suspect, Rodney Reardon.

weapon used: 9-mm semiautomatic handgun

February 1989 – Willie Howard Womack Jr. (26) enraged by his sacking as an errand runner shot and wounded 2 employees of a car dealership in Norfolk, Virginia, before killing himself.

weapons used: AK-47-style rifle, .32-cal. derringer, .22-cal. pistol

What could be done?

1. The Federal Government could ban the import or sale of paramilitary weapons to civilians.
2. A Federal Law could be introduced to force buyers to provide detailed background information about themselves, with charges for making false statements.
3. A waiting time could be set to allow time for checks on background to be made.
4. Private transfers of guns should only be allowed through licensed gun dealers so that up-to-date records of ownership are kept.
5. Individual States could license all gun owners and keep information so that records can be easily investigated.

> **IT IS EASIER TO BUY A GUN IN THE UNITED STATES THAN IT IS TO GET A LICENCE TO DRIVE A CAR.**

*Q*UESTIONS

1. Whose human rights are at risk in violent America?
2. Why is there so much violence in the USA?
3. How might the US Constitution be said to be to blame for violence in the USA today?
4. What actions could the US Government take to reduce the level of violence?

*A*CTIVITY

Organise a class debate on the subject of, 'The people of the USA have an inalienable right to keep and use arms.' Your teacher will help you with the organisation of the debate.

The Drug Menace

Many of the violent crimes committed in the United States are related to drugs. But apart from crimes, which result from drug habits, many millions of Americans have their lives ruined by drugs. It is probably the biggest social problem in the country today, and President Bush has said that he will fight the drug menace. In February 1990 Bush met with the leaders of the three South American countries which are the source of virtually all of the world's cocaine – Peru, Bolivia and Colombia. This was an attempt to step up the war against the drug lords.

But many US drug experts do not think that the war against drugs can be won simply by waging war on the suppliers. An attack has to be made on the demand for drugs by the 14.5 million users who spend an estimated $100 billion on illegal drugs every year. Education does not seem to have much effect, and more police and prisons to cope with bigger jail sentences for offenders would be very costly. The US Government has a very difficult problem to solve, but there are signs that it is not doing everything possible to solve it. Government studies of the drug problem show that it is getting worse among the poor non-white 'underclass'. This increasing proportion of the population receives little interest or sympathy from politicians, and the queues of addicts at drug treatment centres are becoming longer and longer.

This large group of people lives in despair, more and more cut off from ordinary American society. Many addicts are poor, unemployed and have no future outside the ghetto. Many are also involved in crime. They are increasingly bitter about their position in the land of freedom and opportunity. It would be easy to say that drug users have only themselves to blame. But the Government must also bear part of the responsibility for the despair and helplessness felt by many of these people. The drug menace, and the failure to attack it successfully, are a threat to the human rights of many millions of people.

COCAINE KIDS

Terry Williams of the City University, New York, spent four years studying a teenage cocaine-selling group. In his report, *Cocaine Kids*, he says:

'Many teenagers are drawn to work in the cocaine trade simply because they want jobs, full time or even casual labour. The drug business is a safety-net of sorts where it is always possible to make a few dollars...'

'Money and drugs are the obvious immediate rewards. But there is another strong motivating force, and that is the desire to show family and friends that they can succeed at something. A kid who can routinely handle money, control personal use of cocaine, deal with buyers and control a weapon, may make it out of the street and into the world of the superdealer...'

In fact, only one of the original group of eight was still dealing when Williams completed his study. The others had got out of a very dangerous business.

(From *Cocaine Kids* by Terry Williams, City University of New York, 1989.)

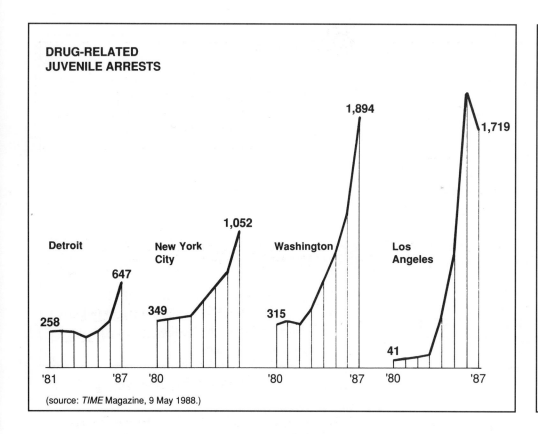

DRUG-RELATED JUVENILE ARRESTS

Detroit: 258 ('81) ... 647 ('87)
New York City: 349 ('80) ... 1,052
Washington: 315 ('80) ... 1,894 ('87)
Los Angeles: 41 ('80) ... 1,719 ('87)

(source: *TIME* Magazine, 9 May 1988.)

THE BIG SUPPLIERS
1989 production in tonnes

Coca leaves

Peru	110 000
Bolivia	70 000
Colombia	20 000

Opium

Burma	1 300
Afghanistan	750
Iran	300
Laos	250

Marijuana

Mexico	4 750
Colombia	2 700
Jamaica	400

(source: *TIME* Magazine 28 August 1989.)

"I'm Going to Detroit"

The hardscrabble town of Marianna, Ark. (pop. 6,200), near the Mississippi River, has no movie theater but plenty of boarded-up storefronts. Summer work for teenagers can mean wrenching labor in the rice and soybean fields. Young black men know that if they want something better, they have to go elsewhere.

Enter the four Chambers brothers – Larry, Billy Joe, Willie Lee and Otis – who blew into their old hometown driving gleaming BMWs and Camaros, sporting gold chains and fancy clothes. When they offered ambitious young men $2,000 a month to return with them to Detroit, they had no shortage of takers. Over four years, some 150 young men, most between the ages of 17 and 21, made the trip north. Recalls Michael Vondran Jr., 17: "People were saying, 'I'm going to Detroit, I'm going to Detroit.' No one really knew what they were getting into."

What the young recruits found was not what they had been promised. At the height of their empire, the Chambers gang controlled about half of Detroit's crack trade, running 200 drug houses, supplying some 500 more and raking in $3 million a week. They key to their success was the supply of green kids from Marianna, who were subjected to a regimen far more harrowing than Marine boot camp.

The young men who, became runners, couriers and dealers were threatened and abused. The trick in the crack trade, police say, is to keep people in line. If the Chamberses' recruits tried to flee, the brothers knew where to find them. "A Chicago kid might be able to leave, but not a kid from Marianna," says the town's police chief, Mark Birchler.

Youths caught sampling the cocaine were roughed up. The punishment for stealing could be permanent: one Marianna boy returned with mangled fingers. To exact obedience, the brothers sometimes deliberately shorted the boys on the crack that was parceled out for them to sell. When the receipts came up short, the boys were forced to work off their shortages, which kept them in bondage for months at a time. "They ran everything on fear and intimidation," says Birchler.

Not everyone stayed intimidated. In February tips from disaffected Marianna youths led to criminal indictments in Detroit against the four Chambers brothers, as well as 18 others, including many from Marianna.

Today Marianna is a town traumatized by its past. Some of the young men who left as country bumpkins returned as hardened criminals. About half of those indicted are still at large, and people are terrified that the Chamberses will try to get even. There have been several fire bombings, including one directed at a woman who testified against a Chambers brother. Yet one fact about Marianna remains the same. Says Councilman Roy Lewellen: "I can't think of eight black teenagers who are employed."

(source: *TIME* magazine, 9 May 1988.)

1. Why is the drug problem, 'the biggest social problem in the USA today'?
2. Which groups of people are most at risk from the problem?
3. Why might the US Government not be doing everything possible to solve the problem?

*A*CTIVITY

In a group, draw up a list of suggestions which you would put to the US Government to tackle the problem of drugs. Refer to the information about the problem contained in this Unit.

Equal Rights for Women–The Women's Movement

In a 1989 telephone poll of 1000 US women, the following issues were given as being the six most important in the USA today:

Equal pay with men	**94%**
Creche facilities at work	**90%**
Protection from rape	**88%**
Maternity leave from work	**84%**
Ending job discrimination	**82%**
Abortion	**74%**

Non-professional women, poor women and women in minority groups feel their needs have been largely ignored by the women's movement. They want:

PROBLEMS FOR WOMEN IN THE USA TODAY
- The Wage-Gap: women earn 66c, men $1, for the same work
- 59% of women work in low-paid jobs
- More than 60% of adults below the poverty line are women
- After divorce, women and their children suffer a 73% fall in their standard of living (ex-husbands enjoy a 42% rise in standard of living)
- Working wives still do 75% of household chores

Access to education
Better health care
Safe neighbourhoods for their children

MEDIAN WEEKLY EARNINGS (1987) in US$		
		$
ALL WORKERS		373
MALE		433
	White	450
	Black	326
	Hispanic	306
FEMALE		303
	White	307
	Black	275
	Hispanic	251

MEMBERS OF US CONGRESS (1989)		
	MEN	WOMEN
Representatives	410	25
Senators	98	2

*Q*UESTIONS

1. In what ways are women's human rights denied in the USA today?
2. What special problems are suffered by poor and minority group women?

*A*CTIVITY

Find out more about the work of the Women's Movement in the USA.

'All men are created equal'?

The USA is one of the wealthiest countries in the world. Most Americans enjoy a lifestyle and standard of living which is the envy of people in many other countries. There are many opportunities for people to be successful and wealthy.

From what you have read in this Unit you will have seen that there are also large numbers of Americans who live in poverty and despair. They appear to be less equal than the others. Torture, illegal imprisonment and slavery may not be features of life in the United States in the 1990s, but human rights are under threat. A country in which so many people live in misery and are denied the basic rights of equality, decent housing, reasonable standards of living, employment and freedom from the threat of violence and the drug menace, cannot honestly claim to be a country in which everyone enjoys equal human rights.

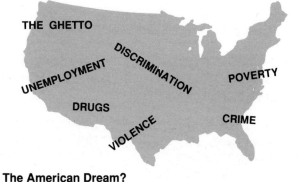

The American Dream?

A Soviet view of Human Rights in the USA
VSEVOLOD SOFINSKY, Soviet expert at the UN Human Rights Commission, comments

Another decade of rights and wrongs

WHEN the covenant was still just being developed, many capitalist countries frankly admitted that it could not be fulfilled under capitalism....

And when you look at their reports [to the UN] – sometimes delivered years late – you can see why.

They reveal failure to comply with the covenant and in some cases outright violations of the rights it proclaims.

The Western countries suffer mass unemployment, and in some cases no unemployment benefits are paid.

In most Western countries, the pay gap between men and women is getting wider. Women get half what men do in some Canadian industries.

In some Western countries the majority of workers remain unorganised, as employers hinder unionisation in every way.

Western governments have reported millions of adults illiterate. The covenant proclaims the right to education. But in Japan secondary and higher education are very expensive, and hardly within the reach of the masses.

National minorities and the indigenous population in Western countries suffer even more from violation of their rights, with higher unemployment rates and poorer education....

The covenant has been signed by 81 states, including all the countries of the socialist community. Many others are considering signing.

But the United States has not done so. It has failed to sign the overwhelming majority of international laws on human rights.

The rampage of racism, the policy of genocide towards the country's Indian population, police repressions against dissenters and attacks on trade unions are routine in the USA.

Unemployment there has reached a post-war record. Women average 62 per cent of men's pay – not surprising since Congress repeatedly turns down the Equal Rights Amendment.

Black workers in the USA are paid on average 88 per cent of what white workers get. Black women get 79 per cent of white women's pay.

Officially 35 million Americans live in poverty. There are six million beggars and three million homeless. A government report in 1984 said hunger was widespread and would remain so for a long time to come.

One US Congressman said in October 1984 that the United States had a more effective system for looking after stray dogs and cats than for the homeless people.

The International Covenant on Economic, Social and Cultural Rights was certainly an important step on the road to putting the UN Charter requirements on human rights into practice.

But there is clearly a glaring contradiction between the convention and reality in some far from poor countries.

(source: *Soviet Weekly*, 21 December 1985.)

Q UESTION

What are the main problems for human rights in the USA, according to Vsevolod Sofinsky, a Soviet human rights expert?

A CTIVITY

'All men are created equal'. Write a paragraph saying whether or not you agree with this description of life in the USA today. Your paragraph should contain reasons to back up your point of view.

KEYWORDS

The following Keywords are used in this Unit. Make sure you have understood what they mean.

melting pot
salad bowl

discrimination
prejudice

HUMAN RIGHTS IN THE SOVIET UNION

Equality of Citizen's Rights

❝Citizens of the USSR are equal before the law, without distinction of origin, social or property status, race or nationality, sex, education, language, attitude to religion, type of occupation, domicile, or other status.❞ *(Article 34)*

❝Women and men have equal rights in the USSR.❞ *(Article 35)*

❝Citizens of the USSR of different races and nationalities have equal rights.❞ *(Article 36)*

Basic Rights of Citizens

❝Citizens of the USSR have the right to work (i.e. to guaranteed employment and pay...)❞ *(Article 40)*

❝Citizens of the USSR have the right to maintenance in old age, in sickness, and in the event of the complete or partial disability or loss of the breadwinner.❞ *(Article 43)*

❝Citizens of the USSR have the right to health protection.❞ *(Article 42)*

❝Citizens of the USSR have the right to housing.❞ *(Article 44)*

❝Citizens of the USSR have the right to education.❞ *(Article 45)*

❝Citizens of the USSR have the right to cultural benefits.❞ *(Article 46)*
(Constitution of the Soviet Union)

The Soviet Union has, until recently, been a one-party Communist State. In the Soviet Union great emphasis is placed on the rights of the whole people, and the rights and freedom of individuals are considered to be less important. The Government of the Soviet Union emphasises the right of all the country's people to have equal economic rights. Issues such as individual freedom receive less attention than the rights to work, to have adequate food and adequate housing.

In 1990 the American news magazine, *TIME*, chose Mikhail Gorbachev as its 'Man of the Decade', in recognition of all his efforts to promote peace throughout the world and bring about change in Eastern Europe.

Q UESTIONS

1. Which rights are considered most important in the Soviet Union?

2. Why are the rights of individual people considered less important than those of the people as a whole?

National and ethnic minorities

The many ethnic minority groups in the Soviet Union have a wide variety of customs and traditions, language and dress, and ethnic pride. The Russians are the largest group (51 per cent) in the Soviet population. Because of high birth rates among other groups and their own almost zero population growth, the Russians are likely to be in a minority of the whole USSR population by the end of the twentieth century.

The growth of national pride and the demand for freedom from Soviet rule grew rapidly in the 1980s. Many people in the fifteen Soviet republics felt that they were being denied the most basic and important human rights – freedom and independence – and they demanded release from Soviet domination. These demands for freedom followed closely on the moves towards democracy in the countries of Eastern Europe which had close links with the Soviet Union, such as Poland and Romania.

The unrest and demands for freedom caused great problems for the Soviet Government which had come to depend on the food and goods produced in the republics. One of the Soviet Union's most difficult problems for many years has been its inability to produce enough food to feed its people.

Independence for some of the republics would make this problem much worse, weakening the Soviet Government and threatening the position of Mr Gorbachev. Many of the ethnic minority groups believe that they have been exploited for many years and kept under control by force and military strength. Mr Gorbachev's policies of *glasnost* and *perestroika* have given them hope that they will soon regain their human rights.

Of a population of 289 million, 12 ethnic groups account for 89%:

Russians 51%	Tartars 2%
Ukrainians 15%	Armenians 2%
Uzbeks 6%	Tadzhiks 1%
Byelorussians 4%	Georgians 1%
Kazakhs 3%	Moldavians 1%
Azerbaijanis 2%	Lithuanians 1%

There are also more than 100 other ethnic groups.

THE IMPORTANCE OF THE REPUBLICS
(WHAT THEY PRODUCE)

REFRIGERATORS
57% Russian S.F.S.R.
12% Ukraine
11% Belorussia
6% Azerbaijan
6% Lithuania

WHEAT
48% Russian S.F.S.R.
25% Ukraine
21% Kazakhstan

MOTORS
32% Ukraine
23% Russian S.F.S.R.
13% Belorussia
11% Armenia

COTTON
60% Uzbekistan
16% Turkmenistan
11% Tadzhikistan
9% Azerbaijan
4% Kazakhstan

GAS
75% Russian S.F.S.R.
12% Turkmenistan
6% Uzbekistan
5% Ukraine

BEEF
48% Russian S.F.S.R.
24% Ukraine
8% Kazakhstan
6% Belorussia

POULTRY
55% Russian S.F.S.R.
22% Ukraine
6% Kazakhstan
4% Belorussia

TELEVISIONS
46% Russian S.F.S.R.
34% Ukraine
12% Belorussia
7% Lithuania

CORN
56% Ukraine
26 Russian S.F.S.R.
5% Moldavia

COAL
55% Russian S.F.S.R.
25% Ukraine
19% Kazakhstan

Source: PlanEcon

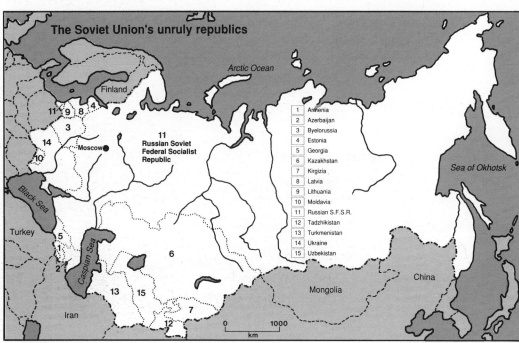

The Soviet Union's unruly republics

1	Armenia
2	Azerbaijan
3	Byelorussia
4	Estonia
5	Georgia
6	Kazakhstan
7	Kirgizia
8	Latvia
9	Lithuania
10	Moldavia
11	Russian S.F.S.R.
12	Tadzhikistan
13	Turkmenistan
14	Ukraine
15	Uzbekistan

Lithuania was the first of the 15 Soviet republics to declare itself independent in March 1990

Independence Day for Lithuania
From
RON POPESKI,

VILNIUS, Sunday. THE Soviet Baltic republic of Lithuania declared itself a sovereign state today, becoming the first of Moscow's restive republics to attempt peaceful secession.

The move, approved by the Parliament in the capital Vilnius, was announced on Lithuanian radio.

Earlier the Parliament elected a nationalist leader as president and voted to change the republic's name to the Republic of Lithuania, instead of the Lithuanian Soviet Socialist Republic.

The declaration of independence said the Republic of Lithuania was a sovereign state on the basis of its pre-Second War constitution.

Lithuania, like its sister Baltic republics of Latvia and Estonia, was part of the Russian empire but gained independence in 1918 – only to lose it again in 1940, after Josef Stalin's Red Army occupied the republic...

"The Supreme Soviet of the republic of Lithuania, expressing the will of the people, has decided and now solemnly declares that the execution of sovereign powers, which was curtailed by foreign powers in 1940, has been reinstated," the resolution said.

(source: *Glasgow Herald*, 12 March 1990.)

How the Kremlin has moved: Soviet troops have been dispatched to quell unrest throughout the empire

Spades and gas used on protesters

Eye-witnesses have said that soldiers used spades and poisonous gas on protesters in a nationalist demonstration in Tbilisi, Georgia, on 9 April. At least 19 people are known to have died, but unofficial sources put the number at over 100.

AI has urged the authorities to find out if any of those who died was deliberately killed, rather than arrested.

Unofficial sources have claimed that among those killed were 11 militiamen who were reportedly trying to protect demonstrators from members of Special Units of Internal Troops of the USSR Ministry of Internal Affairs.

The official news agency TASS said that the security forces acted "strictly in accordance with instructions on the non-use of weapons, and precautionary measures were taken, especially with regard to women and children". AI has asked for information about the instructions.

(source: *Amnesty* No. 39, June/July 1989.)

Latvia ends communists' lead role

LATVIA yesterday became the second Soviet republic to abolish the Communist Party's constitutionally guaranteed supremacy, local activists said.

The Latvian parliament voted 220-50 to follow the example of Lithuania and much of Eastern Europe, eliminating from its constitution a section that gives the Communist Party the "leading and guiding force of Soviet society," said Viysturs Koziols of the Latvian People's Front newspaper *Atmoda*.

He said the decision came after a stormy debate lasting more than three hours.

The change is expected to reduce the party's grip on all spheres of life in the Baltic republic...

(source: *The Scotsman*, 29 December 1989.)

Protest in Vilnius, Lithuania, August 1989

Vilnius, August 1989

QUESTIONS

1. Why might the Russians be concerned about the growth in population of ethnic minority groups in the Soviet Union?

2. What basic human rights do ethnic and national minority groups feel they are denied?

3. For what reasons would the Soviet Government be concerned if many Soviet republics became independent?

ACTIVITY

Collect newspaper cuttings about one of the republics which is campaigning for independence. Look for evidence of human rights violations in these cuttings.

Jews in the Soviet Union have suffered more than most other minority groups. Because of their identification with Israel and the strong, close links of the Jewish faith, the Jewish religion in the Soviet Union has been seen as an obstacle to the progress of Communism.

In the early years of Soviet Communism, many Jewish schools and synagogues were closed and many Jewish customs were banned. Because of this discrimination against them, many Jews applied to leave the Soviet Union, but visas were often refused. These refusals have been condemned as a denial of human rights, particularly in the USA which has a large Jewish population. In the 1970s the USA was able to obtain permission for many Jews to leave the Soviet Union as part of an agreement to supply much-needed US grain to feed the Soviet people. Between 1974 and 1989, more than 180 000 Soviet Jews went to the USA.

The loss of such large numbers of people caused concern in the Soviet Government because many of those who emigrated were skilled people. By the mid-1980s the number of Jews allowed to leave fell to around 1000 each year. Mr Gorbachev now allows more to leave each year. In 1986, 221 Soviet Jews arrived in Israel. In 1990, 185 000 arrived; in 1991, 400 000 were expected to make the journey. Recently there has been a rapid increase in anti-Jewish feeling in the Soviet Union as a result of increasing feelings of nationalism throughout the country.

The future success of *perestroika* depends on economic and technical help from the USA and Europe. Once again, the Soviet Union will have to allow Jews to leave the country and gain their full human rights, as part of the payment for this assistance.

QUESTIONS

1. In what ways have Jews suffered human rights problems in the Soviet Union?
2. Why can the Soviet Union not afford to lose large numbers of Jews?
3. How might *perestroika* help Soviet Jews?
4. What criticisms have been made by western countries of the treatment of Muslims in the Soviet Union?
5. How does Alim Akhmedov answer these complaints?

——— Muslims are free to work and worship ———

Candidate of Philosophy ALIM AKHMEDOV examines how Islam and socialism work alongside each other.

IF YOU WERE to believe the mass media in the West and in some Muslim countries you would think that Soviet Muslims are persecuted, deprived of religious facilities and made to give up their language and culture.

Another common theme is that they allegedly represent some sort of counter-society – a time bomb that is bound to explode.

Such stories are very far from the truth.

In the years of Soviet government the peoples of Central Asia have made great progress, in industry and agriculture and in the development of their national cultures.

Having freed Muslims from social and national oppression, socialism has given them full political, economic and personal rights, including the right to practice the religion of their choice.

There are thousands of mosques in the Soviet Union and, since the adoption of the 1977 Constitution, 69 new ones have been opened.

Muslims live mainly in the Central Asian Soviet republics – Kazakhstan, Azerbaijan, Georgia and Armenia – and in autonomous republics of the Northern Caucasus and the Volga Region.

At the time of the October Revolution in 1917, Central Asia and Kazakhstan – where most Muslims lived – were at a low economic, cultural and educational level.

Poverty and disease plagued the majority of the population and many peoples were even on the verge of extinction.

The communist party set about ending this state of affairs and ensuring full equality, progress and prosperity for all the peoples of Russia.

In Uzbekistan there are now, for example, over 10,000 schools. In most of them lessons are taught in Uzbek and in the rest – as the republic is a multinational one – subjects are taught in Karakalpak, Russian, Kazakh, Tajik, Turkmen and Kirghiz...

The Supreme Mufti of the Yemen Arab Republic, Ahmad Mohammed Zabara, said: "Over 100 different peoples inhabit the USSR. They are all equal and enjoy the same privileges.

"The religions are also equal and exist in conditions of full freedom."...

Priests are trained both in Islamic educational establishments in the Soviet Union and in the shariat departments of Islamic universities in Arab states...

Soviet Muslims, like their fellow countrymen, voluntarily and conscientiously take part in the building of their new society and in the management of its affairs...

(source: *Soviet Weekly*, 24 May 1986.)

The Dissidents

In the Soviet Union, as in many other countries, people are free to complain and protest about many things. Complaints about long queues and shortages of goods in the shops and about poor standards of housing are found in the Soviet newspapers. But there are some kinds of protest which until recently have not been allowed.

Dissent is protest against the basic political and moral beliefs of a country. The people who dissent – called **dissidents** – disagree with the Government about its beliefs and policies and write books and newspaper and magazine articles to publicise their views. For many years these unofficial writings, *samizdat*, were published secretly and passed around by 'underground' methods. These writings were banned by the Government, who saw them as attacking the State and betraying the Soviet Union.

The new climate of openness encouraged by Mr Gorbachev since 1985 has brought many of these ideas out into the open. Many of the dissidents who had been imprisoned or exiled are now free. But the story of the dissidents and how they were treated is an important example of how Soviet citizens have been denied their human rights. There is no guarantee that this would not happen again in a post-Gorbachev USSR.

In some cases dissidents were removed from their jobs or moved ('internal exile') to other areas of the Soviet Union and separated from their family and friends. These areas were usually 'closed' to foreign visitors. In other cases, such as that of the famous writer, Alexander Solzhenitsyn, dissidents were exiled from the Soviet Union altogether. Some were arrested and put on trial, accused of 'anti-Soviet propaganda'. They could be imprisoned or sent to labour camps, or even to psychiatric hospitals on the grounds that they were mentally ill.

'The formula of development "at the expense of others" is on the way out. In the light of existing realities, no genuine progress is possible at the expense of the rights and freedoms of individuals and nations, or at the expense of nature.'

(Mr Gorbachev, addressing the UN, December 1988)

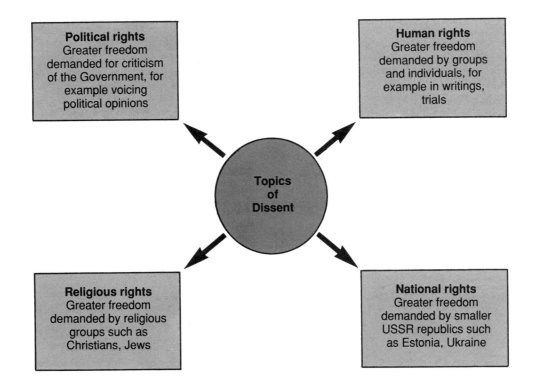

Political rights
Greater freedom demanded for criticism of the Government, for example voicing political opinions

Human rights
Greater freedom demanded by groups and individuals, for example in writings, trials

Topics of Dissent

Religious rights
Greater freedom demanded by religious groups such as Christians, Jews

National rights
Greater freedom demanded by smaller USSR republics such as Estonia, Ukraine

One of the most famous Soviet dissidents was Andrei Sakharov.

Human Rights
Andrei Sakharov

A Soviet nuclear scientist, 'father' of the Soviet Hydrogen Bomb. Member of the Soviet Academy of Sciences. He was awarded the Nobel Prize for Physics in 1975. Supporter of human rights in the Soviet Union.
Removed from his job as a nuclear physicist. Arrested in 1980, before Olympic Games, and 'resettled' in the city of Gorky, 400 kilometres east of Moscow. In 1985, after several hunger strikes by Sakharov, his wife, also under internal exile for 'anti-Soviet activities', was allowed to visit the USA for specialist eye treatment.

Statements

'There are few people in the USSR who react seriously any more to slogans about building Communism.'
'All my activities stem from a desire for a free and worthy destiny for our country and our people. I consider the United States the leader of the movement toward a free society.'
'I don't find that socialism has brought a better social order.'
'The action against me is part of a widespread campaign against dissidents. Its specific cause was probably my statement about events in Afghanistan.'

Here is how Sakharov described his 'internal exile':

❛ 'I live in an apartment guarded day and night by a policeman at the entrance. He allows no one to enter, but family members, with a few exceptions... There is no telephone in the apartment. A radio-jamming facility has been set up in the apartment just for me. In terms of everyday life, my situation is much better than that of my friends sent into exile or, particularly, sentenced to labour camp or prison. I still do not know which branch of Government or who personally made the decision to have me exiled. Every time my wife leaves, I do not know whether she will be allowed to travel without hindrance, although she is not formally under detention.' ❜

*Q*UESTIONS

1. Who are the dissidents?
2. What do they protest about?
3. Describe what has happened to dissidents in the Soviet Union?
4. Why is there hope that their situation might improve in future?

*A*CTIVITIES

1. Find out more about dissidents like Andrei Sakharov and their treatment in the Soviet Union. You will find information in the school library and in the local library, and from newspapers and magazines.

2. Imagine you are a dissident in the Soviet Union. Write a letter to a UK newspaper outlining your complaints about the Soviet Government and describing how you have been treated.

Psychiatric hospitals in the Soviet Union

In March 1989 a group of twenty-six American psychiatrists, lawyers and interpreters toured Soviet psychiatric hospitals and interviewed more than two dozen patients. These patients appeared to be in the hospitals for 'political reasons'. The group concluded that while there had been some improvement there was still evidence of: unjustified confinement in psychiatric hospitals; continued use of drugs for control rather than cure; officials guilty of abuse in charge of hospitals.

In 1983, Soviet psychiatrists resigned from the World Psychiatric Association rather than be expelled for human rights abuses. They were re-admitted in 1989 after stating that the abuses had stopped. Nevertheless, the West German-based International Society for Human Rights listed many cases of improper confinement. Other critics noted that the Soviet Union still used diagnosis such as 'sluggish schizophrenia', one

A US Comment on Human Rights in the Soviet Union
The Issue That Will Not Fade

Despite recent progress, Moscow has far to go on human rights

When Mathematician Naum Meiman's wife was allowed to leave the Soviet Union to undergo cancer treatment last January, he thought it was a sign that his twelve years as a Jewish refusenik were about to end. But his wife died in Washington a few weeks later, and since then Meiman, 76, a founder of the Soviet human-rights movement, has remained, isolated and in need of surgery he cannot get in the Soviet Union. Soviet authorities point to his once classified work for the Soviet Academy of Sciences 30 years ago as an excuse to prevent him from joining his only relative, a daughter in Colorado.

Meiman's story encapsulates the human-rights situation in the Soviet Union. Those who apply to leave risk harassment, loss of jobs and the prospect of years of empty waiting. Although Jewish emigration has grown from 914 in 1986 to about 8,000 this year, it is only a fraction of the 51,322 permitted to emigrate in the peak year of 1979. The State Department estimates that 400,000 Jews, out of a population of 1.8 million, would like to leave. To focus worldwide attention on Soviet human rights, a large Washington demonstration is being planned by a coalition of U.S. Jewish organizations, for Sunday, the day before Mikhail Gorbachev will arrive for his summit with Ronald Reagan.

The President has called the Soviet dissidents the "unseen guests" at the summit, and his Administration has made human rights a crucial test of U.S. Soviet relations. State Department officials note the surge in Jewish emigration and point with satisfaction to the even larger burst in Armenian emigration, which is expected to grow from fewer than 247 Armenians last year to more than 6,000 in 1987. By year's end, an estimated 12,000 ethnic Germans will have been allowed to move to West Germany, vs. only 783 in 1986. In a pre-summit gesture of goodwill Soviet officials told Western diplomats last week that they would approve emigration requests for 73 Soviet citizens. (Meiman was not on the list.)

U.S. officials observe that the Soviets are showing a new willingness to discuss human rights. Says a State Department analyst: "When we met with [former Foreign Minister] Andrei Gromyko, we'd try to raise human rights and he would say it was an internal matter. Now the Soviets bring up the issue." To be sure, they often seek to turn it to their advantage by complaining of what they consider American abuses, including unemployment, homelessness and the imprisonment of anti-nuclear protesters.

The Kremlin's new eagerness to discuss human rights spawned a meeting in Moscow last month between Deputy Secretary of State John Whitehead and Deputy Foreign Minister Anatoly Adamishin – the highest-level direct talks ever held on the subject. Although such a dialogue was an encouraging sign, Whitehead came away skeptical about the degree of Soviet progress. "Are people free to move about the country," he asked rhetorically, "to listen to free media, to leave when they want, to take jobs where they want? No, the freedoms we treasure in this country do not exist there." Until that glaring imbalance is corrected, human rights will continue to be a major stumbling block in U.S. Soviet relations.

By Nancy Traver/Washington

(source: *TIME* Magazine, 14 December,1987.)

"Now, if there are no further comments, let us continue ..."

QUESTIONS

1. Describe how women in the Soviet Union are denied human rights.
2. What improvements in Soviet women's human rights are highlighted by Lidia Lykova?
3. Why might her views not be completely free from bias?

QUESTIONS

1. Read the news extract 'The Issue That Will Not Fade' (page 55). What criticisms are made of the Soviet Union's human rights?
2. What sign is there that things might be improving?

KEYWORDS

The following Keywords are used in this Unit. Make sure you have understood what they mean.

national minority
exile (internal/external)
ethnic minority
dissident

HUMAN RIGHTS IN CHINA

'Citizens enjoy freedom of speech, correspondence, the press, assembly, association, procession, demonstration, and the freedom to strike, and have the right to "speak out freely, air their views fully, hold great debates and write big-character posters".'

(Chinese Constitution, 1978)

In 1980 the '**four big rights**' – to speak out freely, air views freely, hold great debates, and write big-character posters – were removed from the constitution, following a clampdown by the Chinese Government after a period of protest by people demanding **democracy**. At the trial of one of the leading protesters, Wei Jingsheng, editor of a political journal who was sentenced to fifteen years imprisonment for giving away state secrets and carrying out counter-revolutionary activities, the following official statement was made by the court:

'Freedom of speech of the individual citizen must be based on the four basic principles of insisting on the socialist road, the dictatorship of the proletariat, the leadership of the party and Marxism - Leninism - Mao Zedong thoughts. The citizen has only the freedom to support these principles and not the freedom to oppose them.'

The movement away from giving more freedom to individuals has continued more recently with the Government's reaction to the demand for democracy by the supporters of the Tiananmen Square hunger strikes. The strength of the Communist Party in China has been shown in the way it has clamped down on protest. It has ignored pleas from western countries for greater freedom in China and has criticised the movement towards democracy in Eastern Europe. The clampdown has been a serious setback for human rights in China.

China in crisis...

This declaration, issued by four student leaders in Tiananmen Square just before the shooting began, represents the movement's final ideas: thoughts which so terrified the Chinese Government that it took refuge in massacre. Three of its authors are believed to be in hiding for their safety. The fourth, Liu Xiaobo, may already have been seized by the secret police.

The June 2nd Hunger Strike Declaration

1: The purpose of our hunger strike
We are on hunger strike. We protest, we appeal, we repent. We are not in search of death; we are looking for real life. In the face of irrational and violent pressure from the Li Peng government, the Chinese intellectuals must cure their soft-boned disease of being vocal but of never being active for thousands of years. We must act to protest against martial law, to call for the birth of a new political culture, to make up for our past mistakes of being soft and weak for so long.

We all share responsibility for the Chinese nation being left behind many others.

2: Our main slogans
• We have no enemy. Don't poison our wisdom and the democratisation of China with hatred and violence.
• We all need introspection. Everyone is responsible for the fact that China has been left behind by many other countries.
• We are first and foremost citizens.
• We are not in search of death – we are looking for real life.

3: The location, duration and rules of the hunger strike
A) Location: under the monument to the People's Heroes in Tiananmen Square.
B) Duration: 72 hours, from 1400hrs 2 June to 1400hrs 5 June.
C) Rules: boiled water only, no food, no nutritious drinks (such as sugar, glucose, fat or protein).

4: The hunger strikers
Liu Xiaobo
Zhou Duo
Hou Dejian
Gao Xin

Written by these four, Tiananmen Square, Peking, 2 June 1989

A profile of four protest leaders

■ **Liu Xiaobo:** PhD in Literature, lecturer in the Chinese department of Peking Teachers' University. Author of several books on Chinese culture, he worked closely with student leaders from the start of the demonstrations and has also been a primary contact with those outside China. As a result, he had been criticised by name by the government as a "black hand".

■ **Zhou Duo:** Former lecturer in the Institute of Sociology at Peking University; head of the planning department of Stone (Computer) Corporation, a private electronics company. He acted as a contact between sympathetic intellectual groups and known student leaders.

■ **Gao Xin:** Sociologist, former editor of *Teachers' University Weekly*; member of the Communist Party.

■ **Hou Dejian:** Pop singer and composer who is popular in China and Hong Kong. On Sunday morning in Tiananmen Square he tried to negotiate a truce with military commanders to protect the students there. Then the shooting began.

The Chinese text of the hunger strike declaration made by four student leaders on 2 June
(source: *The Independent*, 10 June 1989.)

Peking massacre 'was not a tragedy'

From WILLIAM KAZER, Peking

CHINA'S Communist Party chief Jiang Zemin said yesterday that the Peking massacre in June was not a tragedy and that the leadership was united in this view...

"We don't think it was a tragedy," said Jiang Zemin, in reply to a question about the assault that killed hundreds, if not thousands, of people in Peking on June 3 and 4.

He and other leaders did not voice a word of regret for the deaths of unarmed civilians in the attack during the 90-minute press conference, televised live and clearly designed to bolster the image of the new top line-up.

"This was a counter-revolutionary rebellion. Its nature is very clear and there are no differences among our party leaders on this."...

Meanwhile China launched its strongest attack yet on France for aiding fugitive dissidents.

The *People's Daily* accused France of supporting pro-democracy activists who met in Paris last week to found the Front for Democratic China and said Paris had endangered relations with Peking.

"These criminals, who have been agitating and plotting to subvert the Chinese government, are openly supported by France," the daily said. France denies helping the dissidents and said it is only offering political asylum. – Reuter

(source: *The Scotsman*, 27 September 1989.)

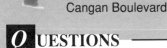

An unidentified man blocks the path of Chinese tanks on Beijing's Cangan Boulevard

COMMUNISM

DEMOCRACY! FREEDOM!

*Q*UESTIONS

1. Why did the four students go on hunger strike in Tiananmen Square?
2. How long did they intend to protest?
3. What rules did they have for themselves?
4. How did the Chinese Government react to the protest?
5. How did a Chinese Government spokesman defend the government's actions?

*A*CTIVITIES

1. Look at the photograph. Describe what you see. Why do you think the man took the action he did? What options were open to the tank commander? How can you find out what happened next? Try to find out.

2. Study the cartoon. Explain what message the cartoonist is trying to put over to readers.

The Dalai Lama, 1984

Tibet

The 1989 winner of the Nobel Peace Prize was Tenzin Gyatso, the fourteenth Dalai Lama of Tibet. He was awarded the prize because of his non-violent struggle against the Chinese occupation of his country. The struggle has continued for over thirty years.

Since the 1950s the Chinese Government has claimed that Tibet is, 'an inalienable part of the Motherland.' Since March 1989 it has been under martial law, occupied by an estimated 300 000 troops of the People's Army. Hundreds of troops are camped outside every monastery, pilgrimage sites are closed, and soldiers guard every alleyway leading to the Tibetan quarter in the capital, Lhasa.

An article in *Scotland on Sunday* (26 November 1989) noted that, '…despite hundreds of arrests and frequent reports of torture (including electrocution, suspension from the ceiling and boiling water poured down the throat) the Tibetans seem firm in their loyalties. "As soon as they lift martial law," said one young Tibetan, "we will protest again. We are not just fighting for political rights. We are fighting for survival."…'

Tibet has been occupied by the Chinese since 1950. The rest of the world has not complained, but the Tibetans themselves refuse to accept Beijing's domination of their land. In March 1959 they launched an uprising to try to drive the Chinese out, but were defeated. China then set out to destroy the culture of the Tibetan people. In 1959 there were 6500 Buddhist monasteries in Tibet, but today very few remain. Many thousands of Tibetans are thought to have been killed.

In March 1989, on the thirtieth anniversary of the uprising, rioting again broke out in Tibet in an effort to gain independence. China imposed martial (military) law and cracked down again on the Tibetans. Soon afterwards the troubles in Tibet were overshadowed by the massacre in Tiananmen Square.

Support for Tibet grows in China

Colonisation policy is challenged in post-Tiananmen wave of sympathy, writes Philip Colley

CHINESE public opinion has begun to shift in favour of the Tibetan dissident movement, in a mood of post-Tiananmen Square sympathy for others suffering under martial law. Many Chinese who were previously prepared to accept their government's position on Tibet are beginning to have their suspicions. As a Chinese student who witnessed the Beijing massacre said: "Now we can believe that what the Tibetans have been complaining about for all these years has actually been happening."

Before June 4, it was unthinkable to the Chinese that the People's Liberation Army could be used against the people, including the Tibetans. With that illusion smashed, sympathy for the Tibetans has increased among Chinese intellectuals at home and abroad…

(source: *The Guardian*, 4 January 1990.)

Fire in the Mountains

The spirit of independence survives in Tibet, but for how long?

The Tibetan holiday was approaching, and the Chinese were prepared for trouble. Hundreds of martial-law troops took up posts in the alleys and stairways of Lhasa's Drepung monastery as the annual Sholdon festival ceremonies began…

Outside the Dalai Lama's vacant summer palace the ceremonies continued – and so did the state of military readiness…

The calm didn't last. A group of about a dozen shaven-headed Buddhist nuns burst into the middle of the circle waving their fists and shouting "Free Tibet!" On the fringes of the crowd, squads of People's Armed Police officers scrambled to stop the protest. At first they could only dash back and forth, seeking an opening through the human wall formed by the audience. When the police finally managed to force their way through the crowd, they wrestled the nuns to the ground and began dragging them away toward waiting security vans. The onlookers roared in anger at the assault on the nuns, and one man took a swing at an officer. The police hauled him away as well. Tibetans in the crowd said the prisoners would surely be beaten, interrogated and locked away for a long time. A furious Tibetan carrying a small child in his arms spat in English: "Chinese police no good."…

(source: *Newsweek*, 25 September 1989.)

Tibetan children dragged from homes

Following the imposition of martial law in the Tibetan capital Lhasa, [Amnesty International] fears that large-scale arbitrary arrests may occur and that those detained may face long-term incommunicado detention and torture.

The decree of martial law, in force since midnight on 7 March, empowers Chinese security forces to take "all necessary measures" to put down disturbances. Its imposition followed days of rioting in early March between security forces and Tibetan protestors. Armed police then conducted house-to-house searches for people suspected of involvement in the unrest of the previous days. Arrests continued during the following days.

Foreign tourists, ordered to leave Lhasa by noon on 9 March, reported seeing Tibetans – including children – being dragged from their homes and driven away in police trucks. By 9 March Tibetan sources estimated that more than 1,000 people had been arrested.

Tourists described how Tibetans pleaded with them to stay, fearing that in the absence of foreign travellers and journalists to act as witnesses, the security forces might behave with impunity.

Six tourists expelled from Lhasa later described "ill-organized" police savagely beating Tibetans on the first day of demonstrations and "firing indiscriminately".

AI has called on the government to issue clear instructions to security forces to ensure that reprisals are not taken against those alleged to be involved in demonstrations. It has also urged the government to publish the names of all those detained under martial law, to release all those not charged with a criminal offence, and to ensure no detainee is tortured.

(source: *Amnesty* No. 39, June/July 1989.)

---

*Q*UESTIONS

1. Who is Tenzin Gyatso?
2. Why did he receive the Nobel Peace Prize in 1989?
3. What actions has China taken in Tibet?
4. Describe some of the tortures reported from Tibet.
5. Why does public opinion in China now support Tibet?

*A*CTIVITIES

1. Find out from a map the location of Tibet.

2. Imagine you are a British TV news reporter in Tibet. You have to prepare an item for the nine o'clock news in the UK. Write a report of 100/150 words describing conditions in Tibet, the reasons for the problems, and a description of a recent incident. (Use the source material given in this Unit to assist you.)

Life in death's shadow

In China, the process of judicial execution can be swift, brutal and publicly humiliating.

Prisoners sentenced to death are paraded publicly, with placards hanging around their necks...

The People's Republic of China has executed over 1,500 of its citizens since 1983. Amnesty has documented that number of cases but believes the true figure to be far higher: some sources have estimated the number of executions to be as high as 30,000. The number of crimes punishable by death was substantially increased in 1982 and 1983. Whilst many of those executed appear to have been convicted of serious crimes of violence, people have also been executed for crimes as various as stealing bicycles, "molesting women", hanging a banner with a "counter-revolutionary" slogan from a hotel window and also for plotting to set up "subversive" organisations.

Execution is by shooting. It is often preceded by "mass sentencing rallies", in which prisoners sentenced to death are paraded publicly, with placards hanging around their necks giving their names and the crime for which they have been sentenced. The prisoners are forced to face the crowd with their heads bowed and their hands tied behind their backs. Some of these rallies are shown on television.

The humiliation of this treatment follows upon a criminal procedure notable for its lack of safeguards for the defendant. The prisoner does not even have the benefit of being presumed innocent. The right to be defended is guaranteed but in practice access to lawyers is limited.

A further, and unusual, difficulty concerns the speed with which proceedings are conducted. On 10 September 1983, two young men were officially reported to have been executed in Nanjing just six days after committing the alleged offence for which they were sentenced to death. On 29 December 1987, a 22-year-old man was executed in Beijing, three weeks after being arrested and six days after his trial. The speed with which executions are carried out has been made possible by amendments to the Criminal Procedure Law 1980, introduced in 1983. They not only reduced the time limit to lodge an appeal from ten days to three but also made it possible for courts to bring defendants to trial without giving them a copy of the indictment in advance and without giving advance notice of the trial or serving summonses in advance to all the parties involved.

The courts can either pronounce death sentences for "immediate effect" or subject to reprieve for two years. Unlike the British system of suspended sentences, this does not mean that execution will only be carried out if the prisoner re-offends. The prisoner must show evidence of "repentance", good behaviour or perform "meritorious service". In other words, the prisoner lives in a state of uncertainty.

The Chinese maintain that the death penalty is a deterrent both to the offender (!) and to others. It is also claimed to prevent private retaliation and to protect people's interests. The Chinese argue that the increased range of offences carrying the death penalty and the changes in criminal procedure introduced in 1983 were made necessary by a dramatic upsurge in crime. It should be noted that a significant drop in the crime rate was recorded in 1982. Further, Wang Fang, Minister of Public Security, stated in August 1988 that major crimes had been increasing at the rate of 20,000 a year since 1985. This calls into question the effectiveness of the death penalty as a deterrent.

(source: *Amnesty*, April/May 1989.)

QUESTIONS

1. How many Chinese citizens have been executed since 1983?
2. Which crimes are punishable by death?
3. How are prisoners executed? Describe their treatment before execution.
4. How are defendants denied human rights?
5. Why are more offences now punishable by death?
6. Why might the death penalty not be considered a deterrent?

The threat to family life

China has the largest population of any country in the world. It is estimated that one quarter of the world's people are Chinese. To deal with its problem of over-population, China has been trying to reduce its population growth rate. In the 1950s it was 2.2 per cent, in the 1970s it was down to below 1.5 per cent. It is hoped to reduce it to zero by the end of the century.

Several methods are being used to bring about the fall in the birth rate which is necessary to reduce the population growth rate. These policies can be seen as a threat to the human rights of families, and in particular to women in China.

1. *Marriage age.* The legal age for marriage has been raised from 20 to 22 for men and from 18 to 20 for women. Although it is legal to get married at these ages, the 'recommended' ages for marriage are 28 for men and 25 for women.

2. *'One is enough'.* A massive propaganda campaign has been started to encourage families to have only one child. This policy is backed up by a number of benefits to couples who carry it out and by a number of penalties for couples who ignore it.

A monthly bonus of 5 yuan (8% of the average town wage) has been offered to all single-child families who pledge not to have further children. They will also receive preference in the allocation of housing and in educational opportunities for the child.

These privileges are automatically withdrawn on the birth of a second child. If a third child is born, the family begins to suffer penalties. Wages can be reduced by 5–10% after the third child and up to 20% after a fifth. The press has reported cases of couples holding official positions who have been penalised financially for having third and fourth children.

3. *Family planning.* Article 53 of the Chinese Constitution 'advocates and encourages family planning'. Birth control pills are distributed free of charge and other methods of family planning are also freely available.

Couple flees China's one-child policy

By Jim Fox   Special for USA TODAY

BUFFALO – Sai-zhen Wang was pregnant and her choice was clear: Get an abortion, her fifth, or flee China so she could have her second child. She ran. Wang, 34, and her husband, Jin Mu Li, 37, stowed away last year on a ship to Canada. With them was a nephew, Chun Kong Cheung, 19.

Twice the men were jailed for entering Canada and the USA illegally. Wang wasn't jailed because she was pregnant. Now the family – Wang, Li, Cheung and 8-month-old May Li, the daughter Wang refused to give up – await a U.S. hearing on a bid for political asylum. U.S. authorities say the family's application is one of the first under a new order allowing asylum for those fleeing China's one-family, one-child policy.

"My doctor said another abortion would kill me," said a tearful Wang, who left her first child, a daughter, 10, with relatives in China. Wang feared the frail girl wouldn't survive the trip.

Li, before he and Wang were married in 1979, served in the Chinese army. His "reward" was being allowed to go back to his hometown, where he worked in a leather goods factory. He was promoted to "team leader," in charge of maintaining machinery.

Wang worked in an electric-meter factory. Cheung was a farm worker.

Because of overpopulation, Chinese authorities require couples who have had one child to use contraceptives. If the devices fail or, as in Wang's case, they aren't used for religious reasons, women are "encouraged" to get an abortion.

While jailed in Buffalo, Li and Cheung went on hunger strike, attracting the attention of law students at the State University of New York at Buffalo, who volunteered to help them.

U.S. immigration officials issued the family work permits Wednesday, pending their hearing – which might not be for several months.

The family planned to head for New York Friday, to seek friends and employment in the city's Chinatown.

Li suggested he'd take his own life if they can't remain in the USA, "My life wouldn't have any meaning," he said.

Cheung, who fled because "there is no life for me in China," is also seeking asylum because he opposes "the mandatory abortion policy" at home.

He said his father was "branded a counterrevolutionary" for opposing China's policies. The father was sentenced to hard labour and banished with the family to a state-run work farm. Li said the USA is "a real democratic nation, where we'd have a better life."

Families subject to pressure

It is not against the law in China for a couple to have more than one child, says the nation's State Family Planning Commission.

Chinese law is that a couple be "committed to practice family planning," the commission says.

Single-child families do get economic benefits, including preference in education and housing.

China has an extensive education program to encourage couples to use birth control and to teach teen-agers family planning, the commission says.

Family planning centers are set up locally and "family planning motivators" go to rural areas and urban neighbourhoods to teach birth control.

They also deliver contraceptives to homes.

– Mary Romano

(source: *USA TODAY*/International Edition, 3 March 1990.)

QUESTIONS

1. Why is China concerned about its rate of population growth?
2. What steps have been taken to slow down the rate of growth?
3. In what ways does this represent a threat to human rights?

ACTIVITY

Read the newspaper extract about Sai-zhen Wang and her family. List the different ways in which the members of this family have been denied their human rights in China.

China and Hong Kong

Since 1832, when two Scotsmen set up business near Canton, the city of Hong Kong has become a busy overcrowded seaport and a world shipping and financial centre. It is a British colony, but the lease on most of the area runs out in 1997 by which date it must be given back to China. Although China does not recognise the lease, it has never tried to take over Hong Kong by force. In 1984 China and Britain signed a 'hand-over' treaty.

At present, China is offering Hong Kong housing space on the mainland and is interested in good relations with Hong Kong to help its own 'modernisation' plans.

In 1984 about 25 000 Chinese refugees crossed the border into Hong Kong, under a recent quota system. About 10 000 illegal Chinese refugees also tried to get in. Most refugees settle in Hong Kong and this increases its already excessive population of about 6 million.

In 1997 the British colony of Hong Kong is due to be handed over to the Chinese Government and will then become part of China. The people who live in the wealthy colony are afraid that when this happens they will suffer a reduction in their human rights. They are especially fearful since the events in Tiananmen Square.

The ability of the Chinese Government to influence life in Hong Kong even before 1997 was demonstrated in 1989. The Hong Kong Communist newspaper *Wen Wei Po* had been a supporter of the Chinese Government but began to criticise it after June 1990. In July the editor was sacked by an official of the Chinese news agency which subsidises it after he had tried to dismiss the pro-Beijing deputy director of the paper. The people of Hong Kong expect the paper to become just another offshoot of the *People's Daily*. They say that it is clear that they cannot trust Chinese promises of continued free speech after 1997. An article in *People's Daily* warned that even under British rule, 'no one is allowed to make Hong Kong a base to subvert the central government.' It was a strong warning to the colony not to oppose Communist policies.

Britain ready to reopen China talks
By DAVID WALLEN

BRITAIN will urge China to think again about stationing troops in Hong Kong after 1997, when the two sides resume talks on the colony's future in London today.

Earlier talks scheduled for July were called off after the Peking massacre and Foreign Office officials insist that the British side will "put to the Chinese in robust terms" that it was this event which destroyed confidence in Hong Kong and that it is now up to China to do something to restore goodwill...

Britain accepts the two sides have got to learn to talk to each other again if the handover of the territory to China in 1997 is to go ahead smoothly.

(source: *The Scotsman*, 27 September 1989.)

QUESTIONS

1. What will happen to Hong Kong in 1997?
2. Why are the people of Hong Kong worried about what might happen to them?
3. How has China shown it can influence events in the colony even before 1997?

KEYWORDS

The following Keywords are used in this Unit. Make sure you have understood what they mean.

'four big rights'   martial law

democracy

3
CONFLICT AND PROTEST

OPEN DOORS – CLOSED DOORS

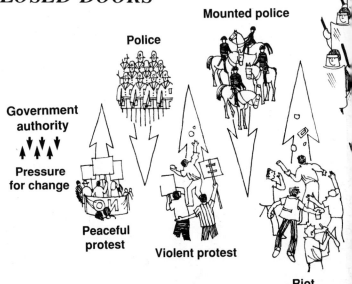

Protest and conflict

In all countries, Governments are involved in making decisions about how the people should be ruled. In some countries, where there is little, if any, voting, the Governments are **dictatorships**, enforcing tough controls on what people can do and say. George Orwell in his book, *1984*, showed how a Government used the tactics of 'Big Brother', the 'Thought Police' and 'Newspeak' as its ways of controlling people and preventing the growth of any protest or opposition. In democratic countries, people can express their opinions about their Government's activities by voting, and there is usually some freedom to make criticisms and to protest about the Government's actions. However, even in democratic countries Governments have methods of controlling protest. Thus protest actions may be met by Government reactions. If discussions fail and no solutions are found, then both the strength of the protests and of the reactions may increase (see diagram).

Whose views?

Descriptions of people's actions and Governments' reactions may vary depending on who is speaking, writing, televising, photographing, or filming.

QUESTIONS

1. In what ways is a dictatorship different from a democratic country?
2. In what ways might protest actions be increased?
3. What methods can Governments use to control protests and criticisms?

Common knowledge

He's a terrorist, You're a guerilla, I'm a freedom-fighter

A BOMB is planted in a shopping centre. When it goes off, the shop window explodes and flies across the mall in a million glass shards. Innocent people are shredded by the splinters.

The people who planted the bomb make demands of the government. "Unless you agree to our demands, we will continue our campaign to liberate our people."

Now, depending on who the bombers are, and who the government is, and what the campaign is about, the bombers will be described in one of three ways: as terrorists, guerillas, or freedom-fighters.

The contras in Nicaragua were described as guerillas - a word which neither approves of nor condemns them. The mujahedin, the Afghanistan rebels who fought the Soviets were called freedom fighters (anyone who fought the Soviets were freedom fighters). The IRA are described as terrorists (for their bombings of the innocent and uninvolved).

However, the *Soviet press* would have described the Contras and the mujahedin as *terrorists*, and the IRA as *freedom-fighters*.

So, as the innocent and the not-so-innocent die in shootings, and booby traps, and random explosions around the world, language subtly programmes our reactions to the events.

(source: *The Indy*, 26 April 1990.)

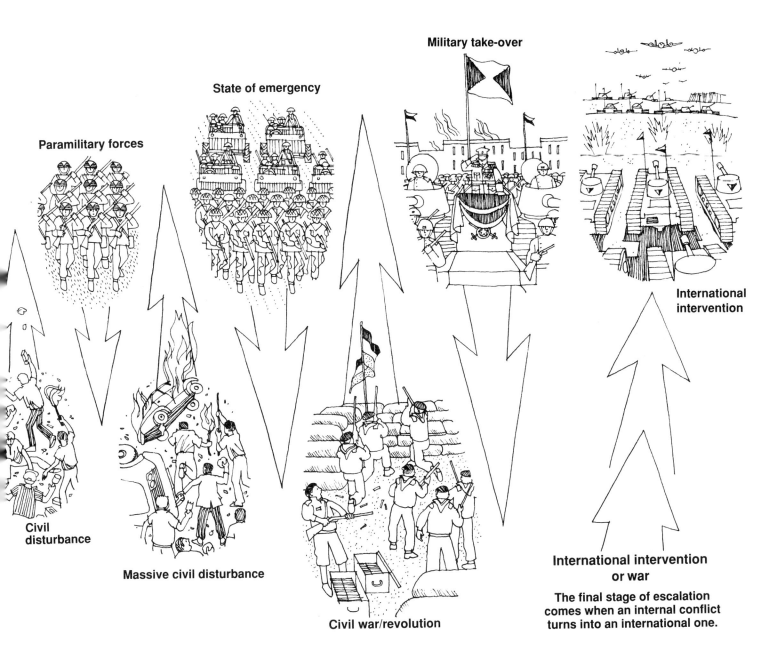

Paramilitary forces

State of emergency

Military take-over

International intervention

Civil disturbance

Massive civil disturbance

Civil war/revolution

International intervention or war

The final stage of escalation comes when an internal conflict turns into an international one.

A CTIVITIES

1.   Form groups and select any two forms of Government control.

2.   Your group should try to find out more about these two methods of control. For example, what variations are there, and in which countries do they exist?

3.   Write a summary of your findings.

4.   Can your group produce a list of examples of countries in the world where actions/reactions such as those in the diagram are currently happening?

5.   What is your group's opinion of the views put forward in the extract 'Common knowledge'?

6.   'Government-controlled, computerised identity cards are a threat to civil liberties.' Research and debate this motion.

Protecting rights and freedoms

Freedoms and civil liberties in the USA are guaranteed by the Constitution, a document written in 1787, and the Bill of Rights of 1791. For example, Amendment 1 of the Constitution states, 'Congress shall make no laws respecting the establishment of religion... or abridging the freedom of speech; or of the press.'

The high principles of the documents have not always been upheld in the past. For example, slavery existed in the USA until 1865 and women had no vote until this century, when there has also been discrimination against minorities, and suppression of unpopular speech. During the Cold War era in the 1950s, hundreds of people were investigated for 'Un-American activities' by anti-Communist Senator Joe McCarthy and his Committee, who tried to prove that these people were Communists, threatening freedom in the USA. An Immigration Law came into effect during this time which barred foreigners from visiting the USA because of their left-wing political beliefs. Although this ban was lifted in 1990, permanent residence in the USA can still be prevented. Gradually, though, the Supreme Court has backed freedom of speech, racial equality and the rights of the accused.

Dealing with protest

Protest demands for change and claims for rights have not always been supported by the US Government. During the 1960s the protest marches by Civil Rights supporters were sometimes put down violently by local police and the armed National Guard. The shooting of Martin Luther King, the black Civil Rights leader, led to serious rioting in several US cities, where troops were brought in to quell the protests.

In the 1960s and 1970s, there was strong Government reaction to anti-Vietnam war protests. In 1967 there were demonstrations involving thousands of people in Washington, San Francisco and Chicago.

Also, 125 000 protesters demonstrated in New York, opposing America's involvement in the war. Violence and rioting occured in several cities and at Kent State University several students were shot and killed by National Guards.

Covert action

Sometimes the US Government, and particularly the President, may wish to keep secret some of its dealings. In 1972, for example, seven men, later linked with President Nixon's advisers, were arrested for 'bugging' the rooms of the Democratic Party in the Watergate building in Washington.

In 1989, Colonel Oliver North and General John Poindexter, appointees of President Reagan, were found guilty of illegally selling arms to Iran and using the money to fund the US-backed right-wing Contra rebels in Nicaragua.

Into the 1990s

In recent times the US Government has taken strong action on various social problems such as illegal immigration and drugs. Despite the welcome carved on the Statue of Liberty, many immigrants, especially the illegal immigrants (aliens) who are estimated to number three million a year, are often robbed or held hostage until 'fees' are paid to the smuggling organisation.

In an effort to limit the trafficking of drugs in the '90s, the American Government not only gave aid to Colombia in South America to fight the 'drug barons', but also increased police and drug squad powers of search. This drive against drugs and drug-related crime has led to protests about civil liberties being set aside and the rights of the individual overruled.

QUESTIONS

1. What examples are there of limits being placed on people's freedoms in the USA in the past?
2. Give examples of situations when there has been violent reaction to protest in the USA.
3. What is 'covert' action?

ACTIVITIES

1. In groups, find more information about one of the following: a) Irangate, or b) illegal immigrants, or c) The CIA.
2. Write an individual report of your group's research.
3. Prepare a short speech justifying 'stop and search' tactics.

In terms of freedom of the individual to check what information is recorded about himself or herself on files, the USA is ahead of many countries. As computer technology advanced, so the Freedom of Information Act in the USA was passed, which makes it illegal for any agency to 'disclose any record of any person to others, without the agreement of the individual concerned'.

The price of law and order: Boston, USA

"L.A. LAW"

Chalk one up for "L.A. Law." Only a week after the hit TV series aired a new episode involving a wrong-address drug raid by pumped-up television narcs, the District of Columbia police force managed to act out the real thing. The victims were George and Katrina Stokes, who live in a crack-infested neighbourhood of southeast Washington. The Stokeses were home watching television early one evening when a heavily armed D.C. SWAT team came crashing through their door. George Stokes was ordered to the floor at gunpoint, somehow sustaining a gash on his head in the process. His wife, understandably terrified, fell down the cellar stairs as she tried to run away from the band of black-uniformed intruders.

Like their television counterparts, the D.C. drugbusters soon found they had the wrong house. Worse yet, a camera crew from a local television station was on hand to record the whole event.

(source: *Newsweek*, 23 April 1990.)

Conflict USSR

Government controls

Up to a few years ago scenes such as this one in Moscow during the 1990 May Day parade would have been unthinkable. Under previous leaders of the Soviet Union such as Stalin, Krushchev or Brezhnev, the May Day parade was mainly a chance to show off to the world the military strength of the USSR, and the marchers were mostly Communist Party members and supporters. The Communist Party's control was total, and any protests or revolts would be put down by the Army, and the KGB (Secret Police). The media was also under strict Government control. Protesters could be arrested, imprisoned, exiled to remote parts of USSR, or executed.

May Day Protest

THE SOVIET Union's traditional May Day showpiece in Red Square turned into a humiliating farce for President Gorbachev and the communist leadership yesterday.

Thousands of jeering radicals launched an unprecedented demonstration at the parade through Red Square in a stinging attack on 72 years of Communist rule.…

Demonstrators jeered and shouted, "shame, shame" and "Politburo resign", their fists in the air, as Mr Gorbachev slipped into the Kremlin. Soviet flags, their hammer-and-sickle insignia torn out, dotted the square.

Other marchers yelled "Down with the KGB" and "Freedom for Lithuania," as they hoisted the red, yellow and green flag of the breakaway republic, locked in a struggle with the Kremlin since its 11 March declaration of independence.

(source: *The Scotsman*, 2 May 1990.)

Glasnost

As leader of the USSR, Mikhail Gorbachev has encouraged a policy of *glasnost* (openness). This allows not only open criticism of many aspects of Soviet life by individuals and the media but also criticism of political actions and leaders, including the Communist Party itself. Indeed, by 1990, leaders of the Soviet Communist Party had voted to end the one-party rule in the USSR, and to allow a multi-party political system.

May Day protesters in Red Square, 1990

Glasnost and the Soviet minorities

By allowing much more open criticism of how Soviet affairs were organised, President Gorbachev found that discussion included not only how to improve the Soviet Union itself, but also the possibility of the republics and their ethnic groups breaking away from the Soviet Union. Instead of representing **minority** interests within the Soviet Union, they wished to assert their own national status. The rise of nationalism and outbreaks of violence gave rise to the possibility of the Soviet 'disunion'. In several states such as Georgia, Armenia, and Azerbaijan, Soviet troops had to be brought in to quell riots and protests, during which people were killed.

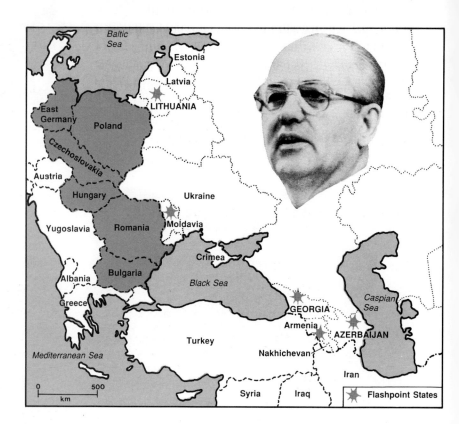

Government reaction

Case study – Lithuania (Soviet Republic in the Baltic Sea region. Population 3.8 million people. Capital city – Vilnius)

Lithuania

February 1990
Voters in free elections in Lithuania voted for pro-independence party, *Sajudis*, defeating the Communist Party.

March 1990
Declaration of independence by the Lithuanian Parliament.

April 1990
Some factories close. Petrol rationing introduced.

May 1990
Lithuanian Parliament rejects Soviet request to end independence laws.

August 1990
More factories close due to lack of oil and gas supplies. Lithuanian parliament votes to end independence temporarily, and to negotiate with USSR.

January 1991
Demonstrations and protests continue.

Soviet Union

February 1990
Warnings by Soviet leaders that independence would be illegal.

March 1990
Soviet Union rejects the declaration.

April 1990
Soviet Union enforces a blockade of oil and gas to Lithuania, which has none of its own.

May 1990
Soviet Union threatens to enforce further economic sanctions.

August 1990
Soviet oil and gas supplies to Lithuania begin again, a few days after the Lithuanian Parliament decision.

January 1991
Soviet troops take over radio stations. 13 Lithuanians killed.

Each stage leads nearer to confrontation and possible military clash. For the Soviet Union, revolts in the republics and the solution of these difficulties is one of the major problems of the 1990s.

Q UESTIONS

1. In what ways did Soviet Governments keep close control over protesters?

2. What changes have taken place in the USSR as a result of *glasnost*?

3. For what reasons is there the possibility of Soviet 'disunion'?

A CTIVITIES

1.   Form groups and update the Lithuania Diary.

2.   Find out what other protest groups are now challenging the Soviet leadership, indicating what the aims of these groups are and how successful they have been.

Conflict China

Violent Government reaction to protests in China has not in the past been unusual. In the 1950s, during the 'Great Leap Forward' to speed up industrial and agricultural production, many protesters were killed. In the 1960s the Chinese leader, Mao Zedong, launched a 'Cultural Revolution' to attack what he saw as 'selfishness, and Westernisation' in society. Thousands died during the turmoil and civil unrest which followed. In the 1980s, the leader of China's

Communist Party, Hu Yaobang, began to encourage open protests and criticism in China, as a way of improving democracy and economic production. However, this policy, similar to Mao's 'Let a hundred flowers bloom' in the 1950s, was not popular with many members of the Government, and when student protests increased, Hu was forced to resign in 1986. His death in 1989 led to further student protests.

Tiananmen Square 1989 (*Case Study*)

China's road to a showdown

CHINA'S Spring of protest, which led to yesterday's clampdown, was triggered by the death on 15 April of sacked Communist Party leader Hu Yaobang, revered by students as a reformist. This is how the protest developed:

17 APRIL Protests begin at Tiananmen Square in Peking as students call for democracy and reforms. Crowds of up to 100,000 drawn to city centre despite official warnings...

26 APRIL *Peoples Daily* publishes major Communist Party attack on protesters, angering students...

2 MAY Leaders of unofficial and illegal student union ride bicycles to government and party headquarters to demand leaders meet them or face further mass protests on 4 May. In Shanghai, some 10,000 protesters march to government headquarters...

13 MAY About 1,000 students, later to grow to 3,000, begin hunger strike for democracy in Tiananmen. Mr Zhao makes televised appeal, ignored by students, to end protest because of Sino-Soviet summit.

15 MAY Mr Gorbachev arrives at Peking airport as protests

continue in Tiananmen Square. Officials move welcoming ceremony from square to airport.

16 MAY Mr Gorbachev and Deng Xiaoping meet at Great Hall in formal reconciliation between Soviet Union and China. More than 250,000 mass in Tiananmen Square and nearby streets. Protests spread to Shanghai and five provincial capitals. Appeal to end protests from state council, highest government body, broadcast on loudspeakers in Tiananmen Square.

17 MAY A million people jam central Peking. Protests reported in seven cities, including Shanghai. Mr Gorbachev visit to Forbidden City cancelled and Great Hall news conference shifted to western suburbs because of crowds...

19 MAY Premier Li Peng tells a visiting Australian official that "chaos has occurred in central Peking and the Chinese government will take steps to stop it." Troops begin to move into the capital. President Yang Shangkun declares state of emergency in Peking, saying in a television address that the capital had been reduced to an "anarchic situation" and the normal work of government was impossible.

(source: *The Scotsman*, 20 May 1990.)

How it was in the Square

(Eye-witness account by Jonathan Mirsky,
reporter for *The Observer* (London).)

It is always curious to read the police report of an event in which one was involved; all the more so when the event was what the Chinese call 'the clear out' in Peking's Tiananmen Square on the night of 4 June and I was one of the 'thousands of ruffians' whom the police 'beat back'.

I was standing on the Golden Water Bridge throughout these events and award the deputy commander only a few marks for good reporting. He got the time exactly right, there were only 80 or so policemen near the bridge, and the stand was indeed burning.

As for the thousands of ruffians with Molotov cocktails I saw at most ten. The army was already in the square, the armoured personnel carrier had already run

down a demonstrator before my eyes leaving a red smear on the paving stones and tanks were rolling over the tents in which the demonstrators had camped.

If there were ruffians on the north end of the square, - much less thousands of them bearing knives and Molotov cocktails - I saw none apart from the handful who threw their petrol bottles at the personnel carrier after it had run down an unarmed man - and at Gal's men.

Everyone else was either a spectator or non-violent demonstrator - or both at once, like many of the million or so people who had milled around Tiananmen since 15 April, the day of the first demonstration.

(source: *Observer* News Service, September 1989.)

IN TIANANMEN SQUARE

TANKS and armoured vehicles patrolled the haunted streets of China's capital early today firing machine-gun bursts at anyone foolhardy enough to venture out, as the full extent of the massacre in Peking unfolded.

A morning news broadcast quoted the military as saying the bloody capture of Tiananmen Square from pro-democracy protesters had been "just an initial victory" and predicting a long fight against "dregs of society".

The shooting of hundreds, possibly thousands of students and citizens in Peking on Saturday night has left the Chinese capital tense and numb.

The exact number of dead may never be known, but the Chinese Red Cross claimed more than 2,000 were killed.

The horrific events of Saturday when soldiers opened fire, turning machine-guns, mortars, flame throwers and tanks on thousands of unarmed protesters, was the unthinkable.

The Chinese government says it warned the protesters to leave the square. But when the orders were disobeyed the government finally cracked, and so too did the army...

(source: *The Scotsman*, 5 June 1989.)

Dealing with protest

Government reaction

The Government ordered troops to clear Tiananmen Square, imposed martial law on Beijing and brought in more troops to enforce these laws. Orders were given for the arrest of thousands of students involved in the Democracy Movement, and Chinese television showed 'counter revolutionaries' being held by security forces. The 84-year-old leader of China, Deng Xiaoping, congratulated the troops on preventing the fall of the Government while the newspaper, *Beijing Daily*, described the protesters as 'ruffians and thugs'. Security checks were increased, and in the Beijing area foreign news magazines were banned.

Even in 1990, although martial law was lifted and several hundred protesters were released, there were still large numbers of troops in the capital, and Amnesty International estimated that there were still 600 people unaccounted for among the thousands still in prison. On the anniversary of the Tiananmen Square action, the Government issued warnings forbidding people to organise protests, shout slogans, lay wreaths, or sleep on the ground in the area of the Square.

KEYWORDS

The following Keywords are used in this Unit. Make sure you have understood what they mean.

dictatorship   **minorities**
glasnost

QUESTIONS

1. What actions did the Chinese Government take to enforce the law after the Tiananmen Square protest?

2. In what way does the account of the *Observer* news reporter differ from that of the official Chinese news agencies as to what happened in the Square?

3. What events have caused major crises for the Chinese Government in the last 40 years?

4. What other protests have been made recently?

ACTIVITIES

1. In groups, select one item per group from China's recent past e.g. 'The Great Leap Forward', 'Let a Thousand Flowers Bloom', 'The Cultural Revolution'.

2. Do some research to find out more about your group's selected item.

3. Choose one of your group to report back your findings to the whole class.

4. In pairs or groups, prepare possible arguments put forward by a) troops and b) students as they confronted each other in Tiananmen Square.

5. Join with your 'paired' group and discuss your viewpoints.

6. Discuss the significance of the cartoon above. What bias, if any, is shown in it?

MEDIA INTERNATIONAL
Media – USA

TV/Radio

In the USA, most households have at least one television. Indeed, with a generally high standard of living, viewers are prepared to pay for TV's technological 'extras' such as laserscan video-disc players, big-screen, stereo TV sets, and digital sound. Almost one million households have laser-video-disc players. Watching television is a popular pastime in the USA, where the 'couch potatoes', as viewers are sometimes called, can choose from more than twenty TV channels.

Show screens the future

By Bruce Schwartz USA TODAY

Coming to a TV in your home: watching a rented movie that was digitally sent to your VCR.

Electronic video is one of the concepts to be exhibited at the Consumer Electronics Show, opening Saturday in Las Vegas.

The show's featured theme: the home theater, "a convergence of lifestyle and technology," says NEC's Brian Williams.

Emc² Inc. will gauge interest in its "electronic video rental store," says co-founder Will Graven.

The proposed technology: shipping a movie digitally through fiber optic lines or satellite into a "new generation" home video/computer unit.

Huge-screen TVs are heading to stores....

(source: *USA TODAY*, 6 January 1990.)

Who owns TV/Radio?

The main TV/radio networks in the USA are Capital cities/ABC and Columbia. Most networks in the USA are commercial, depending on advertising for their income. With millions of dollars involved in advertising, TV and radio have become part of the high-cost **media** and entertainment business in the USA. Large, multi-national, privately owned companies, struggle for control of media companies. In 1989, for example, the Japanese multi-national company, Sony, took over the American Columbia Company in a deal worth over $3 billion, which included films, TV and CBS Records. In 1990, Time Warner became the world's biggest media-entertainment group, incorporating magazine publishing, film production, record production, book publishing and TV networks.

While most TV and radio is commercially based, some radio programmes are financed from US Government funds. 'The Voice of America', for example, broadcasts news throughout the world in about 40 languages, and 'Radio Free Europe' broadcasts in 23 languages. In 1990 Lech Walesa, leader of the Polish movement Solidarity, described this service as 'the sun on the earth'.

By 1990, Cable News Network (CNN), a daily, 24 hours a day live news channel was being beamed into 20 million American homes, and to over 100 countries.

A look at statistics that shape our lives   TV viewing USA

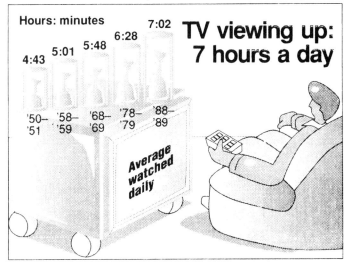

Hours: minutes
4:43 5:01 5:48 6:28 7:02

TV viewing up: 7 hours a day

'50–'51 '58–'59 '68–'69 '78–'79 '88–'89

Average watched daily

Source: Nielsen Television Index

Television goes global

NOW that television programming, complete with commercials, can be sent by satellite to distant and different countries, what is going to happen to global culture? Some fear that the world is about to become one homogeneous mass, watching pornography and American soaps from corner to corner...

Satellite television is only one of the ways in which the western world barges in on other countries. Emigrants from poor countries continually send back news from beyond. In many of the world's rain forests and desert islands, the video revolution occurred before broadcast television. Hollywood, the soaps and endless Taiwanese kung-fu specials, in videotape, have already arrived there. Television broadcast by satellite extends the already teeming market...

(source: *The Economist*, 18 June 1988.)

USA TODAY

TIME

INTERNATIONAL HERALD TRIBUNE

NEWSWEEK

The New York Times

The Washington Post

Newspaper titles, USA

Newspapers/Magazines

National newspapers, such as the *New York Times*, *Washington Post*, and *Wall Street Journal* are fairly well known in America, but most of the 1000 different newspapers are based on local areas, and carry mainly local news. In the 1980s, however, a newspaper called *USA Today* was published using the latest colour printing technology. It prints short news items, and has gained a daily national circulation of almost two million, with additional sales in other parts of the world. The colour magazines *TIME* and *Newsweek* also publish international editions.

The freedom of newspapers and magazines is guaranteed in the US Constitution, which prevents any law limiting the freedom of speech. Recently, though, the increasing number of mergers and takeovers have raised fears that competition will be restricted and people's choices might suffer.

Media issues – USA

Bias

Gore Vidal, the author and critic, claims that there is no real right-wing versus left-wing political debate in the USA, since few left-wing speakers or writers appear in the US media. In 1989 during the Virginian miners strike there was little or no reporting of this event in the US media. Some miners claimed that more attention would have been paid to them by the US media if they had been miners on strike in the USSR.

Advertising

Much of the US media's finance comes from advertising revenue. Adverts shown in prime time,

WHY JOHNNY CAN'T READ AND WRITE

Cartoon by Orlando

when most people are watching television, are very expensive. Many programmes such as sport and drama are broken into sections to allow advertising slots. Indeed, there is a suggestion that football (soccer) should be played in three 25-minute slots to allow more time for advertising during the 1994 World Cup in the USA.

Recently, several hundred US schools have accepted an offer by Time/Warner of video cassette recorders and TV for the classroom, in return for showing the Channel 1 news programme containing adverts to their pupils.

Influence

The worldwide influence of American media through TV, radio, **satellite** and video means that programmes such as *Dallas* are directed at international audiences and may spread the ideas of capitalism to many countries of the world where the governments do not consider such ideas as the appropriate ways of organising their countries.

In America itself, the media is used widely for political influence. In the 1988 elections, for example, entertainment stars such as Frank Sinatra, Woody Allan, Meryl Streep, and Cher all appeared on political programmes.

Media – USSR

Newspapers/Magazines

There are over 8000 newspapers, including 600 dailies, in the USSR. Most newspapers have been increasing their circulation recently, due in part to improved technology but mainly due to the influence of *glasnost* (openness). However, *Pravda*, the main newspaper in the USSR, which is published every day in over 40 cities, has not increased its sales recently and, in 1990, made several changes. A new editor, approved by President Gorbachev, was appointed and the sub-title 'Communist Party of the Soviet Union' has been dropped. The 'openness' policy has meant that differing viewpoints are printed, and more readers are showing interest. Indeed, one of the Soviet newspapers, *Argumenti i Fakty* , which receives thousands of letters each day, recently gained an award by press critics in London for the quality of its journalism. It has started an international edition, as has the glossy *Moscow News*, a current affairs magazine hoping to attract Western advertisers.

Press controls and ownership

Most official newspapers and magazines in the Soviet Union are owned and published by public organisations such as the Communist Party. Information for the media is supplied mainly by the TASS News Agency, which is directly under Government control. During Gorbachev's term in office **censorship** has been loosened, and now it is not only *Krokodil*, a satirical magazine, or the *samizdat* (underground) papers which criticise officials and the Government.

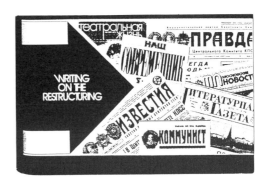

Newspaper titles – USSR

The Soviet press: *circulation figures*		
	1986	**JUNE 1989**
Daily papers		
Izvestiya ("News")	6,900,000	11,336,500
Komsolmolskaya pravda ("Young Communist League Truth")	14,600,000	18,589,000
Pravda ("Truth")	11,000,000	10,920,000
Sovetskaya Rossiya ("Soviet Russia")	3,600,000	4,865,000
Weekly papers and magazines		
Argumenty i fakty ("Arguments and Facts")	not known	21,748,400
Literaturnaya gazeta ("Literary Gazette")	3,000,000	6,450,000
Moskovskie novosti ("Moscow News")	not known	250,000
Ogonek ("Little Light")	561,000+	3,350,000

(source: *Soviet Spring*, January 1990.)

TV/Radio

Several national TV networks and four radio channels broadcast in all republics of the USSR. The main TV channels broadcast about 20 hours per day to about 90 million TV sets in the USSR.

Issues – problems and debate

As censorship is eased in the Soviet media, so more criticism of Government is published and there is more openness about problems in the USSR – corruption, ethnic tensions, environmental concerns, and crime.

The policy of *glasnost* has also influenced the content of TV programmes. There have been televised debates between different candidates in the recent elections, and the Congress of the Soviets was broadcast live in 1990 for the first time. Indeed, might this policy of televising debates lead to even more discussion of a wide range of issues in the Soviet Union? In 1990, President Gorbachev ended the Communist Party's domination of broadcasting. The republics were allowed greater control over production and content of programmes. By 1991 the Russian Republic was producing its own TV news programmes.

Soviet TV Programmes A Round-up

National channels 1 and 2
- *Vremja* ("Time"), a daily 35-minute news programme. Usually starts at 9pm.
- *Mazldunarodnaja panorama* ("International Panorama"), weekly 60-minute current affairs programme. Goes on air on Sundays, and is repeated during the week. Usually 4–5 subjects...
- *Chto, yge, kogda?* ("What? Where? When?), a TV game show. No established regularity – once or twice a month.
- *Podznakompi* ("Under the Sign of Pi"), a popular scientific weekly programme. Normally starts at 10pm...
- *Spokoinoz nochi, malyshi* ("Good Night, Little Ones"), a programme for small children, aired 8–8.10pm daily. Usually includes a cartoon.
- *Eto vy mozhete* ("You can do it"), a monthly programme on interesting inventions, developments and such phenomena as extra-sensory perception and faith-healing. Normally goes on air on Sundays...

(source: *Soviet Spring*, January 1990.)

ETHNIC UNREST

AS SERIOUS ethnic violence persisted in Azerbaijan and Armenia last week, President Gorbachev went on Central Television to explain the reasons for declaring a state of emergency in Nagorno-Karabakh, Baku and some other border areas....

(source: *Soviet Weekly*, 25 January 1990.)

Enough is enough

Elena Titova investigates why an industrial worker has handed in his party card

ALEXANDER Stupak has been in the party for ten years, and now he's had enough. Like hundreds of other communists he's resigned from the CPSU....

He's one of the top workers at the giant Uralmash machine plant in the Urals, and his decision has not been taken lightly....

"I no longer believe that the ruling party, which claims to be the guiding force of Soviet society, is capable of improving the life of the people," he told me at the Uralmash party office.

(source: *Soviet Weekly*, 22 March 1990.)

Progress for *perestroika*

QUESTIONS

1. Why has circulation increased in most Soviet newspapers?

2. What attempts were made to improve the circulation of *Pravda*?

3. In what ways does the Soviet Government control the press?

4. What kinds of problems are now more openly written about in the Soviet press?

5. In what way might television in the USSR be contributing to the changes?

Media – China

Newspapers/Magazines

In 1990, more than 2000 newspapers were published in China. Most of these newspapers are published in the provinces and contain mainly local news.

Some of the larger-circulation newspapers are:

BEIJING RIBA (BEIJING DAILY)
published by Beijing Communist Party

BEIJING WANBAO (BEIJING EVENING NEWS)

CHINA DAILY printed in English
One of the Chinese magazines which is published for the international market is the *Denmin Huabao* (*China Pictorial*), which is printed in about a dozen different foreign languages.

TV/Radio

There are more than 100 million TV sets in China. Virtually all TV and radio programming is controlled by the Government through the Ministry of Radio and Television and the Central People's Broadcasting Station. This broadcasting station operates three TV channels, a Chinese radio broadcasting service, and Radio Beijing, a Chinese radio service broadcast in over 40 languages including English, German, Arabic, Russian, and Esperanto.

Outside a TV shop, Shanghai

Advertising on TV is permitted in China, and a one-hour programme usually carries about ten minutes of advertising. The main Chinese advertisers are drinks and electronics companies, who spend over £3 million on adverts. Japanese companies take almost half of the advertising on TV in China.

Media issue – bias

Most public information in China which comes via the media is controlled by the Government. Thus, in times of crisis, the news can become the official news and alternative views gain little or no access to the media.

Demonstration in Tiananmen Square, 17 May 1989

TV programmes

Friday, May 12

Channel 2
19:46   TV series: Volga Diary (15)
20:02   Cultural Life: Cradlesong
20:33   TV drama: Autumn Whispers
22:55   TV series: The Soul and the Land (2)

Channel 8
19:00   US cartoon: The Littles (21)
19:51   Around the World: 1. Labour created the world 2. Guinness World Records
20:12   Japanese TV serial: Happiness for Tomorrow (19)

CCTV English Service
22:10   News
22:30   Window on the World: Earth – the changing environment

Channel 15
20:00   China National Peking opera Competition
22:15   Kunqu opera: Hujiazhuang Village

Channel 6
18:45   Beijing News and Weather
19:45   Legal Knowledge
20:10   Travelling in China: The ancient city of Kaifeng, Henan, China
20:50   Japanese TV serial: The Third Mother (22,23)

Channel 21
19:30   For Children
21:35   World Sports Special

(source: *China Daily*, 12 May 1989.)

In the months leading up to the Tiananmen Square incidents the Chinese media to some extent supported the demands for reform. In April '89 the *China Daily* published reports of China Youth News TV programmes which criticised Government departments and officials. In May there were protests by over 1000 journalists, objecting to censorship of the news by Government authorities and officials. However, after the military intervention in the Square in June '89 to crush the pro-democracy protests, the media generally followed the Government's view and showed TV pictures of 'criminals responsible for the rebellion' who were arrested, tried and executed.

Media issue – foreign news

As part of a crackdown on the media after the Tiananmen incidents the sale of foreign newspapers and magazines was banned in Beijing. Hong Kong-based newspapers and magazines were also banned in China because they presented different versions of the killings from those given by the official Chinese **news agencies**. Some foreign TV broadcasts are available in China but at that time some satellite transmissions by Western TV stations were cut. Several broadcasts by the 'Voice of America' radio stations were jammed.

'...On Saturday, the *People's Daily* devoted half its front page to a speech by Mr Jiang warning that there could be no place in authority for people disloyal to Marxism and declaring that revolutionary ardour was needed to take China through an "extremely critical time"...'

(source: *The Scotsman*, 1 January 1990.)

'...Meanwhile the official media disclosed that 350,000 people had been disciplined and more than 2,500 of them arrested in a nationwide campaign against the "six evils" of corruption.
Several criminal gangs had been smashed in Guangdong, the southern province bordering Hong Kong, the reports said...'

'...CHINA'S Communist Party chief, Jiang Zemin, vowed yesterday that Peking would pursue its own version of socialism despite "twists and turns" in other countries...'

Q UESTIONS

1.   Which Chinese newspapers and magazines appear in other countries?

2.   In what ways does the Chinese Government control the media?

3.   What advertisements can be seen on Chinese TV?

4.   What signs were there before the Tiananmen Square incidents that some people in the media supported the protesters?

5.   In what ways did the Chinese Government put restrictions on the media after the Tiananmen Square incidents?

A CTIVITIES

1.   Find out how many TV sets there are in Britain.

2.   Draw a graph to compare the size of the population and the number of TV sets in Britain and in China.

3.   Working in groups, three groups should prepare viewpoints supporting more freedom for journalists in China.

4.   Three other groups should prepare viewpoints supporting the censorship by officials in China.

5.   Pairs of groups with opposite viewpoints should now combine to discuss their notes.

KEYWORDS

The following Keywords are used in this Unit. Make sure you have understood what they mean.

media	**censorship**
satellite	**news agency**
consumerism	

Media Report – *Tiananmen Deaths*

The Beijing regime claims that no-one was shot in Tiananmen Square in the early hours of Sunday, 4 June. That claim has already been contradicted by reports in the western press. But, here, for the first time in Britain, is the direct testimony of an anonymous student who escaped from the Square. He describes the deliberate shooting down of students beaten from the Monument to the People's Heroes in the middle of the Square.

If a right-wing Taiwan newspaper had published this eye-witness account of the Tiananmen massacre, the Beijing assassins could have tried to dismiss it as fabrication. But it appeared in "Wen Wei Po", one of Hong Kong's two pro-Beijing pro-Communist dailies...

(source: *New Statesman*, 16 June 1989.)

Voices of Protest – USA

Appalachian miners' strike

In 1989 the coal miners in the Appalachian Mountains area of the USA went on strike for more than four months. They demanded an end to compulsory Sunday working. During the strike the 50 000 miners also complained of media coverage which concentrated on the violence involved in the strike – the destruction of property and stone throwing. Little or nothing, they claimed, was printed about the dangers of coal mining or the poverty in which many miners' families lived. In particular the £2 million fine imposed on the United Mineworkers Union for **civil disobedience** (for slowing up coal trucks near the Pittston mines) was totally ignored by the press.

Appalachian miners' strike, 1989

JESSE JACKSON

BLACK is no longer beautiful in America. Many of the nation's black leaders have decided that they would rather call themselves, and be called, African-American. The decision has blown open an intriguing debate among political activists and intellectuals which has bubbled below the surface of American life for two decades.

Declaring the new outlook at a recent Press conference in Chicago, the Rev Jesse Jackson stated: "Just as we were called coloured and were not that; and then Negro, but not that; to be called black is just as baseless. To be called African-American has cultural integrity. It puts us in our historical context."

The civil rights leader and twice presidential campaigner, explained: "Every ethnic group in the country has a reference to some land base, some historical cultural base. There are Armenian-Americans and Jewish-Americans and Arab-Americans and Italian-Americans. African-Americans have hit that level of cultural maturity."

"Our children are in this cultural vacuum, because if you don't know your history, you don't know your destiny. There is more authority in Martin Luther King's crypt than in the Reagan presidency. His leadership is beneath the dignity and promise of America....

He never saw a weapons system he didn't support. He never saw a civil rights bill he did support."

(source: *The Scotsman*, 27 February 1989.)

MINERS' STRIKE

Like the country music they spawned, the miners have gone from the raw power of songs like Sixteen Tons and Cumberland Gap, to tugging at heart strings. But from the tears in the eyes of the miners' wives at Camp Solidarity when the stereo played Stand By Your Man, the sentiment still has the power to move.

(Source: © 1990, *Washington Post* Writers Group. Reprinted with permission.)

VOICE OF PROTEST – USA "CALIFORNIA GREENS"

LOS ANGELES – California's "Big Green," the most sweeping environmental initiative ever, could start a grassroots rebellion across the USA.

"It's inevitable other states will pick up the ball," says Lucy Blake of the California League of Conservation Voters.

Says the Democratic National Committee's Robin Shepper: "There seems to be a movement because people just don't want to wait."

Among other things, the initiative would prohibit the sale of any food sprayed with any of 30 cancer-causing pesticides. The ban would apply to all fruits and vegetables sold in California, regardless of origin.

The 39-page initiative would appear as a summary on the ballot. It also would:

• Limit emissions causing atmospheric ozone depletion and global warming. Sources: automobiles, power plants, other industries.
• Provide $300 million to protect old redwood forests.
• Prohibit oil drilling within three square miles of shore; establish a $500 million fund for spill prevention and cleanup.
• Make developers plant a tree for every 500 square feet.

(source: *USA TODAY*, 28 April 1990.)

Low-level dump site fight rages

By Rae Tyson   USA TODAY

HUDSPETH COUNTY, Texas
Amid the quiet and isolation of the desert, this county's 2,900 residents – like thousands of others across the USA – are fiercely fighting a government plan to bury low-level nuclear waste in a dozen or more sites nationwide.

"The more we find out about it, the worse it gets," says Mary Alcorn, who operates a 160,000-acre cattle ranch with her husband, Jim. The Alcorn ranch – about 10 miles from the proposed site – is one of its closest neighbors.

Indeed, widespread opposition here and across the USA could help unravel the finely crafted plan for disposing of the nation's low-level nuclear waste after Jan. 1, 1993.

"It's a hot potato in nearly every state," says Michigan Gov. James Blanchard.

Under the federal law, states are responsible for disposing of low-level radioactive waste – contaminated clothing, rags, building materials, sludge – that comes from nuclear power plants, hospitals and university research centers.

(source: *USA TODAY*, 30 March 1990.)

75

Voices of Protest – USSR

In 1957 Andrei Sakharov campaigned for the halting of nuclear tests. By 1966 he was a known **dissident**, openly criticising the lack of freedom in the Soviet Union, and publishing his writings in *Samizdat* (the underground press). Sakharov criticised Soviet intervention in Afghanistan and in 1981 was arrested and banished to Gorky, 400 kilometres east of Moscow, where he lived with his wife under house arrest. After President Gorbachev came to power, Sakharov and his wife were freed. Sakharov won nomination for a parliamentary seat in Moscow, and continued his criticisms of the slow pace of change. He died in 1989. 'It is no accident that for many years, in our country, new promising scientific trends could not develop normally while on the surface ignorance bloomed.'

Boris Yeltsin, the 59-year-old political opponent of Mr Gorbachev, who defeated him in elections for the Communist Party Leadership in 1988, strongly criticises privileges for Communist Party leaders, and Gorbachev's leadership of the Soviet Union. Yeltsin claims that the political and economic reforms are too slow. In the same year he resigned from the Communist Party as a protest at the slow pace of reform. 'Things cannot continue as they are. At this meeting the party has been given one last chance. It is necessary to restructure the Communist Party. There must not be a Party monopoly on power.'

In 1990, Yeltsin was elected Chairman of the Russian Republic which later declared itself to be 'above' the laws of the Soviet Union. In 1991 he was elected President of Russia.

Crossing point: Thousands of marchers cross the Krimsky Bridge on their way to a mass rally outside the Kremlin

Nuclear Protest – *Chernobyl*

Health is the top item on Byelorussia's agenda. And, in the republic affected worst by the disaster at the Chernobyl nuclear power station, local health authorities have proved unequal to the challenge.

One reason is the scale of the catastrophe: although Chernobyl is in the Ukraine, 70 per cent of the area contaminated lies in neighbouring Byelorussia. This was the republic which had the ill fortune to lie directly upwind of the destroyed reactor on April 26, 1986, and in the spring days that followed.

One-fifth of Byelorussia, in an area where 2.2 million people live, is contaminated by radioactive isotopes, particularly caesium-137, strontium-90 and plutonium-239 and 240.

A quarter of the people there are children under 14, and they were the first to feel the effects of Chernobyl. When I visited the children's haematology centre in Minsk over 60 children were receiving treatment for leukaemia. All needed bone marrow transplants.

Journalists writing about Chernobyl know how hard it was to gather objective information about the real state of affairs in the affected area, and how much pressure was brought to bear on them. Reporters "stirring up emotions" and "creating panic" were blatantly curbed by angry party and government officials....

Minsk, the Byelorussian capital, recently saw a massive demonstration. As bells tolled, they marched along the central street carrying black flags and placards with the names of hundreds of populated areas where it is dangerous to live. They demanded that the government take more energetic steps to clear up the effects of the disaster....

(source: *The Scotsman*, 5 February 1990.)

Georgia Protest

..."Noisy meetings and processions" were organised, *Pravda* reported. Self-proclaimed 'leaders' emerged with 'extremist slogans' such as 'Georgia for the Georgians' and 'Long Live the Independence of Georgia'. An unprecedented hunger strike took place in Tbilisi in an attempt to block the constitutional changes. More than 100 demonstrators had to be taken to hospital, and one of the unofficial 'leaders' even managed to climb onto the roof of a government building, where he desecrated the state flag. There were demonstrations and strikes, not only in Tbilisi but also in Kutaisi, Batumi and other towns. The loss of life that has now occurred will make it still more difficult for them to do so in the future.

(source: *Scotland on Sunday*, 16 April 1989.)

Students march towards Tiananmen Square to demand democracy, press freedom and dialogue with the Government, 4 May 1989

Voices of Protest – China

'Rights are not granted from above. People are born with them, but the term "human rights" is taboo in China.' 'The last forty years have been a great disappointment.'
In 1989 the astro-physicist and human rights campaigner Fang Lizhi was refused permission to meet the visiting US President, George Bush. He was accused of committing crimes of counter-revolutionary **propaganda** before and during the student demonstrations. To avoid arrest he and his wife took refuge in the US Embassy building in Beijing. In 1990 several hundred scientists, led by Soviet physicist Yuri Orlov, threatened to boycott conferences in China if the Chinese Government did not allow the couple to go free. In that year Fang Lizhi fled to the USA, then settled in Britain, where he continued to criticise the Chinese Government.

"I swear, for the sake of my country's democratisation to use my young life to defend Tiananmen Square. We are willing to fight."
Chai Ling, one of the student leaders of the 1989 Democracy Movement, was twenty-three years old at the time of these events.

After the Tiananmen Square **protest** had been put down in 1989 the authorities tried to arrest her. As 'China's most wanted woman' she fled to the Australian Embassy in Beijing, and in 1990 appeared in France, promising to continue her protests against the Chinese leaders.

'The Communist Party in China boasts about democracy, but its democracy only represents a few of the people in power.' Ren Wanding took part in the Cultural Revolution in the 1960s although he objected to its extremes and to the army clampdown which followed. In the 1970s he was a protest leader, discussing political changes and producing underground protest magazines. Arrested in 1979, he was imprisoned for four years without trial. In 1989, he wrote the words in italics above.

'We, the Muslims, demand the right to build new mosques, and Islamic schools.' In Xinjiang region about half the population of 15 million is Chinese Muslim. The Chinese Government put a limit on the number of Muslim buildings and this led to racial and religious discontent in the Kashgar area of Xinjiang. In 1990 two Chinese negotiators were killed by protesters, and troops shot about fifty people in the riots which followed.

KEYWORDS

The following Keywords are used in this Unit. Make sure you have understood what they mean.

civil disobedience
dissident
propaganda
protest

4

NATIONAL INTEREST AND POWER

4.1

NATIONAL NEEDS

We all have needs as individuals. These needs change as we grow older and as our circumstances change. Among these needs are food, care, health, protection, shelter, clothing. Just as individuals have needs so also do countries. These needs are often shown as needs of the country's citizens as a group – for example 'the country needs better hospitals'. Often Governments will talk about these needs in terms of the national interest.

Some of the most important of these national needs can be seen in the following diagram:

WHAT THIS COUNTRY NEEDS

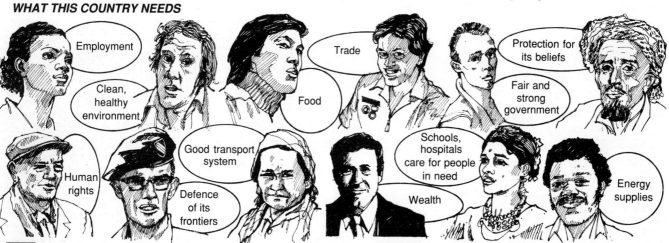

A CTIVITY

Study the above diagram of national needs and in small groups try to decide which of these needs are the most important for a country. Compare your list with other groups in the class and discuss your findings.

Conflict

Sometimes the needs of one country can come into conflict with the needs of another country. These clashes can arise over a conflict of interests about basic things – ownership of land or supplies of food or raw materials such as oil.

Throughout history, countries have often come into conflict over disputed borders or over situations where one country has invaded another to guarantee supplies of food or raw materials which they saw as essential to their own survival. Other conflicts of national interest arise over differences of values or beliefs – countries have fought with each other over matters of religion. In the period since 1945 the major clash of national interests in the world has arisen over the conflict between the two ideologies of Communism and Capitalism. The two leading world powers – the USA and the USSR – have seen their own best interests as being served by defending and spreading their own ideologies. Later in this unit you will see an example of a conflict between Britain and Argentina over a dispute of national interests concerning the Falkland Islands.

Cooperation

Sometimes the needs of a country can also be met by cooperating with another country or with a group of other countries. Rather than fight to gain possession of food or raw materials countries will more usually trade with each other for these goods.

A most important example of international cooperation in the period since 1945 has been the formation of the United Nations in an attempt to solve world problems such as war and peace, world hunger and the destruction of the environment. Later in this Unit you will find another example of international cooperation in the European Community where the countries of Western Europe have agreed to cooperate to meet their shared economic needs. In Chapter 4, Unit 4 you will also find examples in NATO and the Warsaw Pact of countries agreeing to cooperate to meet their defence needs.

In agreeing to cooperate with other countries, a Government may have to sacrifice some form of national need for the benefit of other needs. The British Government has often been in dispute with its European Community partners over such things as farming, where Britain feels that the Community policy on farming is not necessarily good for British farmers or consumers.

1.
Israelis in revenge raid on guerrillas
ISRAELI warplanes destroyed a guerrilla base of a radical Palestinian faction in south Lebanon yesterday, four days after the group killed an Israeli colonel...

(source: *The Scotsman*, 26 January, 1990.)

2.
UK will send 6,000 men and 120 tanks to Gulf
By Christopher Bellamy and Colin Brown

BRITAIN is to send a reinforced armoured brigade, with 120 Challenger tanks and at least 6,000 men, to Saudi Arabia. Tom King, Secretary of State for Defence, said it would be the heaviest and most concentrated military force deployed by Britain since the Second World War....

Mr King said: "Our purpose in sending further forces is two-fold. First, to ensure that no further aggression can possibly succeed and that the defensive shield is sure for Saudi Arabia and the threatened Gulf States. Secondly, to ensure that Saddam Hussein understands that while we seek the implementation of the United Nations' resolutions by peaceful means, other options remain available and that, one way or another, he will lose.

Iraq's evil aggression must be reversed...."

(source: *The Independent*, 15 September 1990.)

5.
UK to compromise on European union
MARGARET THATCHER will today signal her readiness to accept limited steps toward European union to avoid being isolated at the European summit in Dublin, **writes Colin Brown**.

Compromise proposals are being prepared by a Cabinet committee, chaired by the Prime Minister, to enable Britain to retain control over policy on key areas, while allowing the European Council and Commission to determine policy in other areas....

(source: *The Independent*, 27 April 1990.)

6.
US 'may base new missiles in Britain'
THE United States is considering siting a new land-based nuclear missile system in Britain, it was claimed last night...

(source: *The Scotsman*, 6 February 1990.)

7.
Superpowers to unite against Iraq
By Christopher Irvine

TODAY'S snap summit will present a united superpower front to isolate Iraq and seek the formation of joint American/Soviet action to deny what President Bush has called the fruits of Saddam Hussein's aggression....

(source: *Scotland on Sunday*, 9 September 1990.)

Moscow rubs salt in Lithuania's wound
MOSCOW – As factories shut, key medical supplies dwindled and Russian lorry drivers blocked streets in Vilnius yesterday, Lithuania looked more isolated than ever in the face of Kremlin insistence that the pressure would not relent until it rescinds its proclamation of independence of 11 March, **writes Rupert Cornwell**....

(source: *The Independent*, 27 April 1990.)

4.
China lifts martial law but maintains squeeze on Tibet
CHINA yesterday announced the lifting of martial law in Tibet, nearly 14 months after it sent in troops to quell the worst outbreak of anti-Chinese violence in 30 years...

(source: *The Independent*, 1 May 1990.)

A CTIVITIES

1. Here are some examples of countries taking action to follow their national needs. Some actions involve other countries and result in conflict or cooperation. Write a sentence about each one, saying which particular needs are being followed and – if appropriate – whether they result in conflict or cooperation.

2. Choose an example of an international crisis or conflict which is on-going during the time you are studying this topic. Make up a short project on this crisis, showing which countries are involved, what the different countries see as their national interests, and the ways in which they are protecting these national interests.

The Falklands Conflict

In 1982 British and Argentinian forces fought a short but bloody conflict over the Falkland Islands, a group of islands which lie about 640 kilometres south-east of the coast of South America.

The war caused the death of some 250 British servicemen and over 700 Argentinians. Britain lost thirty planes and helicopters and six ships with more aircraft and ships being damaged. Argentina lost 120 aircraft, one submarine and four ships, and left on the Islands many items of military equipment when they surrendered to UK forces on 14 June 1982.

What caused this war? Why had two countries so far apart felt that force was the only means by which they could resolve their differences?

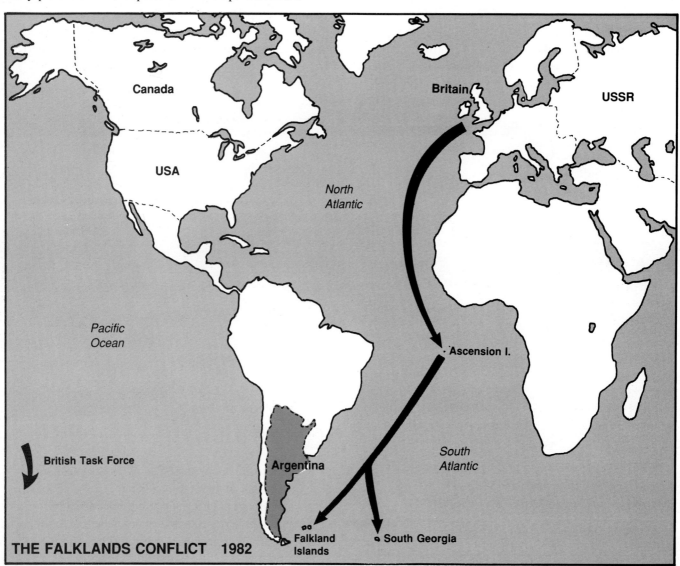

THE FALKLANDS CONFLICT 1982

ACTIVITIES

1. Study the claims and counter-claims on the opposite page and making two separate lists – one for the UK and one for Argentina – write down the various forms of national interest which both sides claimed to be defending.

2. Use your class or school library to find out more about the Falklands Conflict.

3. Hold a class discussion on whether the Falklands Conflict should have happened.

Claim and Counter-claim

UK

• "The Falkland Islands have been British since 1833."

• "The Falkland Islanders want to remain British. Britain has a duty and a right to meet the wishes of its citizens."

• "Argentina invaded the Falkland Islands in April 1982 despite the fact that negotiations had been taking place for many years over the future of the Islands. The UK has to defend her territory and citizens against such acts of unprovoked force."

• "The Government of Argentina was an unelected military dictatorship. The Argentinian leader, General Galtieri, only wanted a success in the Falklands to improve his popularity in Argentina and take away attention from his domestic failures."

Argentina

• "Argentina has a historical right to the Islands, which we call the Malvinas. When Argentina gained independence from Spain in 1816, we rightly claimed the Islands."

• "The UK has never been interested in the Islands. They are over 5600 kilometres from the UK but only 640 kilometres from Argentina. The Islanders have depended upon Argentina for such services as air transport and hospitals."

• "The UK has delayed and delayed negotiations for more than seventeen years and has never shown any strong willingness to protect or invest in the Islands."

• "The UK had ignored the Islands for years and only sent troops to the Malvinas to avoid being seen to be weak by the British public."

Conflict in the Falklands

The European Community

WHO?

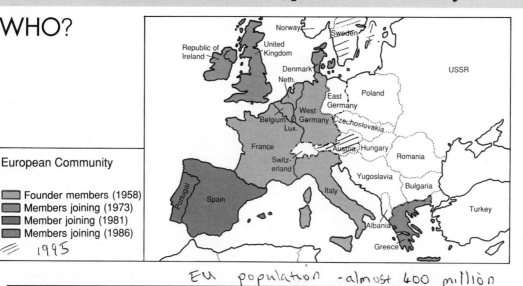

European Community

- Founder members (1958)
- Members joining (1973)
- Member joining (1981)
- Members joining (1986)
- 1995

EU population - almost 400 million

WHAT?

The European Community arose from a desire to establish a peaceful and prosperous Europe after the horrors of two World Wars. The twelve nations of the Community have agreed to merge their economic interests to form a 'common market' where trade may be conducted freely, people can work wherever they want, and money can be invested where it is most needed.

THIS. . .

. . .NOT THIS

Free Trade

Each of the countries of the European Community used to charge taxes – known as *tariffs* – on goods imported into that country. These have now been removed in order to create: a larger home market, cheaper goods, a wider range of goods, and a better standard of living for Community citizens.

Agriculture

It is vital that Europe can produce the food its people need. The Community's Common Agricultural Policy sets common prices for food in order to create a stable market and make sure that farmers are adequately paid.

Freedom To Work

All citizens of the European Community are free to seek jobs in any Community country, on equal terms with the nationals of that country. Work permits are not required and there is no loss of social security rights.

Regional Help

The Community has funds to help regions and groups with economic difficulties.

Finance

The European Monetary System was set up in an attempt to create a common system of currency exchange rates, moving perhaps to a single European currency.

The World

The Community's Common Trade Policy allows it to trade and to negotiate as one united body.

1992 - Free movement of: goods, people, services, capital)

ACTIVITIES

1. Study the above information on the European Community and make a list of the national needs which it aims to achieve through cooperation.

2. Use your class or school library to find out more about the European Community.

KEYWORDS

The following Keywords are used in this Unit. Make sure you have understood what they mean.

needs   **conflict**

national interest   **cooperation**

POWER

In the previous unit we saw that states have national needs which are known as their **national interests**. Some states are in a better position than others to protect or to promote their national interests. The ability to do this depends upon the **power** of a state to protect itself and to influence others. Power can be measured in a variety of ways.

We can look at this in terms of the power which individuals can use in looking after their own needs and in influencing others.

These three cartoons illustrate what can make individuals powerful. A person's power to influence others can come from that individual's:

– size and physical strength
– occupation or position
– wealth.

Of course, possession of weapons can also give an individual power over others. This is a very dangerous form of power and is one that the law takes great care to prevent people from using.

National power

Just as we can measure an individual's ability to be powerful, so we can apply measures to countries to judge how powerful they are. A country can be powerful because of its size, wealth or military strength.

1. Size

A country's size can be measured in terms of its land area. A large country will usually have raw materials and food available within its own borders. A smaller country may well have to rely upon imported raw materials and food. Another indication of a country's size is the population of a country. A country's people form the workforce of that country, and a healthy and well-educated population is a major asset to the economy of a nation. Of course, a large population can also be a source of weakness for a country if that country is too poor to feed and look after its people.

Size and population	USA	USSR	China
Area (km²)	9 million	21 million	10 million
Population (millions)	226	262	1000
Average life expectancy (years)	73	69	65
Percentage of population aged under 20	35	37	40–45

2. Wealth

A rich country with a healthy and well-developed economy is in a strong position to look after its national interests. A strong economy allows a country to be independent and to apply influence on others through trading agreements. The wealth of a country is described in terms of its Gross National Product (GNP). GNP is a measure of the value of goods and services produced each year by a country, including earnings from trade and overseas investments.

Industrial strength	USA	USSR	China
GNP ($US billions)	2100	1200 (estimate)	444 (estimate)
Steel (million tonnes)	135	166	34
Oil (million tonnes)	474	629	110
Computers in use	340 000	30 000	2000
Percentage of workforce in agriculture	3.3	25	85

3. Military strength

Military strength is equally a measure of power and can be described in two ways – in terms of numbers of armed forces and in terms of numbers and types of weapons.

The size of a country's armed forces is very important but we also need to know how they are armed and above all in the modern world the size and capability of a country's nuclear force.

Military strength (1)	USA	USSR	China
Military spending in relation to GNP	6%	12%	9%
Armed forces	2.09 million	4.84 million	4.3 million
Nuclear warheads	7192	6302	500
Nuclear submarines	70	85	1

Military strength (2)	USA	USSR	China
Armed forces on active duty	2.09 million	4.84 million	4.3 million
Nuclear warheads	7192	6302	500
Long-range missiles	1628	2384	2
Warplanes	3988	4885	5500
Tanks	11 560	48 000	11 000
Aircraft carriers	13	2	0
Other major surface warships	210	266	25
Submarines	121	370	92

Definition of a powerful country

A powerful country is one which has the economic and military strength to defend its own interests when these are challenged, and the strength to exert its influence on other countries throughout the world.

Use of power

A country can use its power to protect or promote its national interests in a variety of ways. We can see some of these by looking once again at the example of the Falklands Conflict in 1982.

When Argentinian forces landed on the Falkland Islands, the UK Government used its power in the following ways:

1. Diplomatic power

When Argentinian forces landed on the Islands the UK Government used its diplomatic power to get the United Nations to pass a Resolution which called on Argentina to withdraw and to settle the problem through negotiations. In addition the UK used its friendship with the USA to get that very important country to apply further diplomatic pressure on Argentina.

2. Economic power

The UK Government was able to persuade a number of countries including its partners in the European Community and the USA, Australia and New Zealand, to agree not to enter into any new trade agreements with Argentina until they withdrew from the Falklands. This type of pressure is known as **economic sanctions**.

3. Military power

In addition to applying diplomatic and economic pressure, the UK Government sent a military task force from Britain to re-occupy the Islands by force if necessary. At the end of the crisis it was the use of military power rather than diplomatic or economic pressure which was the most important feature in the re-capture of the Islands.

---

*Q*UESTIONS

1. Why might a large country be more powerful than a small one?

2. Why might a country with a large population be more powerful than a country with a small population?

3. In what ways might a large population be a source of weakness for some countries?

4. What does GNP measure?

5. Why might a wealthy country be more powerful than a poor one?

6. What factors must be considered in measuring the military strength of a country?

Nuclear Strength

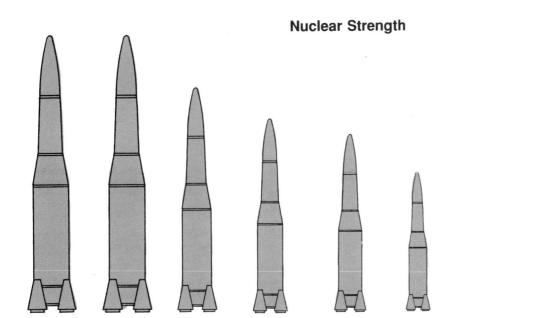

USA & USSR   China   UK   France   India   Canada   Japan   Germany

A CTIVITY

Here is a group of statistics which can be used to measure the power of the countries listed.

Country	Area (sq. km)	Population	GNP per capita	Armed Forces
Australia	7 682 300	16 532 000	$10 900	70 500
Canada	9 215 430	25 625 100	$15 080	84 600
China	9 571 300	1 057 210 000	$300	3 160 000
France	543 965	55 632 000	$12 860	456 900
India	3 287 263	796 600 000	$300	1 367 000
Japan	377 815	122 264 000	$15 770	245 000
UK	244 103	56 930 200	$10 430	316 700
USA	9 372 614	245 602 000	$18 430	2 163 000
USSR	22 402 200	286 717 000	$8360	5 096 000
W. Germany	248 709	61 171 000	$14 460	488 700

Draw a table like the one shown above with the names of the countries down the left-hand side.

The area and population are guides to a country's size. GNP is used to measure a country's wealth and GNP per capita is a measure of that wealth when compared to the population of that country. The size of armed forces gives a guide to the military strength of a country and finally the diagram showing nuclear strength is a further guide to military strength. From the information in the statistics and in the diagram give each country points according to how much power it gains from each of the headings. You should allocate 10 points for the largest and 1 point for the smallest. If one or more countries are equal then divide the points among them. Allocate points for each of the four headings. Once you have completed the table, explain which are the three most powerful countries, giving reasons for your answer.

KEYWORDS

The following Keywords are used in this Unit. Make sure you have understood what they mean.

power

Gross National Product (GNP)

nuclear force

POWER POINTS

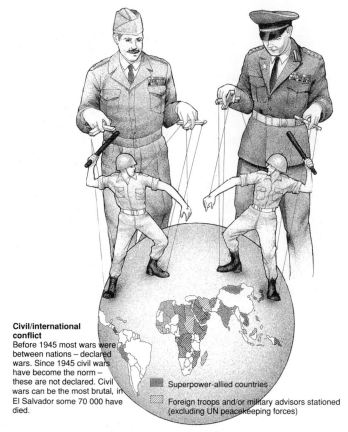

Civil/international conflict
Before 1945 most wars were between nations – declared wars. Since 1945 civil wars have become the norm – these are not declared. Civil wars can be the most brutal, in El Salvador some 70 000 have died.

▓ Superpower-allied countries

▨ Foreign troops and/or military advisors stationed (excluding UN peacekeeping forces)

We have seen in the previous two units those needs which countries feel they must defend and promote as central to their national interests. We have also seen those measures of power which allow a country to follow its national interests.

In the period since 1945 the two most powerful countries in the world have been the USA and the USSR. Because of their overwhelming domination of world affairs, these two countries are known as the **Superpowers**. As Superpowers they have a large range of national needs which they feel they need to protect and defend. In addition they have come to be identified as the leaders of the two opposing ideologies – Capitalism and Communism – which have dominated the modern world. These factors have involved these two great powers in a series of conflicts throughout the world. Sometimes these conflicts bring the two Superpowers into direct conflict. At other times they have confronted each other indirectly, often using other countries to express their rivalry.

In the following 'Conflict Files' we will see examples of the Superpowers involving themselves in other countries in pursuit of what they see as the protection of their national interests. In most of these examples the Superpowers are involving themselves in areas which they see as their 'backyards' and therefore areas which they feel themselves to be justified in controlling.

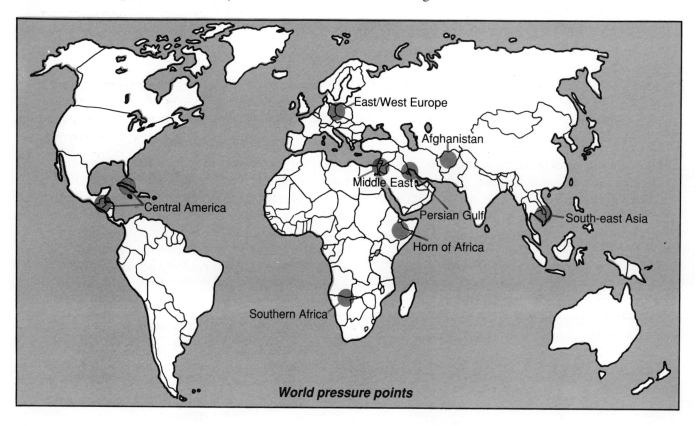

World pressure points

Conflict File – Central America

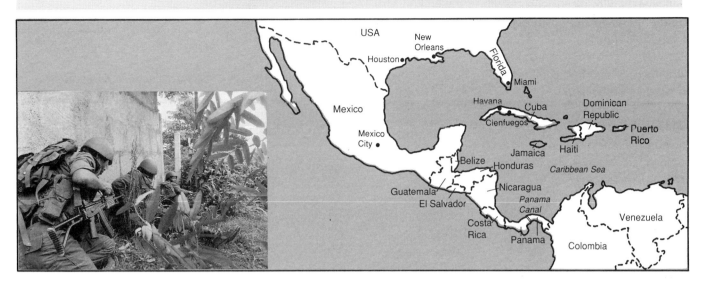

Database: Central America

Central America stretches from Guatemala to the narrow strip of Panama.

Of the region's 23 million people, about half are native Indian. The remainder are white descendants of the Spanish settlers who colonised the area.

The region largely depends upon agriculture, with coffee, bananas, cotton and sugar being the main crops. These make up more than half the region's exports. A small minority of the population in the region own most of the land and the wealth. The region depends heavily upon aid and investment from the United States. The majority of the population are poor and resent the wealthy, powerful minority who have ruled them. Many Central American governments have paid little attention to improving social and economic conditions for their people, to developing democracy or to looking after human rights.

Cuba

Although not strictly part of the region of Central America, the Caribbean island of Cuba has played an important part in the political affairs of the area. In 1959 a revolution in Cuba brought Fidel Castro to power. Since then Cuba has been a Communist state which has relied upon the USSR for economic and military support and which has been eager to see revolutionary change taking place elsewhere in the region.

Capital: Havana
Population: 10 million
Head of State: Fidel Castro
Politics: one-party state – Communist Party of Cuba
Main export: sugar

Guatemala

Under military rule since 1954. Heavily dependent upon the USA for military aid and economic assistance. The Government has been faced with major guerrilla opposition. The guerrilla war and the Government repression have made the country liable to revolutionary change.

Capital: Guatemala
Population: 7.5 million
Main exports: coffee, cotton and sugar
Land ownership: top 2 per cent of the population own 72 per cent of the land

El Salvador

Smallest and most densely-populated country in the region. El Salvador has been greatly affected by internal unrest and civil war as left-wing revolutionary guerrilla groups have fought with Government troops who are largely armed and trained by the USA. Large-scale civilian killings and atrocities have made El Salvador a 'human rights nightmare'.

Capital: San Salvador
Population: 5 million
Main exports: coffee, cotton and sugar
Land ownership: top 2 per cent of the population own 60 per cent of the land

Honduras

The poorest and most under-developed country in the region. Has been controlled by the military who keep close control on any opposition. Honduras has been the centre of opposition to the Government in neighbouring Nicaragua. Those opposed to the Nicaraguan

Government were called 'Contras' and the Contras have been heavily dependent upon US military aid.
Capital: Tegucigalpa
Population: 4 million
Main exports: bananas, coffee and beef
Land ownership: top 4 per cent of the population own 65 per cent of the land

Nicaragua

Nicaragua had been ruled for over 40 years by the Somoza family dictatorship. In 1979 a popular revolution led by the Sandinista Liberation Front overthrew the Somoza Government. The new Sandinista Government took steps to place the country's farmland, banks and businesses under state control. In addition greater efforts were made to build up education and health care.

There were groups in Nicaragua – particularly the supporters of the former President Somoza – who were opposed to what the new Government was doing. These opposition groups became known as the 'Contras' and, based in Honduras, waged, with US aid, counter-revolutionary raids into Nicaragua. The USA also cut off economic aid to the Nicaraguan Government.
Capital: Managua
Population: 2.75 million
Main exports: coffee, cotton and sugar.

Why is the USA involved?

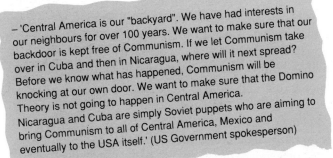

– 'Central America is our "backyard". We have had interests in our neighbours for over 100 years. We want to make sure that our backdoor is kept free of Communism. If we let Communism take over in Cuba and then in Nicaragua, where will it next spread? Before we know what has happened, Communism will be knocking at our own door. We want to make sure that the Domino Theory is not going to happen in Central America. Nicaragua and Cuba are simply Soviet puppets who are aiming to bring Communism to all of Central America, Mexico and eventually to the USA itself.' (US Government spokesperson)

– 'The Governments of Cuba and Nicaragua are the main suppliers of arms to the rebels fighting in El Salvador and Guatemala. Honduras has been the unwilling victim of Nicaraguan attacks. By giving military aid to the Governments of El Salvador and Guatemala and to the Contras in Honduras, we are helping these countries to defend themselves.' (US military spokesperson)

– 'We have major economic interests in Central America. American companies make up 80 per cent of all foreign firms in Central America. The USA is the main trading partner for much of the region. The economy of Central America would collapse without US assistance and we have a right and a duty to look after our interests.' (US business spokesperson)

The above statements show the areas of national interest which the USA feels it needs to protect in Central America. How then has the USA used its power to protect these national interests?

Economic power

The USA has given major economic assistance to the Governments of Honduras, Guatemala and El Salvador. At the same time it cut off aid to the Sandinista Government in Nicaragua.

Military power

The USA has given military aid and advice to the Governments of Honduras, Guatemala and El Salvador. It has been the main source of aid to the Contras who have been largely supplied and trained by American instructors. The USA has also been prepared to use open military force to protect its interests and in 1983 American forces invaded the island of Grenada and overthrew what it felt was a dangerous 'left-wing Marxist' government.

Political power

The USA wish to keep in power governments in Central America which meet with America's approval. This aim would be easier to carry out if these governments also had the support of the people of Central America. Many opponents of American policy criticise the USA for trying to keep in power unpopular governments who do not care for the human rights of their people. To overcome this problem, the USA has been trying to encourage democratic elections throughout the countries of Central America.

Alternative views

Of course not everyone has fully supported American policy in Central America. There are many critics of the USA throughout Central America and in the USA itself.

– 'The USA speaks of Central America as its "own backyard". But Central America is not part of the USA. It is our region and it is up to the people of El Salvador, of Guatemala, of Nicaragua and so on to decide their own future. American involvement only encourages the Soviet Union to involve itself also and we do not want to become a theatre in which the Superpowers play their power games.'

'The USA is only interested in protecting the interests
[of] big business and the profits of the American
[co]mpanies who control the coffee, cotton, and sugar
[a]nd banana plantations here. The USA is not interested
[in] the lives of the ordinary people who live here. We
[w]ant to farm land of our own. We want better schools
[f]or our children, more doctors and more hospitals.'

– 'US policy in Central America is wrong-headed and
short-sighted. We are supporting a range of
governments which have no support among the people
they claim to represent and which have a shameful
record on human rights. By supporting these
governments we are just pushing the people of Central
America into supporting left-wing revolutionary groups.
We are in fact encouraging the very Communism we
are trying to stop. Cutting off aid to Cuba and Nicaragua
only forced these countries to turn to the USSR for
help.'

*Q*UESTIONS

1. Explain the importance of Cuba in the affairs of Central America.

2. What happened in Nicaragua in 1979?

3. What kind of policies did the new Government in Nicaragua put into effect?

4. What was the reaction of the US Government to the new Government in Nicaragua?

5. What were the Contras and what part did they play in the affairs of Nicaragua?

6. What is meant by saying that the USA sees Central America as its 'backyard'?

7. Explain the Domino Theory as applied to US policy in Central America.

8. What is the economic importance of Central America to the USA?

9. Explain how the USA has used its (a) economic power (b) military power and (c) political power to influence events in Central America.

*A*CTIVITY

Study the three viewpoints put forward in the section headed 'Alternative Views'. Hold a class debate on whether the USA has a right to involve itself in the affairs of the countries of Central America.

Nicaragua up-date

In 1990 the Sandinista Government held an election to decide on a new President and on the members of their national Parliament. It was widely expected that President Ortega and his Sandinista Party, which had held power since 1979, would win comfortably. However, the election was won by the opposition Party – the National Opposition Union (UNO) – led by Mrs Violeta Chamorro. This result delighted the US Government who had been opposed to the Sandinistas since they came to power. The USA announced they would lift their economic sanctions and would start negotiations with the Contras in Honduras to end the civil war which had been taking place.

"A Faith In The Dollar, Rather Than The Bullet"
– Anna Torres

TO THE stunned surprise of many, not least the Sandinistas, the Nicaraguan people have voted resoundingly for a change of government. In an election, pronounced free and fair by more than 2,000 foreign observers, including teams from the United Nations, the Organisation of American States and Nicaragua's most relentless opponent, the United States of America, 1.75 million Nicaraguan voters gave their verdict on nearly 11 years of Sandinista rule. The majority pronounced it a failure.

Ever since the CIA formed the Contras by banding together marauding ex-Somoza national guardsmen, disaffected politicians and Indian minorities into a counter-revolutionary army in 1982, Washington's policy towards Nicaragua was aimed solely at ousting the Sandinistas and their despised neo-Marxist policies.

Both Reagan and Bush administrations justified their hostility to Nicaragua on the grounds that the Nicaraguan people did not want the Sandinista style of government. Sandinista politics have been put to the electoral test and they have, as the Americans predicted, resulted in a stunning defeat. When the Sandinistas step down and the US-backed UNO coalition takes office to form a new government on 25 April, US-Nicaraguan relations will be on an entirely different footing.

The electoral upset was astonishing: when the Sandinistas took power in 1979 they did so on a landslide of popular support. They had overthrown the corrupt and hated dictatorship of the American-backed Somoza dynasty and moved quickly to restore dignity to their much-oppressed people with the distribution of land and with literacy and health campaigns. They even held multi-party elections in 1984, long before Gorbachev's perestroika had made that a possibility for Soviet satellite nations of Europe.

The Sandinistas blamed the mess on ten years of economic and political warfare by the US with some justification. The sponsorship of the Contra war, the trade embargo and the US veto on loans from the World Bank and the IMF that might have helped reconstruct this battered land, all played a large part in the disaster. Nicaragua's pitiful survival more and more depended on huge supplies from the Soviet Union – help that was gradually diminishing.

One thing is certain: US fears that Nicaragua would be a focus for communism in Uncle Sam's backyard are finally allayed; in the 1990s the Domino Principle is falling the other way.

(source: *The Scotsman*, 27 February 1990.)

Read the source extract headed 'A Faith In The Dollar Rather Than The Bullet' and answer the following questions:

1. What steps were taken to make sure that the Nicaraguan elections were 'free and fair'?

2. What has been US policy towards Nicaragua since the early 1980s?

3. Find out through your class or school library who the CIA are.

4. What does the article claim the CIA have been responsible for?

5. Why did the USA claim that the election results 'justified their hostility to Nicaragua'?

6. Why was the election result a surprise? You will need to explain what the Sandinista Government had done to gain popular support.

7. Who did the Sandinistas blame for their economic and political problems? Give reasons for your answer.

8. Which country did Nicaragua come to rely upon for help and what was happening to that help?

9. Read the last paragraph. Explain these terms: 'Uncle Sam's backyard' and 'the Domino Principle'.

10. Explain in your own words the viewpoint in the last paragraph.

Conflict File – Afghanistan

In December 1979 the USSR sent its armed forces into its neighbouring country of Afghanistan. For the next ten years the Soviet Army found itself fighting a major guerrilla war against the Afghan Mujahedin rebels who bitterly opposed Soviet intervention in their country. By 1984 the Soviet Union had over 100 000 troops in Afghanistan, enough to control the main cities but not the countryside in which the rebels had their bases.

The rebels were supplied through Mujahedin refugee bases in Pakistan. Some military supplies came from the USA and other Western countries.

The Soviet Union claimed that it had been 'invited' into the country by the Government of Afghanistan who were under threat from rebel attack. Certainly the Soviet Union wished to see a friendly Government in power in Afghanistan and a Government over which they had control. In addition the USSR did not want to see a successful Islamic revolution in Afghanistan similar to the revolution which had taken place in Iran. The USSR has some 40 million Muslims among its population and did not want to see the spread of revolutionary Islamic ideas within its own borders.

The USA was very concerned about this action by the Soviet Union and was especially worried that it might be the first step in a Soviet advance to gain influence in the Middle East oilfields of the Persian Gulf. The war in Afghanistan proved to be very costly for the Soviet Union and proved to be a war that they 'could not win'. Eventually in 1989 President Gorbachev negotiated a Soviet withdrawal and the last Soviet troops pulled out of Afghanistan.

Conflict in Afghanistan

Conflict File – Eastern Europe

We have seen in Chapter 1, Unit 1, the changes which have taken place in Eastern Europe since 1989. This has been a major change of policy for the Soviet Union. Before 1989 Eastern Europe was clearly seen as a Soviet area of influence, as the Soviet Union's 'backyard', where it had freedom to intervene and to decide the politics of the area.

The countries of Eastern Europe – East Germany, Poland, Czechoslovakia, Hungary, Romania and Bulgaria – had been freed from German control during the Second World War by the Soviet Army. The Soviet Union had been invaded by Germany and had suffered terribly during the War, losing some 20 million people. Stalin, the Soviet leader, was determined that the Soviet Union would have greater security in the post-war world and would have a barrier of friendly countries to protect it from any future attack from the West. As a result he put into power in the countries of Eastern Europe Communist governments who owed their positions and loyalty to the Soviet Union. These Eastern European countries became known as 'satellite' countries because of their dependence upon the USSR. They were tied economically to the USSR through the Council for Mutual Economic Assistance (COMECON) and militarily through the Warsaw Pact.

Any country which tried to break away from Soviet control was forcefully dealt with. In 1956 an uprising in Hungary led to a change of Government. The new Government began to change the Communist system and announced that Hungary would leave the Warsaw Pact. Faced with this threat, the Soviet Union sent an army to 'restore order' in Hungary and replaced the 'rebel' government with a leader loyal to the Soviet Union.

Again in 1968 a new Government in Czechoslovakia attempted to reform the Communist system and bring in more freedom. Although the Czechs guaranteed the USSR that they had no intention of threatening Soviet security by pulling out of the Warsaw Pact, the Soviet leadership feared that the changes to Communism in Czechoslovakia might spread through Eastern Europe and even into the USSR itself. As a result in August 1968 Soviet and other Warsaw Pact troops invaded Czechoslovakia and replaced the Government with one loyal to the USSR.

During the early 1980s Poland was faced with major unrest which centred upon the activities of the free trade union 'Solidarity' which seemed to be challenging the power of the Polish Communist Party. The Soviet Union watched these developments with concern but chose to allow Poland to deal with the problem on its own when the Polish Army declared 'martial law' and banned Solidarity.

Eastern Europe was therefore an area where the USSR saw that it had major national interests and used its military, economic and political power to protect these interests. Since Gorbachev has come to power, the USSR has changed its policy towards Eastern Europe and this area has become free to decide its own political future (see Chapter 1, Unit 1).

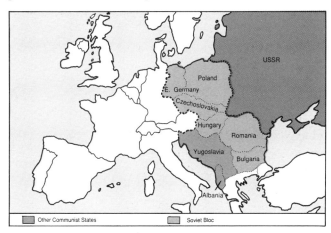

QUESTIONS

1. Describe the Soviet involvement in Afghanistan from 1979.

2. What national interests did the Soviet Union feel it was defending in being involved in Afghanistan?

3. How did the Soviet Union come to have such a major influence in the affairs of the countries of Eastern Europe?

4. What national interests did the Soviet Union feel it was defending in Eastern Europe?

5. In what ways did the Soviet Union use its political, economic and military power in influencing events in Eastern Europe?

6. How has Soviet policy in Eastern Europe changed since Gorbachev came to power?

Conflict File – The Gulf Crisis

In August 1990 Iraq, under the leadership of Saddam Hussein, invaded its neighbouring state Kuwait. This invasion was immediately condemned by almost all the world's leading nations, including both the USA and USSR. It was seen as a major threat to the national interests of the countries of the world, because no country could feel safe if such aggression against a weaker country could be successful. Also, the Persian Gulf area is one of the world's greatest producers of oil. If Hussein controlled the oil supplies of Iraq and Kuwait he would be able to put enormous pressure on the industrialised countries. The situation looked even more serious when it appeared that Iraq would next threaten Saudi Arabia with invasion.

The USA led world opposition to the invasion. It concentrated its efforts in getting the United Nations to pass a resolution condemning Iraq and in getting the UN Security Council to impose economic sanctions by blocking all imports to and exports from Iraq. In implementing this the United Nations acted with a speed and unanimity never before shown. Above all the two Superpowers, the USA and the Soviet Union, were acting together to oppose Iraq.

The United States increased the economic pressure on Iraq by persuading the United Nations to agree that the navies keeping up the economic blockade could use force to prevent supplies leaving or entering Iraq. In addition Turkey and Saudi Arabia cut off Iraq's oil pipelines which passed through their countries. This effectively stopped the main outlets for Iraq's oil exports.

As well as this diplomatic and economic pressure, the United States organised military aid for Saudi Arabia to help defend it against possible attack from Iraq. This multi-national force became known as 'Desert Shield'. Although the main army and air force troops and equipment came from the USA, the United Kingdom, France, Egypt and Syria also sent military help. Iraq, in turn, condemned these actions, claiming that the USA's aim was to gain military control of the Gulf so that it could control Arab oil.

The diplomatic, economic and military pressure on Iraq continued throughout the latter part of 1990. In September the United Nations agreed to a full air blockade of Iraq. In November the Security Council of the UN passed Resolution 678 which gave Iraq until the

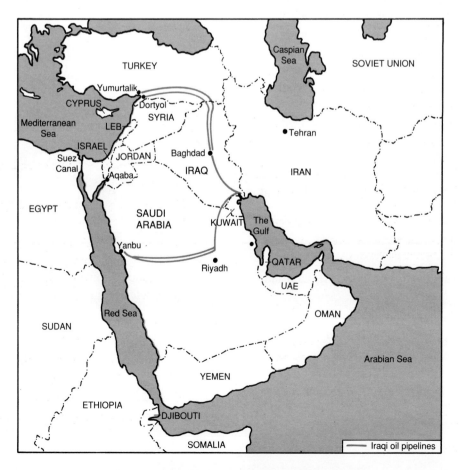

15 January to withdraw from Kuwait or face war. The US-led multi-national force in Saudi Arabia continued to increase its military build-up. Iraq refused to accept the UN Resolutions and claimed it would only enter into talks if these talks also dealt with other Middle East problems, especially those concerning Israel and the Palestinians. By the end of 1990 Iraq was refusing to give up Kuwait and was threatening to use chemical weapons and to bomb Israel if attacked. On the 9 January talks between the USA and Iraq in Geneva failed to find a solution and on the 12 January the UN Secretary-General Javier Pérez de Cuéllar flew to Iraq in a last effort to keep peace. Iraq remained determined they would not withdraw from Kuwait and the last hopes for a settlement collapsed. On the 16 January, one day after the UN deadline, war began when the multi-national force launched a major aerial offensive on Iraq.

THE ROAD TO WAR

1990

2 August	–	Iraq invades Kuwait.
3 August	–	USA announces it is sending a naval force to the Gulf. Iraqi troops appear to be on the point of invading Saudi Arabia.
6 August	–	The Security Council of the UN votes to impose trade sanctions on Iraq.
9 August	–	Iraq seals its borders. Many westerners are held as hostages. Saddam Hussein threatens to hold hostages as human shields against attack.
25 August	–	UN Security Council authorises the use of naval force to support sanctions.
28 August	–	Iraq declares Kuwait as its 19th province.
19 September	–	UN agrees to a full air blockade of Iraq.
22 November	–	Total allied force opposing Iraq numbers almost half-a-million.
29 November	–	UN Security Council resolution 678 passed giving Iraq till 15 January to withdraw or face war.
6 December	–	Iraq orders the release of all hostages.
22 December	–	Iraq says it will never give up Kuwait and will use chemical weapons if attacked.

1991

9 January	–	US-Iraq peace talks in Geneva break up in failure.
13 January	–	Peace talks between UN Secretary-General Pérez de Cuéllar and Saddam Hussein end in failure.
15 January	–	UN deadline passes with no Iraqi withdrawal from Kuwait.
16 January	–	War breaks out.

The war was dominated in the period up to late February by Allied air supremacy which allowed the Allies to bomb military targets in Iraq and Iraqi forces positioned in Kuwait. Iraq retaliated by launching Scud missiles against Israel and Saudia Arabia but for a large part of the war took up defensive positions. On 24 February the Allies launched the land war and quickly swept through Iraqi defences, meeting little opposition. On 26 February Kuwait City was liberated and as thousands of Iraqi troops began to surrender a ceasefire was declared on 28 February.

The war had involved almost 2 million troops – 643 000 Allied and 550 000 Iraqis. The Allies launched more than 100 000 air attacks against Iraq. Up to 100 000 Iraqi troops were killed or wounded and over 175 000 Iraqis were taken prisoner. The Allies lost some 147 troops killed in action and had 13 taken prisoner. Out of a total of 4200 Iraqi tanks, 3700 were destroyed or captured, and 41 out of 42 Iraqi divisions were destroyed or made ineffective.

The war had been successful in meeting all the UN Resolutions, but had left Kuwait and Iraq devastated. Iraqi troops had set fire to more than 950 Kuwait oil wells, causing massive economic and environmental damage. Allied air bombing had destroyed much of Iraq's military and economic base. The rebuilding of Kuwait was estimated to cost up to $150 billion and that of Iraq up to $200 billion.

QUESTIONS

1. Why were many countries concerned about Iraq's invasion of Kuwait?

2. Describe fully the part played by the United Nations in the Gulf crisis.

3. What was unusual about the reactions of the USA and the Soviet Union to the Gulf crisis?

4. What economic and diplomatic pressure was applied against Iraq?

5. Describe the main features of the military campaign against Iraq.

6. What national interests did the USA and its allies feel they were protecting?

7. What national interests did Iraq claim it was promoting by taking over Kuwait?

The Gulf War: A war of technology

The war in the Gulf revealed very early the enormous advances made in the technology of weapons. The first aerial attacks of the war used a variety of aircraft and missiles which made use of advanced technology to locate specific targets and destroy them with pin-point accuracy. Satellites were used to spy on Iraq and send detailed information to allied headquarters. Various devices were used to 'jam' enemy radar and missiles such as the Patriot were used to defend against attacking missiles.

The following newpaper account gives a description of the new technology deployed against Iraq in the first few hours of war.

The RAF Tornado GR1 of Flight Lieutenants Ian Long and Jerry Gegg hugged the ground doing more than 500mph at less than 100ft – "zero feet" in flying terms.

They followed the valleys as the sand dunes flashed by on either side. The plane's computer was locked in to its terrain-following radar.

The radar sprayed a wide beam forward and down, "reading" the hills and hollows and giving a clear-as-day picture on the screen in front of Ian, the pilot.

The aircraft soared and dipped as its auto-pilot followed the contours.

Ahead and to the east were unmanned cruise missles, following similar uncanny guidance systems.

They were programmed to hit Saddam Hussein's presidential palace in Baghdad, the Defence Ministry and other key targets.

Ahead of them again were the Wild Weasels, American F4G fighters, which hunt in pairs – one seeking out enemy radar tracking stations and jamming them, the other destroying them with HARM anti-radar missiles.

To the west, B52 bombers were zeroing in to carpet-bomb Iraqi tank and artillery positions mapped out in the desert by the spy-satellite, Key Hole.

And somewhere out in the dark was a ghostly black plane, still so secret it's talked about only in whispers ... the Stealth "invisible" bomber.

(source: *The People*, 20 January 1991)

Graphic by JOHN SMITH and SANDY MOLLOY

SPYING ON IRAQ

A CTIVITY

1. Conduct a class debate on whether the Gulf War was a 'necessary and just' war.

2. Use your class or school library to find examples of the use of technology in the Gulf War.

KEYWORDS

The following Keywords are used in this Unit. Make sure you have understood what they mean.

**Superpower   indirect conflict
direct conflict   Domino theory**

5

COOPERATION

THE NUCLEAR THREAT

Over the last forty years, a nuclear war between the two Superpowers, the USA and the USSR, has been possible. Despite treaties and agreements the two countries could still fight a devastating nuclear war if international cooperation broke down completely. The danger of a possible nuclear conflict is increased because other countries now have nuclear weapons.

Nuclear war

In 1945 an American plane dropped an atom bomb on Hiroshima in Japan.

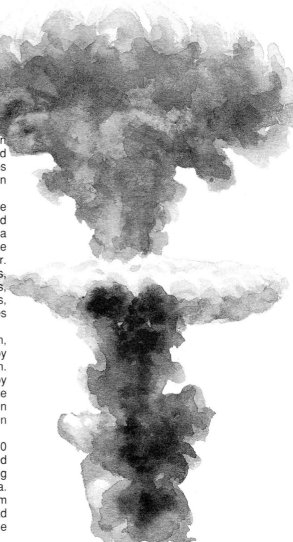

Nuclear war
Hiroshima

August the 6th, 8.15 a.m. The streets are full of people; people going to work, people going to school. It is a lovely summer morning: sunshine and blue sky. Blue sky stands for happiness in Japan. The air-raid sirens sound. No one pays attention. There's only a single enemy aircraft in the sky.

The aircraft flies across the city. Above the centre, something falls. It's hard to see – the bomb is very small; two kilograms in weight, a little larger than a tennis ball in size.

It falls for 10 or 15 seconds, it falls and falls. Then there is a sudden searing flash of light, brighter and hotter than a thousand suns. Those who were looking directly at it had their eyes burnt in their sockets. They never looked again on people or things.

In the street below there was a business man walking to his work; a lady, as elegant as she was beautiful; a brilliant student, leader of the class; a little girl, laughing as she ran.

And in a moment they were gone. They vanished from the earth. They were utterly consumed by the furnace of the flash. There were no ashes on the pavement, nothing but their black shadows on the stones. Scores of thousands more, sheltered by walls or buildings from the flash, were driven mad by an intolerable thirst that followed from the heat. They ran in frenzied hordes towards the seven rivers of the delta on which Hiroshima is built.

They fought like maniacs to reach the water. If they succeeded, they stopped to drink the poisoned stream, and in a month they, too, were dead. Then came the blast, thousands of miles an hour. Buildings in all directions for kilometres, flattened to the ground. Lorries, cars, milk-carts, human beings, babies' prams, picked up and hurled like lethal projectiles hundreds of metres through the air.

Then the fireball touched the earth, and scores of conflagrations, fanned by hurricane winds, joined in a fire-storm. And many thousands more, trapped by walls of flame that leaped higher than the highest tower in the town, in swift or in longer agony, were burnt to death. Then all went black as night.

The mushroom cloud rose 12 000 metres. It blotted out the sun. It dropped its poison dust, its fallout, on everything that still remained not lethal in Hiroshima. And death by radio-active sickness from the fallout was the fate of those who had survived the flash, the river, the blast, the fire-storm.

Philip Noel-Baker

Effects of a Nuclear Explosion

As Philip Noel-Baker's description of Hiroshima suggests, some of the most terrible results of nuclear attack are not immediately visible. A nuclear war could affect human life in five different ways.

(a) Those close to the area where the bomb falls are immediately killed or terribly maimed by the blast and the fireball.

(b) Even more serious are the effects of the nuclear radiation which is released when the bomb explodes. Skin diseases, cancers, diseases of the blood such as leukemia and internal haemorrhages can affect those who survive the immediate effects. Death from these diseases can occur many years later.

(c) The long-term effects of radiation are perhaps the most unpredictable and horrible effects of nuclear war. These can lead to terrible deformities in generations who weren't even born when the bomb fell.

(d) Most difficult to assess are the psychological effects on a nation which is on the receiving end of a nuclear attack. The Japanese people have been so deeply affected that they have built a museum of war which contains deformed human foetuses preserved in chemicals to encourage people to devote their lives to peace, not war.

(e) Recently scientists have shown that there may be another effect of nuclear war, which could be the most devastating of all. A nuclear explosion sends enormous amounts of dust into the atmosphere. As this settled over the area of attack, it would block out the sun, leave the area in permanent darkness and plunge the survivors into a 'nuclear-winter'. A full-scale nuclear war could bring about temporary ice-age conditions over at least half the world. If this lasted long enough, the lack of sunlight could kill off plant life and threaten the very survival of the human race.

The estimated effects of a 20-megatonne bomb on a target such as Grangemouth

① 0–7 km: houses totally destroyed, streets impassable
② 7–10 km: houses irreparably damaged, streets blocked until cleared with mechanical aids
③ 10–25 km: houses severely to moderately damaged, progress in street made difficult by debris
④ 25–40 km: houses lightly damaged, streets open but some glass and tile debris

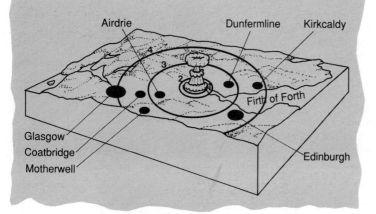

Airdrie · Dunfermline · Kirkcaldy · Firth of Forth · Glasgow · Coatbridge · Motherwell · Edinburgh

---

Effects of a nuclear explosion

The description by Philip Noel-Baker, who helped to draw up the United Nations Charter, gives some indication of the havoc caused by a nuclear bomb which would now be considered a museum item. By the 1990s for example, one US Trident submarine carried a nuclear capacity 6000 times that of the Hiroshima bomb!

Nuclear weapons, even without war, bring their own **radiation** dangers. It is estimated by Greenpeace that about fifty nuclear weapons have been lost at sea. Also, there are problems about what to do with radio-active, out-of-date nuclear weapons, such as submarines. A further danger, recently highlighted, is the effect of radiation on people working on these submarines.

Target Scotland

Scotland's geographic position on the edge of Europe, close to Atlantic and European sea and air routes, gives it a strategic importance for NATO. Consequently enemy **missiles** could be targeted on Scotland's industrial and military bases. The effects of, for example, a 20-**megatonne** bomb on one of these targets could have devastating effects on a wide area.

Q UESTIONS

1. Why is nuclear war still possible?
2. What are the effects of a nuclear explosion?
3. Why could Scotland be a nuclear target?

A CTIVITIES

1. Read the quotation 'Hiroshima,' and in groups, consider what problems would exist for any survivors.

2. Find out what the Government suggests as ways to protect yourself in the event of nuclear war.

3. Discuss, in class group, how adequate these might be.

4. In groups, list six possible targets in Scotland, and write down reasons for your choices.

Modern arms power: An F-5E fighter/bomber and its huge range of weapons

The theory of nuclear deterrence

An important feature of any nuclear arms race is the theory that nuclear weapons can keep the peace. They do this because both sides are deterred from starting a nuclear war. They know that if one side launches a nuclear attack on the other, the other side will be powerful enough to destroy them in return. This has been called the 'theory of Mutual Assured Destruction' or 'MAD'. For deterrence to work both sides have to be sure that the other side will not feel tempted into believing themselves to be strong enough to try a first attack before the other side can use its weapons. Therefore deterrence cannot work if one side feels it can launch a successful attack and destroy all the enemy **nuclear forces** before they can be fired in return. Also it cannot work if one side feels its defences are good enough to survive a counter-attack. **Nuclear deterrence** works only if both sides are equally strong and neither side believes it can win a war. This in turn helps to speed up the arms race as both sides develop new weapons to make sure they do not fall behind.

The United States and the Soviet Union have just 11% of the world's people. But they spend more than half the world's military budget, perform 80% of its military research, account for 53% of its arms exports–and possess 97% of its nuclear weapons.

ACTIVITY

Here is a set of statements connected with nuclear weapons and the arms race.

For

– Nuclear weapons have kept the peace since 1945. No country will use them first because they know that they will be destroyed in return.

– We need the best and most up-to-date weapons to keep the **balance of power** between the Superpowers.

– You cannot hope to achieve world peace and nuclear **disarmament** without being in a strong position to force the other side to disarm.

Against

– Nuclear weapons are far too dangerous to depend upon for world peace. Nuclear weapons have made the world a more dangerous, not a safer place.

– The nuclear arms race creates a vicious circle. This leads to a massive waste of money and scientific research and technology which should be directed towards solving world problems of poverty, hunger and the destruction of the environment.

– Neither side is serious about nuclear disarmament. The arms race creates a lack of trust on both sides and without trust you can never have peace. Neither side trusts the other to make the first step towards real disarmament.

Divide the class into two groups, with one group discussing the 'For' arguments and the other discussing the 'Against' arguments. Each side should note down the main points raised in the discussion.

Then organise a class discussion on the topic, 'Do nuclear weapons make the Superpower rivalry worse or do they prevent this rivalry from breaking into open war?'

The money required to provide adequate food, water, education, health and housing for everyone in the world has been estimated at $21 billion a year. It is a huge sum of money ...about as much as the world spends on arms every two weeks.

The technology of nuclear war

Millions of pounds are spent each year on the technology of war. Countries wish to improve and increase not only the types of weapons but also weapon delivery systems (tanks, guns, planes, missiles) and defence systems.

The Vocabulary of Nuclear War

Nuclear warfare has developed a special vocabulary of its own. Some of these special terms are given here to help you to understand some of the new weapons systems in use today.

ABM Anti-Ballistic Missile: fires nuclear warheads at incoming enemy missiles – a defensive weapon

IRBM Intermediate-Range Ballistic Missile: range of up to 6500 km

ICBM Intercontinental Ballistic Missile: range of over 6500 km

MRV Multiple Re-entry Vehicle: missile with several nuclear warheads

MIRV Multiple Independently-targeted Re-entry Vehicle: missile with several nuclear warheads which are independently aimed at different targets

SLBM Submarine-launched Ballistic Missile

Kilotonne A nuclear bomb with a destructive power equal to 1000 tonnes of TNT

Megatonne A nuclear bomb with a destructive power equal to 1 million tonnes of TNT

Deterrence The theory that possession of nuclear weapons prevents (or deters) an enemy from attacking

Overkill The ability through possession of a vast amount of nuclear weapons to destroy an enemy many times over

Tactical nuclear war A limited war which would use small-scale (tactical) nuclear missiles with a range of about 160 km. This would be a war limited to one specific area such as Europe or the Middle East

Strategic nuclear war A major nuclear war which would use large-scale intercontinental (strategic) nuclear weapons. This would be a global war.

Nuclear weapons

In the event of a nuclear war, nuclear submarines would play an important part because they can stay under the surface of the sea for about three months. They would be able to surface after the original firing of land- or air-based missiles and fire a 200-kilotonne bomb into enemy territory. The present British and American Polaris nuclear submarine fleet, part of which is based in the Firth of Clyde, near Dunoon, will be replaced in the 1990s by the more technologically advanced Trident submarines which have a range of 11 000 kilometres for their twenty-four ballistic missiles.

Cruise missiles can be fired from land, sea, or air. They can be programmed to follow a particular route, sometimes only 20 metres above ground, for a distance of 3000 kilometres. The Cruise computers can 'read' the ground, make the missiles take detours and fly low to avoid enemy radar detection. Many NATO pilots in jet aircraft learn to do this 'low-flying' as part of their training, usually over areas of Scotland and Wales. There have been increasing numbers of complaints about this recently, particularly from farmers in these areas.

On land, countries hold nuclear weapons to back up **conventional forces**. There is a range of missiles such as the Soviet SS missiles which can be mounted on trucks or rail to give greater mobility.

SS Missile

EFA EuroFighter
(artist's impression)

As missile technology improves, so aircraft technology must develop or become outdated. Even advanced aircraft such as the US Blackbird SRY spy planes, capable of speeds of 3200 km/h, were withdrawn in 1990. As one US defence expert put it, "Who needs an expensive million-dollar aircraft, when a satellite can do a better job?"

Despite this, several European countries are going ahead with a new billion-pound aircraft project.

During the 1991 Gulf War, computerised aircraft technology was decisive. US satellites and spy planes provided information about enemy positions, while controllers in AWAC radar planes 'jammed' Iraqi radar, and outlined targets for laser-guided and heat-seeking missiles.

Soldier of the future

As the technology of war advances, so does the equipment and the training needed for soldiers.

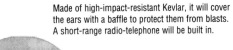

THE SOLDIER OF THE FUTURE

He's armed with high-tech electronics and state-of-the-art materials. And he-or she-will cost less than a fleet of B-2 bombers.

HELMET
Made of high-impact-resistant Kevlar, it will cover the ears with a baffle to protect them from blasts. A short-range radio-telephone will be built in.

VISOR
Polarised to protect the eyes from laser beams, it will be equipped with sensors to detect toxic chemicals and gases.

NIGHT GOGGLES
Equipped with infrared lenses for seeing in the dark. More primitive models were widely used in Panama.

ID TAG
Dog tags giving name, rank and serial numbers will be replaced by a microchip embedded in a molar. (Teeth are the most survivable part of the body.) Scanners will 'read' bar-code data off the tooth, such as blood type, allergies, medical history.

WEAPON
It will be about the length of a sawn-off shotgun, with ammunition in the stock. Projectiles will be darts fired in clusters of three, for wider dispersion.

DARTS
Without heavy casings, they will be equipped with fins that open in flight for stability. They will penetrate their targets with far greater force than conventional bullets.

NAVIGATION
A cartridge the size of a cigarette pack will give this soldier his location on a grid to within ten metres: data will be beamed from three ever present Navstar satellites. Like the goggles, it will increase the soldier's ability to operate at night.

MATERIAL
Researchers are working on clothes that will change colour, like a chameleon, for instant camouflage. The loosely cut shirt and trousers will be worn over a lightweight shield to protect against microwaves, transmitted from enemy vehicles to burn internal organs.

BOOTS
Like fashionable sneakers, they may have inflatable air cushions in the soles.

THE TROOPS
Tomorrow's soldiers will be better educated (more than 90% will be high school graduates) and better paid (so the military can compete with comparable civilian jobs). The percentage of women in the Army will remain at about 10%. With more Hispanics in the armed forces, there will be a greater demand for bilingual instructors.

(source: *TIME* Magazine, 12 February 1990.)

Space war

As the technology of space travel improves, some of these developments have had military applications. Indeed, although the use of space weapons is banned by treaty, much spending on space programmes is in reality devoted to military research. Both the USA and the USSR are developing laser (light beam) weapons, while the USA continues to develop its Space Defence Initiative (SDI), known as 'Star Wars.'

Even more advanced in technology is the plan for the 'Space Pebbles' defence system for the USA. This involves thousands of small missiles or 'pebbles' orbiting the planet. If enemy missiles travelling at twenty times the speed of a bullet were detected making an attack, then a system of sensors and computers would direct these 'pebbles' into the incoming missiles. The estimated cost of such a system is about £10 billion.

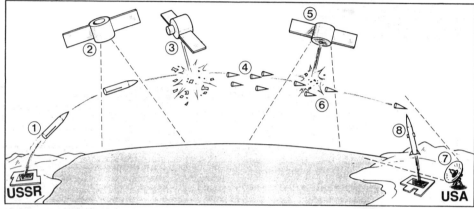

STAR WARS

Key to diagram: ① - Missile launched from Siberia. ② - Detected by US satellite. ③ - Attacked by laser from second satellite. ④ - Some warheads survive. ⑤ - Satellite detects these. ⑥ - US laser attacks them. ⑦ - Radar detects surviving warheads. ⑧ - US missiles attack them.

(source: *New Statesman*, 1 November 1985.)

QUESTIONS

1. What are 'delivery systems,' and why are they important in nuclear war?

2. What are the military advantages of weapons such as:

   a) nuclear submarines? b) Cruise missiles?

3. What is meant by '**conventional**' weapons?

4. In what ways will technology change the soldier's equipment?

5. Describe in your own words how 'Star Wars' would operate.

ACTIVITIES

1. For individual/group research, find information and photos of other weapons of war.

2. Imagine you live in an area of low-flying jets. Write a letter to the Ministry of Defence complaining about the disturbance.

3. Write a letter of reply from the Ministry of Defence justifying these flights.

4. In groups, prepare arguments for and against 'Star Wars,' for class discussion.

5. Find out about, and describe, some of the latest military technology used in the UN war with Iraq in 1991.

Nuclear proliferation

During the late 1960s the arms race reached a stage where countries began to see the need to stop the rapid expansion, or **proliferation**, of nuclear weapons. The Nuclear Non-Proliferation Treaty, signed in 1968, seemed to offer some hope of limiting the spread of nuclear weapons, since almost 100 countries agreed to refuse to exchange nuclear knowledge or equipment. However, the desire of many countries, such as Iraq and

Israel, to join the 'Nuclear Club', and the relative ease with which conventional nuclear reactors, built to provide sources of energy, can provide plutonium for nuclear weapons, has all but broken up the Non-Proliferation Treaty in the 1990s.

Problems of proliferation

More than fifty countries are now capable of producing plutonium for nuclear weapons, and the Stockholm

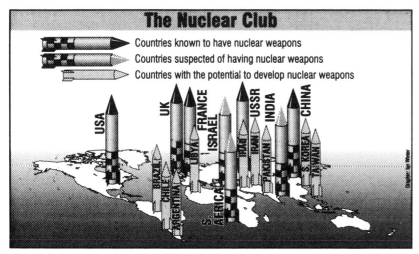

The Nuclear Club

■ Countries known to have nuclear weapons
■ Countries suspected of having nuclear weapons
■ Countries with the potential to develop nuclear weapons

Suspicions have long been held that countries other than the five original nuclear powers - the United States, USSR, Britain, France and China - are developing nuclear weapons ...

Iraq, Pakistan, South Korea and Taiwan have both the ability and the motive to develop nuclear arms.

It is possible that a few South American countries (Brazil, Chile and Argentina) also have nuclear potential.

South Africa is certainly capable of producing nuclear bombs but they have few potential enemy targets.

(source: *The Indy*, 5 April 1990.)

International Peace Research Institute estimates that more than twenty Third World countries are at present trying to buy or build ballistic missiles. In the Middle East, where £20 million is spent annually on military research and armaments, it is possible that another Arab-Israeli conflict could quickly become nuclear since several of those involved now have a nuclear capability. During the Gulf War between Iran and Iraq (1980–88) it is estimated that over 500 missiles were fired, though at that time, they carried non-nuclear warheads. Despite problems of debt, housing, health and education many countries want nuclear weapons for 'defence'. The increase in nuclear weapons means more danger of a nuclear conflict and the resulting devastation.

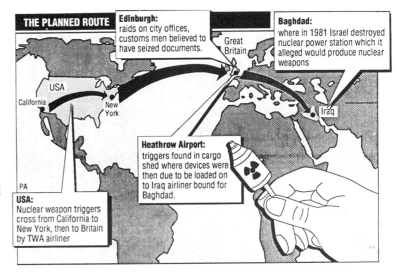

THE PLANNED ROUTE

Edinburgh: raids on city offices, customs men believed to have seized documents.

Baghdad: where in 1981 Israel destroyed nuclear power station which it alleged would produce nuclear weapons

Heathrow Airport: triggers found in cargo shed where devices were then due to be loaded on to Iraq airliner bound for Baghdad.

USA: Nuclear weapon triggers cross from California to New York, then to Britain by TWA airliner

Arms bazaar

How do countries obtain weapons information and technology? World sales of weapons are increasing. Countries wishing to buy weapons or nuclear energy information can buy them from the world's major arms suppliers such as the USA, the USSR, Britain and France. By 1990, for example, Iraq's army had 60 Soviet-built MiG-29 fighter planes, French Exocet missiles and guidance systems, and pilots trained in the USSR and Britain. There is also an 'underground,' secret trade in weapons which have been banned from military import or export by international agreement or by a ban imposed by one country. The USA, for example, bans technology export to the USSR if it could have military use. In 1990, for example, there was an elaborate international plan by weapons dealers to supply Iraq illegally with nuclear triggers, before Iraq's invasion of Kuwait. (See diagram above.)

Q UESTIONS

1. What was the aim of the Nuclear Non-Proliferation Treaty?
2. Why do more countries want nuclear weapons?
3. What are the dangers of 'nuclear proliferation'?

A CTIVITIES

1. Form two groups, one representing countries with nuclear weapons, and one representing Third World countries who want nuclear weapons.

2. Prepare, and discuss 'The dangers of nuclear proliferation.'

Alternative wars

While much attention is focused on the dangers of nuclear war, the developing trends in other types of warfare involving chemical and biological weapons are posing other problems.

Chemical warfare

Despite the fact that the use of chemical weapons has been outlawed by the Geneva Convention of 1925, now signed by 131 countries, the research and stockpiling of these weapons is not banned. Sometimes called 'the poor man's atom bomb' because they are relatively cheap to produce, and potentially devastating in their effect, several countries are reported to have chemical weapons.

Arms of the Rich. Arms of the Poor.

Guerreros/El Tiempo/Bogotá

The Tools of Chemical War

Poison gas comes in many forms, which have different effects on human beings. Some gases used in chemical warfare are nonlethal, but all of them are ugly weapons.

Tear gas: some versions are mild enough for riot use, but the battlefield form can leave its victims helpless …

Mustard gas: a new version of the World War I weapon, it blisters skin, burns lungs and kills relatively slowly …

Blood gas: fast-acting, ideal for surprise attacks. Kills by blocking the absorption of oxygen by blood in the lungs.

Nerve gas: very deadly; interferes with the nervous system. Perhaps the most widely stockpiled chemical agent.

Source: "How to make war," by James F. Dunnigan

Nations reported to have chemical weapons
U.S.
U.S.S.R.
France
Libya
Iraq
Iran
Syria
Afghanistan
N. Korea
Viet Nam
Suspected of having chemical weapons
Burma
China
Egypt
Ethiopia
Israel
Somalia
Taiwan

In 1989, the USA and the USSR were thought to have about 40 000 tonnes of chemical weapons each. There are claims that both Iran and Iraq used such weapons in the Gulf War, while Iraq is accused of using chemical warfare against the Kurds, a minority group in Northern Iraq. Iraq also threatened to use these weapons in the 1990 Gulf crisis.

Biological weapons

Biological Weapons: The Future of War?

If they ever make it out of the laboratory, biological weapons could be the next weapon of choice for some armies, or even for terrorists. Souped up by genetic engineering, bacteria, viruses and toxins could kill or disable in many ways.

Dengue fever: a debilitating tropical virus that could be spread by aerosol.
Plague: the ancient killer could be replicated in bubonic or pneumonic forms.
Anthrax: usually fatal bacterial disease that occurs naturally in animals...
Q-fever: similar to typhus and spread by ticks; long-lasting, but rarely kills.
(FROM VARIOUS PUBLISHED SOURCES)

Disarmament

The dangers of war in modern times, not only to military personnel but to large numbers of civilians, have caused many people to consider alternatives to war as a means of settling disputes.

For some people, the prospect of a nuclear war is so horrifying that they feel strong protest is required.

The dangers and costs of increasing military expenses are forcing some Governments, especially those of the Superpowers, to take a new look at their budgets for military spending.

These moves are encouraged by the United Nations whose aim is to improve prospects of world peace. In 1988 Mikhail Gorbachev, the Soviet leader, told the United Nations that he would cut 500 000 troops and 10 000 tanks from the USSR armies immediately. Both the USA and the USSR agreed to the INF Treaty in 1988, which reduced the numbers of some medium-range missiles, such as Cruise and the SS20s. The important START (Strategic Arms Limitation Talks) meetings in 1990 dealt not only with reductions in long-range missiles and bombers, but also in sea-launched missiles, army inspection visits, and chemical weapons.

QUESTIONS

1. What types of chemical warfare could be fought?
2. Why are chemical weapons called 'the poor man's atom bomb.'?

ACTIVITIES

1. Find out more about INF and START.

2. In groups, consider and note down the problems relating to arms reductions, e.g. quantity, type, inspection.

3. Find out what treaties or agreements have been signed in the 1990s to limit or reduce the prospect of nuclear war.

KEYWORDS

The following Keywords are used in this Unit. Make sure you have understood what they mean.

radiation
missiles
nuclear forces
disarmament
nuclear deterrence

megatonne
proliferation
conventional forces
arms race
balance of power

Faslane peace camp, Scotland, 1990

SURVIVAL!

GLOBAL PROBLEMS
POPULATION, INEQUALITY, POVERTY,
ENVIRONMENT, ARMS/WAR, DRUGS,
SLAVERY, AIDS, APARTHEID,
RACISM, TERRORISM, MINORITIES

As more and more countries build up their stocks of weapons, so the dangers of regional conflicts and indeed global war increase. How wil the world survive? Will it simply be 'the survival of the fittest' in an unequal world as the powerful countries advan and the poorer countries plunge into further crises? Or can countries cooperate to overcome the problems not only of war, but of poverty, inequality, and the continuing destruction of the **environment**?

WARS – RECENT/PRESENT
LEBANON, ETHIOPIA, KAMPUCHEA, LEBANON, SRI
LANKA, PANAMA, NICARAGUA, AFGHANISTAN,
IRAN/IRAQ, EL SALVADOR, SOUTH AFRICA, ANGOLA.

As well as these areas of conflict there are uprisings and rebellions in several other countries.

INEQUALITY

...'For industrial nations, the decade has been a time of resurgence and recovery after the economic turmoil of the Seventies,' says the report, entitled *Poverty and the Environment: Reversing the Downward Spiral.* 'For the poor, particularly in Africa and Latin America, the Eighties have been an unmitigated disaster, a time of falling earnings and rising debt, of falling food supplies and rising death rates.'

During the decade more than 200 million more people have joined the 'absolute poor' – those who do not earn enough 'to meet the most basic biological needs for food, clothing and shelter'. These now number 1.2 billion, almost a quarter of humanity. Two-thirds of them are under 15.

More than 40 Third World nations are ending the decade with lower per capita incomes than in 1980...'

(*Our Common Future*, Bruntland Report 1987)
(sources on this page: *The Observer*, 19 November 1989.)

There is an increasing gap between the developed and the developing nations, known as the North/South Divide.

DESTRUCTION OF RAINFORESTS/HAZARDOUS WASTES/GREENHOUSE EFFECT

ENVIRONMENT

One earth to one world

The world's poor are paying a heavy price for our short sighted disregard for the global environment:

• 20 million people a year die from diarrhoeal diseases related to unsafe drinking water and malnutrition – most of the victims are children;
• rain forests are destroyed and their people devastated – an area the size of Britain is lost every year;
• African countries are becoming a rubbish dump for the West's toxic wastes;
• at least 10,000 people die a year in poor countries due to pesticide poisoning.

Rich countries of the North are directly linked to this mounting environment and development crisis in the South through government policies on issues like aid, trade, debt, agriculture and energy, and through Western banks and companies.

(*Our Common Future*, Bruntland Report 1987)

POVERTY

... [*Worldwatch Report 1987*] attributes the growth of poverty to 'disastrous' trends in international trade and finance. The prices of the commodities sold by Third World countries collapsed in the Eighties, while the cost of the manufactured goods they imported continued to rise. Aid stagnated, debt piled up, and the traditional flow of funds from rich to poor countries changed direction. By 1988 the poor were paying the rich $50 billion a year...

World cooperation

In an attempt to deal with these problems, there have been some movements towards world cooperation. In June 1945, after the Second World War, fifty countries signed the Charter of the United Nations. The Charter has three main aims:

1. To achieve international cooperation for the maintainance of world peace and security.
2. To achieve international cooperation for the protection of human rights throughout the world.
3. To achieve international cooperation for the promotion of economic and social progress throughout the world.

The United Nations and disarmament

One of the continuing problems the UN has to deal with is that of war and conflict. The problem is serious, as the cartoon illustrates.

Since 1945, however, more countries have developed more sophisticated weapons, and the problems of achieving **disarmament** are becoming increasingly difficult.

Over $8000 billion spent on arms since 1945

Range of rockets now up to 10 000 km

New developments: including neutron bomb, cruise missile, chemical and biological warfare

Huge nuclear stockpiles equivalent to over 18 000 million tonnes of TNT: enough for 1.5 million Hiroshimas

As many as 10 independent warheads on one missile

Over 7% of the world's wealth spent annually on arms

Increasing membership of the 'Nuclear Club'

Disarmament and the UN

The United Nations encourages countries to reduce weapons production, so that their resources can be used to solve other problems.

War and Conflict

World War II produced nuclear weapons

and Peace brought ultimate nuclear weapons

. . . so people resorted to argument, and still more argument, until argument led to . . .

Look what 5% less on arms *could* mean

"Every minute 15 children die for lack of essential food and inexpensive vaccines and every minute the world's military machine takes another $1,900,000 from the public treasury."

Since the end of the Second World War nearly 22 million people have died in wars; in the early 1950s half the war dead were civilians but by the late 1980s civilians were about three quarters of the total. In the 1980s, two governments in three spent more on "defence" than on protection against disease and accidents; one in three spent more on military power than on education and health care combined.

The report is not all doom and gloom, however. Although military spending soared while social development slowed during the 1980s, the new spirit of cooperation in the world could start to reverse this. "A mere 5% reduction in world military budgets would free an annual $50,000,000,000 for humanity's protection". With just this reduction, health care for 4,000 million people in the Third World could be provided – enough to immunise every baby and bring clean water and sanitation to all within ten years.

(source: 'World Military and Social Expenditures 1989' by Ruth Siward, in *New World*, April 1990.)

Disarmament treaties

To try to ensure that countries do not continue uninterrupted in arms development, the UN has passed several Treaties.

1963 Partial Nuclear Test Ban Treaty

USA, USSR, and UK agreed to stop testing nuclear weapons in the atmosphere and to conduct such tests only underground. In 1968, however, France exploded its own hydrogen bomb.

Disarmament. The parties to the 1963 Partial Test-ban treaty should be called together to convert that agreement into a comprehensive ban on all nuclear weapons testing, including underground explosions. This was a recommendation by the General Assembly in a resolution with 127 in favour, 22 abstentions and only two against – the US and the UK.

(source: *New World*, April 1990.)

1967 Outer Space Treaty

Signed by 60 countries, banned the sending of nuclear weapons into space or into Earth's orbit.

1968 Nuclear Non-Proliferation Treaty

Signed by more than 90 countries, agreeing to limit the spread of nuclear weapons. Also, by 1990, there were calls by the UN to update and review this treaty, because it was being broken.

QUESTIONS

1. What major problems face the world?
2. Describe some of the environmental problems that will have to be dealt with.
3. What are the main aims of the United Nations?
4. Why will disarmament be difficult to achieve?
5. What treaties has the UN achieved to deal with disarmament?

ACTIVITIES

1. Investigate one of the 'global problems', by finding out the causes, the effects, and possible solutions.

2. In groups, discuss the cartoons and try to decide what message the cartoonist is illustrating.

3. Prepare material for a group discussion on Disarmament.

4. Find out what treaties the UN has agreed to in the 1990s.

The United Nations and the Great Powers

Although the major powers, the USA, the USSR, and China are all members of the United Nations they, like several other members, do not always accept United Nations rules, or requests.

Issues

Regional Conflicts – *Case Study* – Gulf Crisis 1990–1991

In 1990, Iraq invaded Kuwait, claiming that a border dispute had not been settled. This action was condemned by many members of the UN, especially the USA and Britain, who saw their oil imports from Kuwait threatened. The UN Security Council voted to place a trade embargo on Iraq to prevent any country trading with it. This was one of the few times in UN history that the great powers and the UN Security Council had agreed on joint action, though the USSR disagreed with US's boarding of ships in the Gulf to enforce the blockade.

After a visit to Iraq, by UN Secretary General, Xavier Perez De Cuellar, failed to persuade Saddam Hussein to withdraw his troops from Kuwait, Iraq went further by removing the French, Belgian, and Canadian ambassadors from their Kuwait Embassies. These actions were unanimously condemned by the Security Council of the UN as clear breaches of international law, despite Iraq's claim that Kuwait was now part of Iraq.

In January 1991, after Iraq refused a final UN plea to leave, UN forces, mainly American and British, launched a war on Iraq.

The Veto

The UN is prevented from taking quick and possibly successful action to bring about peace and disarmament by the use of the **veto** vote in the **Security Council** of the United Nations. In this fifteen-country meeting, the five Permanent Members – the USA, the USSR, China, France, and the UK – can veto (prevent) any discussion on any topic they disapprove of by voting against it. If any one of these five opposes, then the discussion cannot go ahead.

Membership

From the original membership of fifty, the number of countries in the UN had increased to 160 by 1990.

Changing UN membership (approximate figures by region)

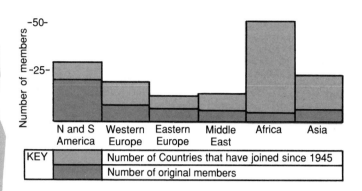

As more and more countries joined the UN so the priorities for discussion and action began to change, as the new members, many from developing countries, made their voices heard. The USA/USSR Cold War confrontation did not appear as a priority for these countries. A second effect of the increasing membership was that the one-country-one-vote method of voting in the UN General Assembly meant that the Superpowers could not rely on their views getting a majority vote. A third effect was that, with the Security Council membership increased to fifteen, the Elected Members can outvote the Permanent Members, provided the veto is not used.

Finance

One serious problem for the UN arises because many countries, including the major powers, do not always pay their assessed dues to the UN. Indeed, in 1988, the UN was in danger of bankruptcy because of this. By the end of 1989, only 72 countries had paid the full contributions, and money owed to the UN amounted to £220 million.

Up to the early 1980s the struggle between the Great Powers tended to dominate other global issues. However, as the Cold War begins to 'thaw' in the 1990s, the USA, the USSR and China are more involved in cooperating with the UN in settling regional conflicts, such as the 1990 Gulf Crisis, in supporting environmental causes, and in taking steps to disarm.

Some Diary Dates – the UN and the Great Powers

USA-UN Diary

1945 One of the founder members of the United Nations, the USA, offers land for the United Nations headquarters to be built in New York.

1950–53 US troops, as part of a UN force, fight against North Korea.

1985 USA accuses USSR delegation to UN of containing spies.

1989 USA is largest payment defaulter of payments dues to the UN, after US Congress votes to withhold money, complaining about the one-country-one-vote system.

1990

USSR-UN Diary

1945 USSR is one of founder members of UN.

1950s USSR uses veto regularly to block discussion on events in Eastern Europe.

1984 USSR vetoes the sending of UN troops on peace-keeping mission to Lebanon.

1988

Gorbachev address: the Soviet leader addressed the General Assembly on 7 December, describing the UN as "this unique instrument without which world politics would be inconceivable today". He announced unilateral reductions of 500,000 troops and conventional weapons; proposed a 100 year moratorium on debt repayment by the least developed countries and write-offs in some cases; a UN peace-keeping force for Afghanistan; and suggested the establishment of a UN centre for emergency environmental assistance in a wide-ranging global survey.
(source: *New World*, January 1989.)

PRESIDENT BUSH ADDRESSES UN: demonstrating the dramatic change of heart in the US – as well as in the Soviet Union – in their approach to the UN, President Bush told the UN General Assembly on 25 September that it was "a vital forum" giving way to a new "welcome shift – from polemics to peace-keeping." In the course of his speech President Bush offered to destroy 80% of American chemical weapons stocks pending negotiation of a ban if the Soviet Union did the same.
(source: *New World*, February 1990.)

China: call for "utmost restraint"

IN AN unexpected move the Secretary-General responded to the violence against democracy demonstrators in Beijing by issuing a public statement on 5 June expressing his sadness at what had happened. The UN Charter precludes UN action on issues that are within the domestic jurisdiction of states but the Secretary-General still called for the "utmost restraint".

In the wake of the violence the World Bank announced in early June that it was holding up a $60 million loan to China. China is one of the Bank's main clients and its development and modernization strategy have been closely coordinated with it.
(source: *New World*, October 1989.)

CHINA-UN Diary

1945 China – Non-Communist country – one of the founders of UN.

1948 China's non-Communist Government flees to Taiwan after victory of Communists in China.

1949 China's application for membership blocked by USA. Taiwan continues to sit in UN as 'China.'

1971 China admitted to UN; Taiwan expelled.

1989

QUESTIONS

1. What actions did the Great Powers and the UN agree on in the Gulf Crisis 1990?

2. In what ways has increasing membership affected the UN debates?

3. Why does the UN have financial problems?

4. What other evidence is there of UN cooperation with major powers?

KEYWORDS

The following Keywords are used in this Unit. Make sure you have understood what they mean.

environment	veto
disarmament	Security Council

ACTIVITIES

1. Find out what the UN Security Council is and what it can do to reduce conflicts. Give examples.

2. Find out from your group research other important dates you could add to the Great Powers UN diaries.

3. Prepare a debate on the subject of 'one-country-one-vote', between those who support this method of voting in the UN, and those who oppose it.

4. In groups, research the subject, 'Gulf Crisis 1990'.

5. Each group should prepare a statement for a TV news broadcast, justifying the actions of one of the following: a) the USA, b) Iraq, c) the USSR, d) Jordan, e) Saudi Arabia, f) the UN.

ALLIANCES IN ACTION

The Cold War

We have seen how countries have needs which are described as their national interests. We have also seen how certain features such as size, wealth and military force give them power to defend and promote their national interests. Finally we have seen how the two greatest powers in the world – the USA and the USSR – have come into conflict with each other in pursuit of their national interests.

In the post-1945 period this conflict or rivalry between the Superpowers dominated world affairs. This rivalry has never yet broken out into open conflict but developed as a period of tension in which the Superpowers competed with each other, with the great danger that open conflict could break out. At other times the Superpowers have made greater efforts to cooperate and to reduce the tension between them.

This tension between the Superpowers became known as the **Cold War**. The Cold War started just after the end of the Second World War, when the USA and USSR, who had been allies during the War, began to compete with each other for influence.

Cold War rivalry spread to other areas of the world, as the Superpowers competed for influence in Africa, the Middle East, South East Asia and Central America.

A CTIVITY

Here are two post-war crises which show examples of the Cold War rivalry between the Superpowers. Use your school or class library to find out about them and write a short note on each:

– Berlin Blockade and Airlift, 1948

– Cuban Missile Crisis, 1962.

THE THREAT FROM THE SOVIET UNION

We, in the USA, believe that, since the Communist Revolution in Russia in 1917, the free world has been under threat from Soviet attempts to bring about world Communism. Since the Second World war the Soviet Union has set out to become the mightiest nation on earth and has used every opportunity to expand its power and influence. It has built up a massive nuclear and conventional military machine and has used it to build a Soviet Empire in Eastern Europe. It has invaded Afghanistan and threatened the oil-producing countries of the Middle East. It has given military aid to Communist revolutionaries in South East Asia, in Africa and in Central America. Wherever there is political unrest and disorder, you will find the hand of the Soviet Union behind it.

As long as the Soviet Union behaves in this way, then the USA has no choice but to unite all free democratic countries in the world to stand against this threat to their freedom and way of life.

We have no wish for war, especially nuclear war. But we have to be strong to defend ourselves. The only way that peace can be kept is by being strong enough to deter the Soviet Union from risking war. We must at all times be prepared to modernise our forces, to keep ahead of the Soviet Union in weapon technology. The only way to nuclear disarmament is by showing the Soviets that we mean business. We have to be militarily strong to persuade the USSR to be serious about reducing their nuclear forces. And then we can have serious talks about mutually reducing our nuclear and conventional weapons. But the Soviets have to show at the same time that they are prepared to stop threatening other nations, to stop threatening our freedom in the West.

Different viewpoints

The Cold War rivalry stemmed to a large extent from the lack of trust which each side had in the other. This lack of trust arose from the view they have had of each other as potential enemies. The following two imaginary newspapers show this.

Read the two newspaper articles –
'The Threat from the USSR' and
'The Threat from the USA'. Now,
working in pairs with one person
representing the USA and the other
representing the USSR, debate how
the Superpowers can begin
disarmament talks.

Make a list of the problems you
come up with during your
discussion. Compare your pair's list
with others in the class and compile
a class list showing the main
problems facing the Superpowers
in reaching agreement on halting
the arms race.

THE THREAT FROM THE USA

We, in the Soviet Union, believe that, ever since our successful
revolution in 1917, we have been under threat from the USA and its
friends. Why did American, British and French troops invade Russia
only months after our revolution in 1917? We have been under threat
ever since. During the Second World War we were invaded by Nazi
Germany and lost 20 million of our citizens in the struggle to free
our country from invasion.

It is only natural that we want friendly countries on our borders
in Eastern Europe. After all, the USA has friendly neighbours on its
borders in Canada and in Mexico.

The Americans accuse us of encouraging revolution throughout the
world. This is false. It is the people of the oppressed nations in
Africa, in Asia and in Central America who rise up themselves in
revolution and look to us for help. The Americans claim they are the
protectors of freedom in the world, but it is they who support the
evil dictators and military governments against whom the people are
rebelling. The USA is only interested in freedom for their large
companies to make their profits by exploiting the poor in the world.

The USA accuses us of building up our military strength to achieve
world domination. This is again false. We need our military strength
to defend ourselves, not to threaten others. Look at a map of the
world and you will see that we are encircled by hostile military
bases and hostile military alliances. We have been invaded this
century – not the Americans. We do not intend to allow it to happen
again. It is the Americans and the West who have led every stage of
the arms race. They developed the first atomic bomb. They are the
only country ever to have used nuclear weapons. They fought a major
war for ten years in Vietnam. They introduced nuclear weapons into
Europe. They claim to want peace and nuclear disarmament but only if
they remain the stronger. Once they stop the arms race, then we will
sit down as equal military partners and start talking about getting
rid of weapons. Until then we will look after our security through a
balance of power between ourselves and the West.

Alliances

A major feature of Superpower rivalry has been the
construction of two major Alliances in Europe.

In 1949, alarmed by what they felt to be Soviet
expansion in Eastern Europe, the USA, Canada and the
countries of Western Europe formed themselves into a
defensive alliance called the **North Atlantic Treaty
Organisation (NATO)**. They agreed that an attack on
any one country would be seen as an attack on them all.
Thus the Soviet Union would be deterred from
attacking West Germany, for example, because such an
attack would bring about a response from all the
NATO countries. The USA described NATO as being
essential to halting (or containing) the spread of
Communism – this became known as the 'theory of
containment'.

In 1955 the USSR and the countries of Eastern
Europe formed themselves into a similar defensive
alliance called the **Warsaw Pact**. By the mid-1950s
Europe was divided into two hostile alliances with
both sides claiming to be defensive groupings.

The end of the Cold War?

By the end of the 1980s there were signs that the Cold War confrontation between the two powerful military alliances – NATO and the Warsaw Pact – was lessening.

Why the change to cooperation?

As well as the reasons given in the quotes by the two leaders of the main countries in each alliance, the basic problem of the cost of the advancing technology of weapons was making many countries look seriously at ways of moving on from the past. Indeed President Gorbachev had already hinted that NATO and Warsaw Pact were both becoming obsolete.

Steps to cooperation

In 1990, the political changes in Eastern Europe encouraged both alliances to consider cutting some of their armed forces. The CFE Treaty (Conventional Forces in Europe) will reduce a wide range of weapons in both alliances.

Mr Bush said the historic events of 1989, including the opening of the Berlin Wall and the collapse of communist dictators across eastern Europe, had closed the curtain on the post-war era.

"Events of the year just ended, the revolution of '89, have been a chain reaction – change so striking that it marks the beginning of a new era in world affairs," he said in his speech to congress...

(source: *The Scotsman*, 1 January 1990.)

...President Gorbachev gave an interview to Soviet television. These are extracts:

What influence did the emerging new situation have on the summit?

Changes are taking place for the better. East European countries are changing, as is the Soviet Union. Western countries are also changing. Substantial changes are in progress in politics, economics, the social sphere and integration processes, too.

The world is ending the Cold War and – we believe and hope – entering a long period of peaceful development.

You said "is ending the Cold War": does that mean the Cold War is not over?

I should like to say that the Cold War is over. That is correct in principle...

(source: *Soviet Weekly*, 9 December 1989.)

NATO holdings	Proposed CFE limits		Warsaw Pact holdings
24,000	20,000	20,000	40,500
30,000	28,000	28,000	53,000
18,000	16,500	16,500	42,500
6,000	5,200	5,200	11,000
2,400	1,900	1,900	5,000
257,000	195,000	195,000	596,000

Total armed forces

3,606,000	4,000,000

KEY
- NATO
- Warsaw Pact
- Excluded from negotiations
- Central area: Manpower proposals
- Main battle tanks
- Armoured combat vehicles
- Artillery
- Combat aircraft
- Attack helicopters
- US/Soviet stationed manpower

Changing forces: How NATO and the Warsaw Pact stand now, and the cuts the Conventional Forces in Europe talks hope to achieve

(source: *The Scotsman*, 7 June 1990.)

With agreements already signed to reduce medium-range nuclear weapons in Europe (INF Treaty), and in, 1991, discussions well advanced on the Strategic Arms Reduction Treaty (START) covering long range nuclear missiles, there seems to be an end to the Cold War.

The age of dinosaurs is past.

Caution!

Despite these changes, however, there is still the possibility of dangerous confrontation between the Superpowers in the 1990s. The Soviet Union still has a vast destructive nuclear capability, while the USA continues with modernisation of Trident nuclear submarines, and the Star Wars project.

Q UESTIONS

1. What reasons are given by the two Presidents for the changes in the NATO – Warsaw pact confrontation?
2. What cautions are there about the new 'non' Cold War?

A CTIVITIES

1. Find out the cost of some of the weapons of NATO and the Warsaw Pact.
2. Form groups and prepare information for a debate on the topic 'The Age of Dinosaurs is past,' relating this to NATO and the Warsaw Pact.

Effects on NATO

NATO, formed as a military alliance in 1949 to defend its members against Communist aggression from Eastern Europe, found itself, forty years later, facing a much reduced threat from Eastern Europe. NATO leaders in the '90s face several possible options.

What to do?

NATO could not continue as it had done previously. Some members, such as Belgium, were expressing doubts about keeping troops stationed in Germany. In 1991, Britain cut its troops by 40 000, while the USA

The challenge of turning swords into ploughshares

Under threat: From left, Star Wars, LHX helicopter; Midgetman; Advanced Tactical Fighter; MX missile; C17 transport plane; Steaith bomber.

itself was cutting its military budget and reducing the number of bases in Europe, such as those at Fairford and Greenham Common in England, and possibly the Holy Loch nuclear submarine base in Scotland. The USA also wanted to remove about 30 000 of its troops from Europe. These American defence cuts could affect a wide range of weapons.

Since about 10 million people in the USA work in defence or defence-related industries, the employment and economic prospects for some areas, such as California, seemed less bright than previously. However, some electronics companies were switching from producing weapons to producing computerised war training machines, while other companies in the arms business concentrated their export sales on areas such as the Middle East. Also, the easing of restrictions on the sale of high-technology exports to eastern Europe by COCOM (The Coordinating Committee on Multilateral Exports Controls) allowed more computer technology to be sold by Western European companies to Eastern Europe, provided they could not be used directly for military purposes.

The future

Some members believed that NATO should change its military role to smaller, rapid reaction forces, since there was no longer a clear frontline, and become more of a political alliance. Britain, however, continued to stress the need for the alliance.

THE NEED FOR NATO

MARGARET THATCHER today outlined her vision of a new world order with closer links between East and West. But she warned the Soviet Union bluntly that the Nato alliance would stay.

"You don't cancel your home insurance policy just because there have been fewer burglaries in your street in the last 12 months," she told Nato foreign ministers meeting in Turnberry.

"If we succeed, we ensure that Nato remains as relevant, indeed as pivotal, in the next phase as in the past," she said.

But some "absolutely fundamental" principles must remain: the need for a secure defence, the need for Western countries to continue standing together, the need for US forces to remain in Europe and the need for a continued nuclear deterrence based on the Continent...

(source: *Evening News*, Edinburgh, 7 June 1990.)

QUESTIONS

1. What changes are affecting NATO in the 1990s?
2. In what ways did the USA reduce some of its commitment to NATO?
3. Why are some exports to Eastern Europe banned?

ACTIVITIES

1. Study the diagram 'Under Threat'. Are the weapons shown still 'under threat'? Find out.
2. Write a reply to Mrs Thatcher's speech.
3. Research 'The Peace Dividend'.

Effects on the Warsaw Pact

Warsaw Pact Attack!

This extract shows the NATO view of how another World War might have started. The attack would have been launched by the military alliance of Communist East European countries – the Warsaw Pact. (The Treaty of Friendship, Cooperation, and Mutual Assistance signed in Warsaw in 1955.)

ATTACK!

World War III was supposed to begin with Soviet tanks pouring through the Iron Curtain and into West Germany. Central Europe would be the main battle-ground, torn apart by small scale "tactical" nuclear weapons as the conflict escalated.

If the situation worsened, or if the Soviets launched a massive nuclear surprise attack, then America had the capability to target 20,000 Soviet sites for nuclear destruction.

Missiles would fall like rain and that would be the end of the world as we know it...

(source: *THE INDY*, 19 April 1990.)

From confrontation to cooperation?

By 1990, however, this military scenario began to look less and less likely. Several Warsaw Pact countries had become non-Communist. The Soviet Union itself was withdrawing conventional forces of troops and tanks from Eastern Europe, while several of the Warsaw Pact allies were making deep cuts in their own military forces.

In this situation the Warsaw Pact military alliance, far from threatening to pour its troops into West Germany in a war, was in serious disarray, incapable of launching any major combined attack. Indeed, by 1991, the Warsaw Pact had ceased to exist as a military alliance. A Soviet official stated that the proposals for reduction in arms by both alliances 'were an attempt to transform European military-political alliances from confrontation to cooperation.' (*Soviet Weekly*, 3 June 1989.)

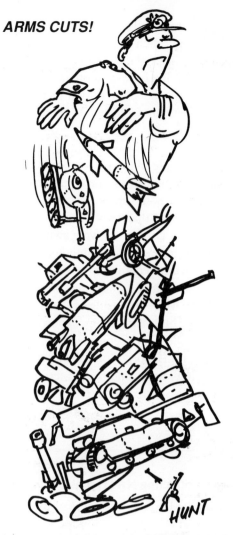

ARMS CUTS!

HUNT

QUESTIONS

1. What three factors changed the unity of the Warsaw Pact alliance?
2. Which Warsaw Pact countries were involved in the arms reductions?
3. What types of military reductions were being made?

ACTIVITIES

1. Form groups. Study the statistics 'Warsaw Pact Reductions.'
2. Discuss what you think the effects of such large reductions would be on these countries.
3. Write a report of your conclusions.

Warsaw Pact conventional arms reductions

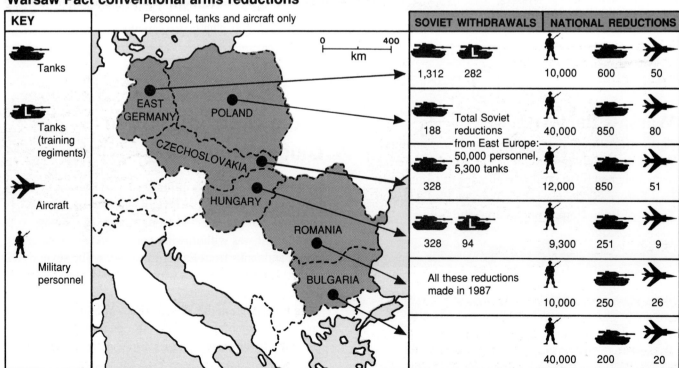

KEY	SOVIET WITHDRAWALS		NATIONAL REDUCTIONS		
Tanks / Tanks (training regiments) / Aircraft / Military personnel	Tanks	Tanks (training)	Personnel	Tanks	Aircraft
	1,312	282	10,000	600	50
	188	Total Soviet reductions from East Europe: 50,000 personnel, 5,300 tanks	40,000	850	80
	328		12,000	850	51
	328	94	9,300	251	9
	All these reductions made in 1987		10,000	250	26
			40,000	200	20

Personnel, tanks and aircraft only

0 — 400 km

EAST GERMANY, POLAND, CZECHOSLOVAKIA, HUNGARY, ROMANIA, BULGARIA

(source: *Guardian Weekly*, June 1989.)

Cooperation

CASE STUDY: GERMANY + GERMANY = UNITED GERMANY

Background

For over forty years, the two Germanies, created after the Second World War, confronted each other from opposite sides of the East-West border, and (after 1961) the Berlin Wall. This confrontation came about not only because of their different political and economic systems, but also because they were members of opposing alliances. (See map p. 111.)

The Fall of the Wall – Effects

The breaking up of the Berlin Wall in 1989 brought about a new situation in Germany. The immediate effect was that thousands of people, especially East Germans, crossed over to sample life in the West.

By 1990, firm plans were drawn up for a new united Germany and its *lander* (regions). In the same year a treaty was signed to form the basis of a United Germany.

United States of Germany
Länder and ex-*Länder* in the Germanies

Total population: 78m

WEST GERMANY | EAST GERMANY

SCHLESWIG-HOLSTEIN 2.6
BREMEN 0.7
HAMBURG 1.6
MECKLENBURG 2.3
BRANDENBURG 2.7
LOWER SAXONY 7.2
BERLIN 3.2
NORTH RHINE-WESTPHALIA 16.7
SAXONY-ANHALT 3.0
SAXONY 4.9
HESSE 5.5
THURINGIA 2.5
RHINELAND-PALATINATE 3.6
SAARLAND 1.1
BADEN-WÜRTTEMBERG 9.3
BAVARIA 10.9

1. Both East and West Germany to have a market economy, free competition, and private enterprise.
2. European Community laws to take effect in East Germany.
3. Currency for both to be the Deutsche Mark.
4. Existing treaties by either state with other countries to remain.

A United Germany: Europe's Economic Powerhouse				
	Germany	UK	France	Italy
Population (m)	78 (61)	57	56	57
Area (1,000 sq km)	357 (249)	244	544	301
GDP (bn £)	854 (726)	435	571	492
GDP per capita (£)	10,948 (11,850)	7,639	10,271	8,587
Exports (£m)	211 (191)	85	96	75
Imports (£m)	168 (148)	100	99	81
(Bracketed figures in column 1 refer to W Germany)				

(source: *Sunday Times*, 12 November 1989.)

Such a united Germany could become not just one of the strongest economies in Europe but also in the world.

Viewpoints

EAST GERMAN WORKER – "I voted for uniting the two Germanys. We in the East will be able to get more high quality consumer goods such as TV, and washing-machines, though this may create unemployment here. I shall regret having to pay higher rents, higher food prices and not having my job guaranteed."

WEST GERMAN WORKER – "Now the 'real' Germany can play its full part in Europe. West German firms can expand, as Volkswagen has done, and build factories in Eastern Europe. This should help employ many East Germans and prevent them coming to this area, where there is a danger of lower wages if too many arrive."

NATO or NEUTRAL?

The uniting of Germany makes a problem for the military alliance. When the West German Army (*Bundeswehr*), is combined with East Germany's army (*Volksarmee*) in NATO, it can be seen, especially by many people in the Soviet Union, as unbalancing Europe in military terms. The suggestion of a 'neutral' Germany met with little approval either in Germany or in NATO.

QUESTIONS

1. What are the main points of the 1990 East German-West German economic Treaty?

2. What evidence is there in the table of statistics of the economic power of a united Germany?

Europe's trade alliances

All Change!

The political changes in Eastern Europe and the uniting of the two Germanies has brought new challenges to Europe's main trading alliances, the **European Community (EC)**, and the **European Free Trade Association (EFTA)**. These changes have also altered the economic map of Europe. Most notably, Eastern Europe's trade alliance, the **Council of Mutual Economic Assistance (COMECON)**, ended in 1991 as a result of economic difficulties brought about by political change.

The twelve-member **European Community** is aiming for three main targets in the 1990s. First, the creation of an internal market with virtually no barriers from 1992 onwards.

Secondly, some members of the EC, especially France and Germany, would also like to see closer **monetary union** and closer political union, despite opposition from Britain. Indeed, in 1990, Chancellor Kohl of Germany called for closer union by 1993, leading to a 'United States of Europe.' This would create a world economic superpower.

Thirdly, the European Community is increasing its trade links with the members of EFTA. In 1991 Sweden applied to join the EC. The EC has also made loans to Poland and Hungary, both former members of COMECON.

Superpower Statistics

The importance and impact of the 12-nation EC is not yet generally understood. A perspective on the people and products (gross national products are in 1988 U.S. dollars):
- The EC: population 322 million, GNP \$4.72 trillion.
- The USA: population 240 million, GNP \$4.86 trillion.
- The USSR: population 286 million, GNP \$2.4 trillion.

(source: *USA TODAY*, 15 July 1989.)

The European Community 1992

FREE MOVEMENT OF PERSONS

European Community nationals and foreign tourists will no longer be subject to checks at the frontiers between the Member States but will be able to move freely within the Community. Increased cooperation between the government departments responsible for dealing with drug trafficking and terrorism could make this possible. Workers, employees and the self-employed; mechanics and accountants; teachers and researchers; doctors and architects – all of them will be able to work in the Member State of their choice on the same terms and same chances of success as nationals of the country in question.

FREE MOVEMENT OF CAPITAL

Pending the development of a common currency, the ecu, the Community's citizens will be able to travel throughout the Community with the currency of their choice, without restrictions.

FREE MOVEMENT OF GOODS

Goods will move freely throughout the Community, without being delayed at the one-time internal frontiers, thanks to the disappearance of fiscal and administrative constraints, along with paperwork.

FREE MOVEMENT OF SERVICES

Companies will be able to offer their services throughout the Community, while consumers will be free to choose the best offer at the best price. European television without frontiers will offer a larger number of channels, programmes and services, thanks to more satellites and the introduction of new technologies. European creativity will be encouraged.

(source: European Commission, 1990.)

QUESTIONS

1. What are the three main trading alliances in Europe?
2. In what ways is the European Community changing in the 1990s?
3. Describe four aims of the 1992 EC 'Internal Market.'

ACTIVITIES

1. Use the library to research and list the membership and aims of the three European economic alliances.
2. Design a graph to illustrate clearly the statistics of 'Superpower Europe.'

KEYWORDS

The following Keywords are used in this Unit. Make sure you have understood what they mean.

North Atlantic Treaty Organisation (NATO)
Warsaw Pact
Council of Mutual Economic Assistance
(COMECON)
European Community (EC)
European Free Trade Association (EFTA)
monetary union
Cold War

6

THE DEVELOPING WORLD – WHY HELP?

UNIT UNIT UNIT
6.1
UNIT UNIT UNIT

THE THIRD WORLD

Where or what is the Third World?

The areas shaded on the map are the poorest areas of the world – the countries of Central America, Southern America, Asia, Africa and the Middle East. The poor countries have traditionally been known as the **Third World**. (The First World is the capitalist countries of the USA and Western Europe, the Second World is the USSR and the countries of Eastern Europe.)

They are also called the **developing countries**, while the richer countries are known as the **developed countries**. They have also been called the **underdeveloped countries** or **less-developed countries** or the South (as part of the North–South division of the world). Of course the poor countries do not provide one uniform group any more than do the rich countries. There is a great variety of levels of development. There are those countries which are the poorest in the world. They have been called the **Least Developed Countries (LDCs)**. Among such countries are Afghanistan, Bangladesh, Botswana, Chad, Ethiopia, Haiti, Malawi, Nepal, Sudan, Uganda and Yemen. Above this group of countries are those which rely on one or two raw material exports for their wealth. And above them are the newly industrialised countries, such as Brazil, Taiwan and South Korea. Finally there are the oil-exporting countries of the Middle East, plus Venezuela and Nigeria.

The Peters Projection World Map

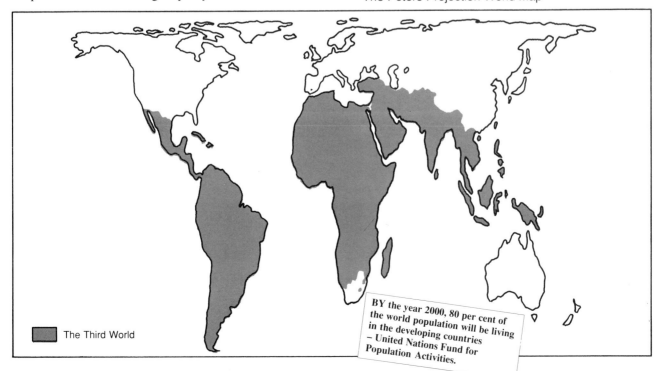

The Third World

BY the year 2000, 80 per cent of the world population will be living in the developing countries – United Nations Fund for Population Activities.

117

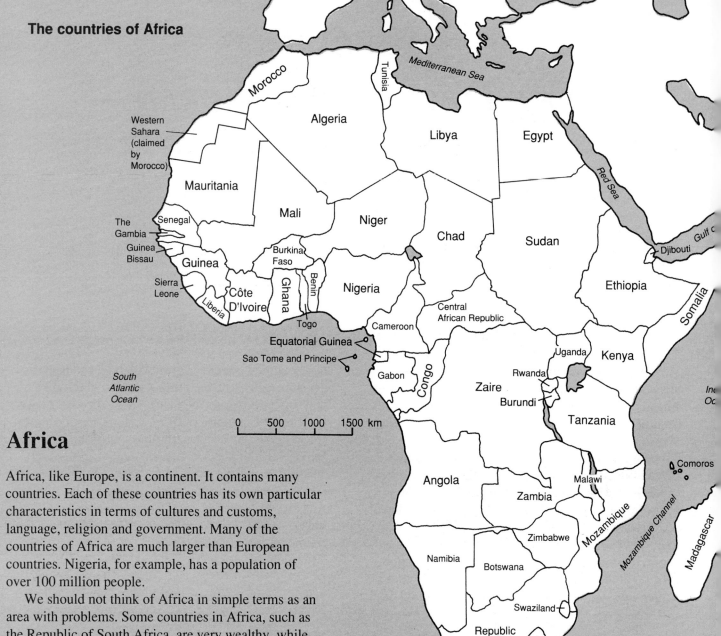

Africa

Africa, like Europe, is a continent. It contains many countries. Each of these countries has its own particular characteristics in terms of cultures and customs, language, religion and government. Many of the countries of Africa are much larger than European countries. Nigeria, for example, has a population of over 100 million people.

We should not think of Africa in simple terms as an area with problems. Some countries in Africa, such as the Republic of South Africa, are very wealthy, while others, such as Ethiopia and Somalia, are very poor. Countries such as Egypt see themselves as part of the Middle East and do not identify with their African neighbours south of the Sahara desert. While many African countries do suffer from problems, the problems of a country such as Nigeria in West Africa are different from those of an Eastern African country such as Tanzania, a Southern African country such as Namibia or a country in the Horn of Africa such as Somalia.

It is also wrong to think of Africa only in terms of problems. There are areas of Africa which do not suffer from the terrible famines and diseases which are highlighted in the world's press. Some of these countries are at a more advanced stage of development than others. It would also be a mistake to think of the causes of problems in Africa as being entirely the fault of those countries which previously 'owned' African countries as colonies. Former **colonial powers**, such as Britain, France, Germany and Belgium, must bear some of the blame, along with other rich countries in the West. But natural disasters and problems of climate also contribute to many of the problems we will look at.

In this chapter we will look at aspects of several different countries. At all times you should remember that what happens in one country does not necessarily apply in others. You should find out more about the situations in different countries and make comparisons where necessary.

Rich World – Poor World

The developed and developing countries

Most of the countries in Africa are 'developing' countries. What does this mean? Development is a process of change in the condition of people's lives. Developing countries are those in which an attempt is being made to improve the quality of people's lives so that they do not merely exist and scratch out a living. The aim is for them to use their own talents and skills to make the most of their country's resources and to raise their standard of living.

There are many roads to development and different countries have chosen different routes. Each country also has different ideas about what it aims to achieve. Much depends on where the country is starting from, what potential it has in resources and people, and how it relates to other countries. The chart below shows some of the main features of developing and developed countries.

Developing countries	Developed countries
Population mostly young	More even spread of population (but increasing % of elderly)
Low life-expectancy	
High birth-rate	High life-expectancy
Large % of people in farming	Low birth-rate
	Low % of people in farming
Cash incomes low	
Low output of manufactured goods	Cash incomes high
	High output of manufactured goods
Large rural populations (but cities growing fast)	Large urban populations
Poor standards of health	High standards of health

Caution: there are wealthy people in developing countries, just as there are poor people in developed countries.

QUESTIONS

1. Study the map of the world on page 117. Identify the areas of the world which are in the Third World.
2. What alternative names are used for the Third World?
3. What is an LDC?
4. How many of the LDCs mentioned are in Africa?

QUESTIONS

1. Why is it unwise to think of Africa in simple terms?
2. What is a 'colonial power'?
3. Briefly describe four causes of problems in African countries.

ACTIVITY

Imagine you live in a developing country. Write a letter to a friend in a developed country explaining how your country is different from theirs. You should include advantages as well as disadvantages of living in your country.

KEYWORDS

The following Keywords are used in this Unit. Make sure you have understood what they mean.

Third World	**developing country**
less developed country	**developed country**
underdeveloped country	**colonial power**
least developed countries (LDCs)	

AFRICA: NEEDS AND PROBLEMS

Why is there so much poverty in African countries? In this Unit we look at some of the problems facing these countries. These problems, some internal and some caused by outside influences, combine to keep many African countries poor.

ACTIVITY

Study the information on food, debt, trade and war. Prepare an individual report to be presented to a conference on 'The problems of Africa'. (Your report should be about 120 words long.)

Africa: The roots of poverty

FOOD Food production in Africa is not keeping pace with the growth in its population. One reason is the inappropriate agricultural and aid policies which promote mechanised farming and concentrate on men rather than the women who grow most of the food. Another is that the best, fertile land is devoted to growing cash crops for export such as cotton and coffee. African governments should place a greater priority on food self-sufficiency. But it is hard for them to forgo the foreign exchange earned by cash crops when they are in such dire need of money as well as food.

Per capita food production
(Index 1975 = 100)

DEBT Africa is plagued by debt to Western banks and international institutions. By 1985 Africa had amassed a collective public debt of 63,000 million dollars, or $150 dollars for every African citizen. This required $1,800 million dollars a year to be spent on interest payments.

In addition to this debt to private Western banks, Africa is in debt to the International Monetary Fund (IMF). Countries in financial trouble are only granted a loan by the IMF if they 'stabilise' or 'adjust' their economies. This involves cuts in public expenditure, in food subsidies, in government wages – in anything that interferes with the operation of the 'free market'. Unfortunately developing countries' financial troubles are usually *external* (for example, a drop in the world price of the sisal or sugar on which the economy depends). So a dose of *internal* medicine is of questionable value. What is more, IMF policies always rebound on the poor first, since they need public expenditure and subsidies the most.

TRADE Many African economies are almost totally dependent on one commodity: copper accounts for 90 per cent of Zambia's export earnings and coffee for 69 per cent of Ethiopia's. This leaves them at the mercy of world markets, of fixed prices in London or New York. For example, the world price of copper fell by 60 per cent in real terms between 1974 and 1984. Even countries with more than one commodity to sell have been badly hit by the slump in world prices: commodity prices in 1987 were at their lowest point for 30 years.

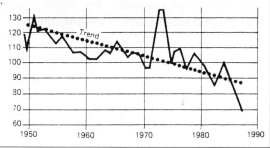

Trend

WAR Military spending consumes Africa's precious resources: sub-Saharan Africa spends four times more on the military than it does on health. This is both a cause and a result of military dictatorship: 28 of the 42 countries in sub-Saharan Africa were ruled by the military in 1986. The worst African famines have been caused as much by war as by drought – from Biafra in 1966 through Ethiopia in 1984 to Mozambique in 1987. The single most destructive influence is the military destabilisation sponsored by apartheid South Africa, which supports rebel groups in the Frontline States which flank it. The most damaging effects have been seen in Angola and Mozambique, whose governments have been under siege since coming to power in 1975.

(source: *New Internationalist*, Third World Calendar 1989 (July).)

HOW TO FEED THE WORLD

Food aid is necessary in a crisis but it is no long-term solution. Here are five ways to address the causes of world hunger.

Stop using money against the poor

Debt has been crippling the Third World over the last five years. Countries can be forced to sacrifice as much as half their export earnings as repayments on debts to Western banks. And before the West offers new loans it insists on drastic cuts in welfare spending which hit the deprived hardest. Debt repayments should never amount to more than 10 per cent of a country's export earnings.

■ In 1983 developing countries paid the Western banks 21 billion dollars in debt servicing – seven billion dollars more than they were able to borrow that year.

Aim for social justice

Hunger only affects the poor – there are no hungry countries, just bigger or smaller numbers of hungry people within countries. A government's commitment to social justice is not the icing on the cake – it is the cake itself. The only way to end hunger is to reduce poverty and inequality, and make feeding people a priority.

Give back the land

Much of the world's cultivable land is owned by people with large farms – particularly in the Americas. Left to itself this will become worse, not better, since it is the large farmers who can borrow and afford mechanisation and fertiliser. Land reform is not only essential for reasons of justice – it also increases food production, since smallholders farm much more efficiently than big landowners. But sharing out the land will not work if inequality persists elsewhere in society.

Control the corporations

The world is now a supermarket for the rich world's consumers – and the managers of that supermarket are the multinational agribusiness corporations. These companies control production prices, often holding small farmers under contract for their export crops. This way they can buy harvests at controlled prices while leaving the risks of bad weather and plant disease on the shoulders of the individual farmer.

■ Multinational corporations are estimated by the United Nations to control 85% of world cocoa, 85–90% of tobacco, 85% of tea, 85–90% of coffee, 60% of sugar, and 90% of forest products.

Put food first

Developing countries are still locked into a farming system created for the benefit of the rich world. Their best land and resources are used to grow cash crops for export rather than food. The trend away from crops for local consumption must be halted, and farmers paid more for their harvests.

■ Almost everyone in the Sahel region of Africa eats non-irrigated drought-resistant crops such as millet and sorghum. Yet of the billions of dollars in aid given to the region after the drought in the early 1970s only 16% was spent on improving the cultivation of these food crops.

(source: *New Internationalist*, Third World Calendar, 1987 (February).)

Refugees too weak to walk are carried into Korem Relief Camp, Wollo Region, Ethiopia

Some of these words are true of Africa. Which do you think?

Poor	Rich
Plenty	Hunger
Disease	Good Health
War	Peace
Pollution	Clean Air
Industry	Farming
Democracy	Dictatorship
Open Spaces	Traffic Jams
Censorship	Freedom
Happiness	Misery
Sophisticated	Simple

(source: Commonwealth Institute Scotland.)

A quiet hunger

THE widow leant back against the mud wall of her compound and gestured at the bowl of baobab leaves in front of her. 'Since our millet ran out,' she said, 'we've been living on those.' Suddenly the tranquillity of the scene took on a sinister aspect, as if it were haunted by the ghosts of her hunger.

The widow lives in a village that has never yet experienced mass famine. It lies in the south-east of Burkina Faso – a good two hundred kilometres away from the famine regions of the Sahel in West Africa. It will probably never hit the headlines. Yet few of these villagers are free of the fear of hunger.

Hunger is not a one-act drama. It wears people down over the years and we witness only the final scene. To a Pakistani it might mean selling a little more land to pay off debts to the village moneylender. To a Brazilian it might mean coaxing life from sandy soil that becomes more infertile with every planting. To a Kenyan it might mean the shortfall, the gap between the last harvest and the next becoming wider every year.

And the stars of this drama are not only the victims shaking their fists at the sky. There is the local merchant who buys up grain at harvest time and then sells it back at an inflated price to the same farmers when their food runs short. There is the government which puts its energy into export crops for the West, which sees development as a matter of prestige, building dams and conference centres for the cities instead of mills and wells for the villages. There are the Western banks and the International Monetary Fund, which force developing countries to act as laboratories for the most extreme monetarist experiments. There are the superpowers which sell their weapons and then use conflict in the poor world as part of their global chess match. And, ultimately, there is you and me for allowing this unholy machine to go on working.

Recognising that the world food problem is not just caused by lack of rain may make it harder to understand. But it also brings hope. Because this means there is something we can do about it.

By Chris Brazier
(source: *New Internationalist*, Third World Calendar, 1987 (January).)

QUESTIONS

1. Describe, using one sentence for each, five ways of tackling the problem of world hunger.

2. Read the extract 'A quiet hunger'. Which groups of people might the widow in the story blame for her hunger?

3. Which of these groups do you think deserves most blame? Give reasons for your answer. (Discuss your views with others in the class.)

Population

Population growth is often seen as just the poor world's problem. Birth rates are already falling and they will fall faster when the poverty of developing countries is revealed.

Top of the table

Countries with largest population
(1983, in millions)

1.	China	1019	11. Mexico	75
2.	India	733	12. W.Germany	61
3.	USSR	273	13. Vietnam	59
4.	USA	234	14. Italy	57
5.	Indonesia	156	15. UK	56
6.	Brazil	130	16. France	55
7.	Japan	119	17. Phillipines	52
8.	Bangladesh	95	18. Thailand	49
9.	Nigeria	94	19. Turkey	47
10.	Pakistan	90	20. Egypt	45

Population growth rates
(1983, in per cent annually)

Highest		Lowest	
Libya	4.1	W.Germany	0.1
Kenya	3.9	Denmark	0.0
Jordan	3.8	Hungary	0.0
Congo	3.7	Switzerland	0.0
U.A Emirates	3.7	UK	0.0
Ivory Coast	3.6	Austria	0.1
Saudia Arabia	3.6	Belgium	0.1
Zimbabwe	3.6	E.Germany	0.1
Ghana	3.5	Italy	0.1
Kuwait	3.5	Sweden	0.1

Why people in the Third World have large families

High infant mortality

When one in four children dies due to diseases caused by poverty, so having more children is a sensible compensation.

Security in old age

There are few welfare schemes in developing countries – the only way to safegaurd your old age is to have children who will provide for you.

Boosting family

Children are not a financial burden to many people – they are a boon. They help in the fields when young and later might get a job and share their wages with the family.

New Internationalist Third Worl Calendar, 1987 (January).

Women's oppression

Men's power often means women have no control over their own fertility.

No contraception

Many people – especially in the countryside – have not heard of contraception or have no way to acquire it.

World population growth is slowing down and will stop in the year 2110, according to the United Nations.

The way forward

In the rich world population growth only slowed down as the quality of people's lives improved . . . before the advent of realiable contraception. The population of many Western countries is virtually static. In the Third World the pattern is likely to be the same. Making contraception available is important but it is not a complete solution. People will not use it until their poverty is relieved. The quickest way to reduce population growth could be for the world's resources to be shared more equitably.

1.   You have been asked to make a speech explaining why people in developing countries have large families. Write, in brief headings, a list of the main points you would make to your audience. You should also suggest a way forward.

2.   Organise a debate in the class on the motion: 'This house believes that people in the Third World are irresponsible in having so many children.'

COUNTING ON CHILDREN

On average 3.9 children are born to each woman in the world – but there are wide regional variations

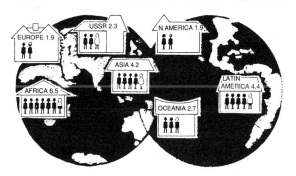

There are also wide variations within regions. In Asia the figure for China is 2.8 while in Pakistan it is 6.3

New Internationalist Third World Calendar 1985 (April).

Health

New Internationalist Third World Calendar 1985 (May).

Children's health

Which way will we choose?

ONE WAY . . .

Infant mortality per 1 000 live births

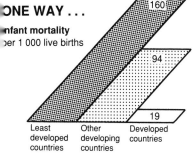

| Least developed countries | Other developing countries | Developed countries |

160, 94, 19

Total energy expenditure
A European child has much more energy to spend on walking and running than a child from a malnourished community in Africa at a time when this is important to the development of physical and mental skills.

African child 79 units*

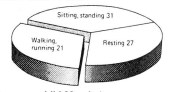
Sitting, standing 31
Walking, running 21
Resting 27

European child 98 units*

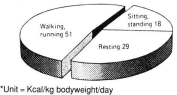
Sitting, standing 18
Walking, running 51
Resting 29

*Unit = Kcal/kg bodyweight/day

. . . .OR THE OTHER

Just four simple methods would save the lives of half the 40,000 children who die every day – if they were fully implemented.

Breastfeeding
is safer and more nutritious than powdered milk. It reduces the risk of diarrhoea and chest infection by half.

Oral rehydration
is a simple mixture of salt, sugar and water. It is the most effective weapon yet in the battle against diarrhoea which kills five million children a year.

Immunisation
against common diseases like tetanus, measles and whooping cough. These carry off 4 1/2 million children a year.

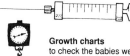

Growth charts
to check the babies weight in case of malnutrition, which is often invisible. An average child in a poor community faces six weight – losing illnesses a year.

Implementation need not be a great problem. For governments that cannot address the root causes of infant mortality and child malnutrition – that is poverty and inequality – these four simple techniques at least offer an acceptable, apolitical start.

New Internationalist Third World Calendar 1986 (July).

SCHISTOSOMIASIS a water-borne disease also known as Bilharzia

The deadly cycle

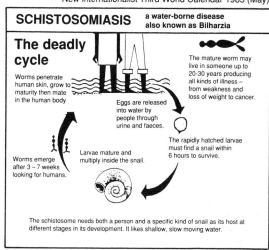

Worms penetrate human skin, grow to maturity then mate in the human body

The mature worm may live in someone up to 20-30 years producing all kinds of illness – from weakness and loss of weight to cancer.

Eggs are released into water by people through urine and faeces.

Worms emerge after 3 – 7 weeks looking for humans.

Larvae mature and multiply inside the snail.

The rapidly hatched larvae must find a snail within 6 hours to survive.

The schistosome needs both a person and a specific kind of snail as its host at different stages in its development. It likes shallow, slow moving water.

Breaking the cycle

IN HUMANS
by health education and drug treatment for those infected

IN SNAILS
by physically removing them or killing them chemically or by biological competitors.

IN THE ENVIRONMENT
by better sanitation improving water supplies and destroying likely breeding ground for snails. A combination of methods works best.

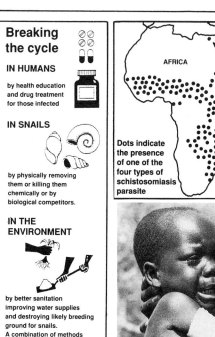

AFRICA

Dots indicate the presence of one of the four types of schistosomiasis parasite

A child victim of war

1. Why is there concern about disease in developing countries?

2. What could be done to prevent (a) high levels of infant mortality, and (b) the deadly disease, **schistosomiasis**?

3. How is the Third World affected by **toxic waste**?

4. Explain how war and corruption make the Third World's problems worse.

DUMPING POISONS

Western industry produces vast amounts of toxic waste, much of which is dumped in the Third World.

● Since 1986 over 3 million tons of toxic waste have been shipped from Western Europe and North America to other countries.

● About 125,000 tons of toxic waste are sent to the Third World from Europe each year.

Mobutu's millions
Corruption in Zaire

ZAIRE is one of the world's poorest countries. But its President, Mobutu Sese Seko, is one of the world's richest men. And it's Western governments that keep him in clover.

Last year auditors from the World Bank and International Monetary Fund (IMF) found that between $300 and $400 million earned by Zaire from exports had gone missing. Zairean officials could not, or would not, account for it. Confidential figures from the Zaire Central Bank show that more money is spent on Mobutu's presidency than on schools, roads, hospitals and other social services combined. Some observers put his personal fortune at more than five billion dollars. He said last year: 'I would estimate it to total less than $50 million. But what is that after 23 years as head of state of such a big country?'...

(source: *New Internationalist*, December 1989.)

Clean water comes to a village in Kenya

Why don't they help themselves?

'THIRD WORLD POVERTY?' said the man at the bus stop. 'People like you always go on about that. But why can't they help themselves?'

We'd exhausted the weather and rising prices and, when the bus still showed no sign of coming, we'd fallen to talking about something important. He was in his sixties, and had a dapper little moustache that seemed to change shape as he spoke.

'They try.'

'Then why do we have to give them all this aid when we're in such a bad state ourselves?'

'But we don't give them much... and besides...' I spluttered into silence. I didn't know the facts well enough. Besides, the bus was coming round the corner at last – the moment was gone.

The truth, I learnt later, is that against all the odds the people of the poor world *are* helping themselves – they finance three-quarters of their own development by their own work and earnings. But the dice are loaded against them. The worst economic recession in over 50 years has been trouble enough to us in the West, but it is crippling the economies of the Southern continents. Take inflation, for instance – it averages six per cent in the rich world, but stands at 34 per cent in developing countries.

What's more, the problems of the poor South are largely due to their relationship with us in the North. The world powers encouraged their colonies to concentrate on producing one or two commodities, and they have found it impossible to diversify since independence – 90 per cent of Zambia's exports are copper, for instance, and sugar is 90 per cent of the exports of Mauritius. This leaves them totally dependent on prices in the international commodity market, which are now at their lowest in real terms since the 1930s.

Even in normal times commodity prices fluctuate wildly from year to year, making it impossible to plan. Sugar prices rose from 17.5 cents a kilo in 1970 to 104.5 cents in 1974, then plummeted to 22 cents in 1977. Yet the rich world refuses to buy the poor countries' raw materials at set prices and set times, which would really give them a chance to plan for the future, knowing how much they would make and how much they could spend. Meanwhile, in order to progress, the Third World has to import manufactured goods which become more and more expensive. Tanzania had to export twice as many bales of sisal in 1976 as it did in 1974 to buy the same farm tractor.

Wherever you look the poor world is frustrated in its desire to help itself. The decisions that controls their destiny are taken far away on the floors of commodity markets and in the boardrooms of multinational companies.

Now that I've got this clear, I'm hoping to meet the moustached man at the bus stop again.

(source: *New Internationalist*, Third World Calendar 1985 (July).)

A CTIVITY

Study the game: 'High Risks' (p.125). Using dice and counters, this game can be played either by individuals or in groups. Your teacher will suggest how you might use the game.

KEYWORDS

The following Keywords are used in this Unit. Make sure you have understood what they mean.

population growth
infant mortality
schistosomiasis (bilharzia)

toxic waste
poverty

Understanding the Third World's problems

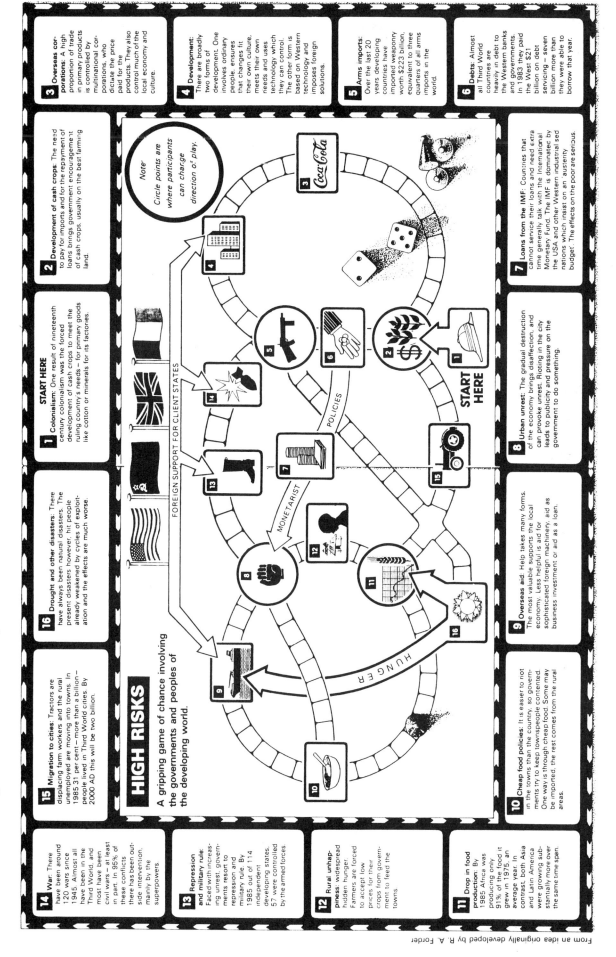

3 Overseas corporations: A high proportion of trade in primary products is controlled by multinational corporations, who dictate the price paid for the products. They also control much of the local economy and culture.

4 Development: There are broadly two forms of development. One involves ordinary people, ensures that changes fit their own culture, meets their own needs and uses technology which they can control. The other form is based on Western technology and imposes foreign solutions.

5 Arms imports: Over the last 20 years developing countries have imported weaponry worth $223 billion, equivalent to three quarters of all arms imports in the world.

6 Debts: Almost all Third World countries are heavily in debt to the Western banks and governments. In 1983 they paid the West $21 billion on debt servicing – seven billion more than they were able to borrow that year.

2 Development of cash crops: The need to pay for imports and for the repayment of loans brings government encouragement of cash crops, usually on the best farming land.

7 Loans from the IMF: Countries that cannot service their loans and need extra time generally talk with the International Monetary Fund. The IMF is dominated by the USA and other Western industrialised nations which insist on an austerity budget. The effects on the poor are serious.

START HERE

1 Colonialism: One result of nineteenth century colonialism was the forced development of cash crops to meet the ruling country's needs – for primary goods like cotton or minerals for its factories.

16 Drought and other disasters: There have always been natural disasters. The present disasters however, hit people already weakened by cycles of exploitation and the effects are much worse.

Note: Circle points are where participants can change direction of play.

START HERE

8 Urban unrest: The gradual destruction of the economy brings disaffection, and can provoke unrest. Rioting in the city leads to publicity and pressure on the government to do something.

FOREIGN SUPPORT FOR CLIENT STATES

POLICIES

MONETARIST

HUNGER

15 Migration to cities: Tractors are displacing farm workers and the rural unemployed are moving into towns. In 1985 31 per cent – more than a billion – people lived in Third World cities. By 2000 AD this will be two billion.

HIGH RISKS

A gripping game of chance involving the governments and peoples of the developing world.

9 Overseas aid: Help takes many forms. The most valuable supports the local economy. Less helpful is aid for sophisticated foreign machinery, and as business investment or aid as a loan.

10 Cheap food policies: It is easier to riot in the towns than the country, so governments try to keep townspeople contented. One way is through cheap food. Some may be imported, the rest comes from the rural areas.

14 War: There have been around 120 wars since 1945. Almost all have been in the Third World, and most have been civil wars – at least in part. In 95% of these conflicts there has been outside intervention, mainly by the superpowers.

13 Repression and military rule: Faced with increasing unrest, governments resort to repression and military rule. By 1985 57 were controlled by the armed forces out of 114 independent developing states.

12 Rural unhappiness: widespread hidden hunger. Farmers are forced to accept low prices for their crops from government to feed the towns.

11 Drop in food production: By 1985 Africa was producing only 91% of the food it grew in 1975, an average year. In contrast, both Asia and Latin America were growing substantially more over the same time span.

(source: *New Internationalist,* Third World Calendar October 1987.)

TRADE AND AID

The map below shows how the countries of the world are linked by trade. All countries are dependent to a large extent on being able to buy goods from other countries and, in return, sell goods to them. The world market becomes busier and busier each year.

The Third World is very much a part of this world market. But it suffers from many disadvantages compared with the industrialised countries of the West and the newly industrialised countries in Asia. Most of the products which the Third World has to sell are **primary products** or raw materials. The products the Third World countries need to buy are mostly manufactured goods from the developed countries. The making and selling of manufactured goods such as farm machinery, clothes and food products produces high profits for the industrialised countries. The selling of raw materials, on the other hand, produces low profits and depends on the prices offered in the world market place.

The roots of poverty

How did this situation arise?

The real problems for Africa began in the nineteenth century when the important powers of that time – Britain, France, Germany, Portugal and Belgium –

divided Africa amongst themselves. The colonial powers, as they were called, exploited the resources of the African countries in order to support their own manufacturing industries. Thus, Kenya became an important country for producing coffee beans, the Sudan concentrated on cotton and Ghana produced cocoa. The Congo later became an important source of copper. These developments depended very much on the use of the cheap labour available in the colonies. The raw materials were shipped to the colonial power where they were manufactured into high profit products.

During the twentieth century, as the African countries gained political independence from the former colonial powers, they found themselves caught in an economic trap. The multi-national companies based in Western countries took over the role of the old colonial powers and controlled the prices paid to developing countries for their products. Many developing countries had only one product to sell. When prices for their products fell, they could not pay for the goods they needed to import or for developing new industries and social services in their own countries. They then had to borrow – either from the World Bank or from wealthy countries. This led to even greater problems. In many cases the **aid** they received was **tied**. This could mean that they were restricted to trade agreements with countries which gave aid, or that they had to accept the

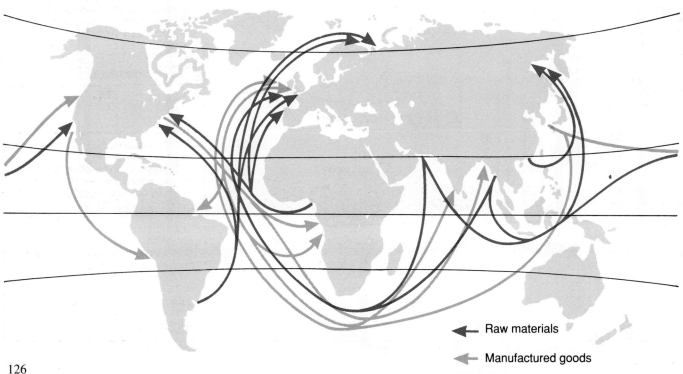

← Raw materials

← Manufactured goods

126

presence of foreign troops in their countries. Borrowing from the World Bank meant increasing debts which were difficult to repay.

In this Unit you will find out more about trade and aid and how the African countries are caught in a trap from which it is very difficult for them to escape.

INTERNATIONAL TRADE!

80%

Poor countries need money to buy goods from abroad which they require for their own development. Trade is therefore vital. Third World countries already finance 80 per cent of their development from their own work and their own trade earnings.

QUESTIONS

1. What disadvantages do African countries have in the world marketplace?
2. Explain how this situation arose. (You could design a diagram to help your explanation.)
3. Why is the developing countries' share of world trade falling?
4. How has the world recession of the 1970s and 1980s affected the developing countries?
5. In what way is debt a problem for developing countries?
6. What four things will developing countries have to do to survive the crisis they are in?

Share of developing areas in world merchandise trade, 1970 – 85

(Percentage shares)

ALL PRODUCTS	28
EXPORTS	26
	24
	22
	20
IMPORTS	18
	16
	14
	12

1970   73   76   79   82   85

But the developing countries' share of world trade is declining. Their exports are mainly raw materials – or 'commodities' – and values of these have fallen by one fifth in real terms during the past five years. It means that they have to sell 20 per cent more coffee, cotton or minerals to buy the same number of tractors, water pumps etc

Also the demand for the Third World minerals and crops is uncertain. Developed countries are spending more than $1,000 million a year on research into human-made substitutes for natural products.

But the world economic recession of the 1970s and 1980s has led to an alarming upsurge of protectionism amongst the richer countries. The European Community's protectionist agricultural policy has made it virtually impossible for Third World countries to sell food to Europe.

NO ENTRY

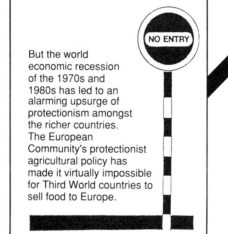

Many poor countries have therefore put their energies into industrializing with the help of foreign loans, to produce manufactured goods not so vulnerable to unstable commodity prices.

Official development aid to poor countries should, in theory, help. But most of it takes the form of government loans, tied to political or economic conditions.
Much of the aid is aimed at helping companies belonging to the rich countries – 80 per cent of West German aid to developing countries is allocated in this way.

The interest poor countries have to pay on their debts to Western banks means they are exporting the money that they so desperately need for their development. The Third World debt is one million million dollars (1986) – that is as much as the total value of the exports of the US, EEC, Canada, Australia and Japan combined.

In order to survive the crisis poor countries will have to:
● Develop strong OPEC-style cartels to bargain for better and more stable prices for their commodities. This has proved difficult so far.
● Trade amongst themselves. South-South trade is seen by many as the only solution.
● Increase self reliance by developing their own import substitution industries.
● Dramatically reduce imports of all but the most essential items – that will mean cuts in weapons systems and luxury goods.

TRADE – THE FACTS

Drowning in a sea of troubles ... Too many Third World countries are still stuck producing primary commodities, unable to move into the more profitable area of processing and manufacturing. This leaves them prey to commodity speculation thousands of miles away, unable to plan from one year to the next. They could break out of the trap and realize the potential of trade – if only rich countries did not club together to prevent them.

ntre illustration: Hector Cattolica

(source: *New Internationalist*, February 1990.)

HOW IT HURTS

Commodity prices fell throughout most of the 1980s. The fall was particularly severe for agricultural (as opposed to mineral) products. This played a big part in the 'Debt Crisis', as poor countries had to borrow to make up the difference. It also forced them to compete with each other – which sent the price of their commodity exports down still further.

Commodity price index and total Third World debt, 1970-1987.

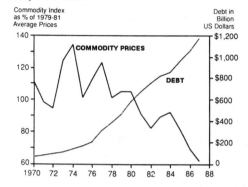

WHO IT BENEFITS

The world divides clearly between countries that have got richer during the 1980s and those that have got poorer (measured by increases or falls in GDP*). A total of 48 countries have been getting poorer during the 1980s – almost as many as those that have got richer

The countries that have got richer, like South Korea or Malaysia, increasingly export manufactured goods for world markets, not primary commodities. Those that have got poorer, like Ethiopia and Zaire, are almost all totally dependent on the export of primary commodities.

	Number of countries with **rising GDP** per capita 1980–7	% of primary commodities to total exports 1987	Country examples
High-income countries	22	28	US, EEC, Singapore
Upper-income countries	9	50	S. Korea, Brazil
Lower-income countries	14	50	Mauritius, Malaysia,
Low-income countries	9	52	China, India, Pakistan
Total	**54**	**42**	

... and falling GDP

High-income countries	3	87	Saudi Arabia, Kuwait
Upper-income countries	5	76	Trinidad, Argentina
Lower-income countries	18	55	Guatemala, Chile
Low-income countries	22	86	Zaire, Mozambique
Total	**48**	**74**	

GDP*:"the value of the total annual production and goods and services of a country, less any income from foreign investments."

A CTIVITY

Study the section: 'Trade – The Facts'. Use this information and the information on the previous page to write a document to be presented to the United Nations explaining how the developed countries treat developing countries unfairly in world trade.

Who gives aid?

AID TO DEVELOPING COUNTRIES IN £ billion at 1987 prices

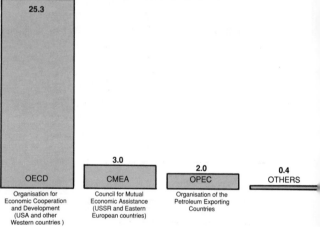

Study the information given above and on page 129.

Q UESTIONS

1. Which group of countries gives most aid to developing countries?

2. How generous do you think developed countries are?

3. Why might the UK and USA be criticised for not giving enough aid to developing countries?

4. Explain the message in the cartoon.

5. How has Bob Geldof helped developing countries?

How generous are the developed countries?

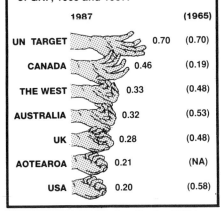
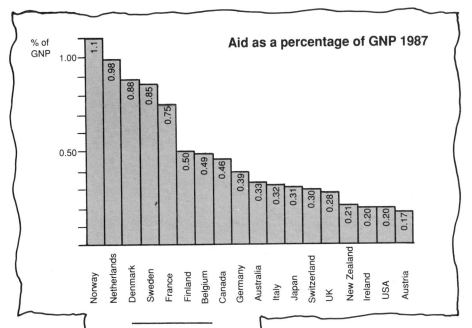

Aid as a percentage of GNP 1987

% of GNP

Country	%
Norway	1.1
Netherlands	0.98
Denmark	0.88
Sweden	0.85
France	0.75
Finland	0.50
Belgium	0.49
Canada	0.46
Germany	0.39
Australia	0.33
Italy	0.32
Japan	0.31
Switzerland	0.30
UK	0.28
New Zealand	0.21
Ireland	0.20
USA	0.20
Austria	0.17

AID – GLOSSARY

Bilateral aid – direct from the Government of one country to another.

Multilateral aid – from an international organisation, e.g. the UN, EC.

Tied aid – aid given on condition that the receiving country enters into trade and/or military agreements with the giving country.

Land of the rising Sum

JAPAN has become the world's topmost aid donor giving $9.6bn in direct aid to multilateral agencies like the World Bank. Japan has given the Third World $600m more than the U.S. according to the Organisation for Economic Co-operation and Development (OECD).

Bob Geldof

FOR A BETTER WORLD

GOOD IDEA — CFC Free Deodorant

MAKES SENSE — Lead Free Petrol

Interest Free 3rd World loans

The Superpowers and Africa

During the period of the Cold War from the 1960s until the 1980s, wars in the Third World were almost inevitably caught up in the rivalry between the Superpowers. Southern Africa and the Horn of Africa are the two areas in which the United States and the Soviet Union have had a strong influence. The Soviet Union has given military equipment to Angola and Mozambique to oppose the Republic of South Africa, while the USA has supported South Africa because of the interests of many large US companies in that country. The USA also believes that South Africa helps to prevent the spread of Communism in southern Africa, especially in Angola, and has supplied weapons to Angolan rebel forces.

In the Horn of Africa, the Soviet Union has supplied the Government of Ethiopia with arms and advisers in a war with Eritrea which began in 1961. The USA has supported cross-border raids into Ethiopia by rebels based in the Sudan. The involvement of the Superpowers in the affairs of African countries has a number of purposes. As part of the Cold War it was part of the 'shadow boxing' between the two Superpowers in various parts of the world. The USA wanted to contain the spread of Communism and protect the economic interests of many US multi-national companies, while the Soviet Union was keen to increase its influence. The Soviet Union saw its role in Africa as helping to overthrow the colonial powers, aiding nationalist liberation movements, supporting sympathetic governments and aiding anti-Western forces.

Both Superpowers also saw opportunities for arms sales and for tying African countries to trade deals. Many African countries have accepted Soviet aid, though they would not necessarily support direct Soviet influence in the countries. They are, however, suspicious of Western aims in southern Africa where countries such as the USA and Britain have strong economic links with the Republic of South Africa.

Now that the Cold War has apparently come to an end, there is an opportunity for the two Superpowers to cooperate in Africa and to bring to an end the wars which have increased the problems of refugees, famine and poverty in Africa. The Angola Peace Agreement in 1989 showed what can be achieved when the USA and the Soviet Union cooperate. An end to war in Africa would mean the loss of arms sales for the Superpowers but would give greater opportunities for development.

130

British aid

In the past quarter-century Britain's total assistance to poorer countries has been more than £16 billion. The total aid from all countries has been about £340 billion. These are very large sums of money. Yet some may argue that the continuing problems of poorer countries demonstrate that this money has been wasted. The answer is that aid must be seen in perspective.

In 1988 world aid was just over £31 billion. This is only slightly more than we spend every year on the Health Service in Britain and about half what we spend on social services. It represents £8 a year for each person in poor countries.

British aid gives high priority to health programmes, particularly primary health care and population, education and training, improved water supply and sanitation, housing, basic infrastructure such as roads and power, and developing and conserving the environment. It reaches the poorest people in their village and local communities and provides humanitarian assistance for the growing number of refugees and the victims of natural and human-made disasters.

In the last ten years Britain has increased its aid and contribution through the European Community's aid programmes. The European partnership brings greater coordination of European aid efforts and ensures that Europe has a worldwide view on how it can assist development.

The voluntary agencies

Voluntary agencies such as Oxfam and Save the Children Fund help poor countries when they are faced with desperate situations because of floods, famines or the effects of war. But mostly voluntary agencies see their main job as helping the long-term development in the developing countries. There are about 100 British agencies which work mainly in developing countries. They are charities which raise money for their work from the public and from private sources. They are independent organisations which decide their own policies and priorities independent of Government influence, although increasingly the voluntary agencies rely on Government financial help. They are also involved in many joint projects with the Overseas Development Administration (ODA) which is responsible for Government aid programmes.

Aid is good for trade

There is one objective, which is the promotion of development. This is entirely compatible with also serving our political, industrial and commercial interests.'

(British Government statement on aid, 1987)

A large amount of **bilateral aid** – from one country to another – is in the form of loans and credit to enable the developing country to buy the products of the developed country. In many cases British business depends on aid to ensure that contracts for engineering work and supplying machinery are won in Third World countries.

Q UESTIONS

1. Study the cartoons on the previous page. Write one sentence about each of them, explaining the cartoonist's message.
2. In what ways have the Superpowers been involved in Africa?
3. Why have they been involved?
4. What reasons are there for optimism about the future?
5. Describe how Britain helps poorer countries.
6. Why are the voluntary agencies important?
7. 'Aid is good for trade.' Explain this statement.

KEYWORDS

The following Keywords are used in this Unit. Make sure you have understood what they mean.

poverty
primary product/ commodity
aid (bilateral, multilateral, tied)
voluntary agency
economic recession

THE UNITED NATIONS AND AFRICA

The United Nations Organisation is involved in helping countries in Africa in many different ways. Help is given mainly through its **Specialised Agencies** such as the World Health Organisation (WHO) and the Food and Agricultural Organisation (FAO). The **World Bank** also pays an important part in giving loans.

In 1986 a Special Session of the United Nations discussed what would be done to help its African members in financial trouble. The participants called for a special partnership between African countries and other members of the international community. African nations south of the Sahara agreed to try harder to overcome their financial difficulties. The other members pledged that they would support their efforts by arranging greater access to their markets, providing more financial help and finding ways for African nations to repay their debts without taking away funds needed for economic growth. Two years on, a mid-term review in September 1988 found that Sub-Saharan Africa's social and economic development is still in a negative phase. Radical change is needed.

(source: *New World*, Jan/Feb 1989.)

'The United Nations considers that Africa's development is extremely important, not only to the people there but indeed to everyone in the world. As with any community, when some members go through hard times, all members are affected. Indeed, it is vital that all of us support the efforts of the African nations to surmount their present difficulties and resume the road to development.'

Javier Perez de Cuellar
Secretary-General of the United Nations

(source: *New World*, Jan/Feb 1989.)

...In response to Africa's economic and social crisis - the most severe to hit any world region in modern times - the United Nations held a Special Session in 1986 to devise a strategy for putting the continent on the road to recovery. This was the first such session ever held for a specific region, and the reasons for doing so were compelling: of all the developing regions, Africa's debt burden is the most debilitating. It is the only area where infant and child deaths are increasing. And it is the only continent where the gap between food production and needs is widening.

The Special Session adopted a five-year UN Programme of Action for African Economic Recovery and Development (UNPAAERD). Under the Programme, African states committed themselves to far-reaching and socially costly policy reforms, while the international community, particularly the developed world, agreed that adequate, long-term international support was needed to help these reforms succeed.

At the half-way point in the Recovery Programme, in the autumn of 1988, the UN conducted a sober assessment of its results. This review found that many African states had undertaken the vital economic reforms suggested in the Programme. However, contrary to expectations, overall resource flows to Africa actually declined between 1985 and 1987. Therefore, by the time of the mid-term review, Africa's economic circumstances were bleaker than when the Programme was first adopted.

Africa's per capita gross domestic product had continued to fall, while its debt rose to more than US$ 220 billion, or three times the continent's annual export earnings. The value of Africa's exports had fallen a further 20 per cent, largely because of declining prices on the world market. The human toll has been just as severe, with malnutrition rising in some countries and structural adjustment programmes bringing painful social consequences, such as job losses, reduced expenditures on social services, and higher costs of living.

Despite the decline in overall resource flows, some significant steps were nevertheless taken by the international community. Africa's international partners moved to increase financial support, resulting in a modest rise in official development assistance. The Toronto Summit of Western leaders agreed to take action on sub-Saharan Africa's debt, while the International Monetary Fund (IMF), World Bank, and African Development Bank (AfDB) announced that they may provide US$ 3 billion a year in additional financing to Africa.

(source: *'The UN system and Sub-Saharan Africa'*, published November 1989 by UN Non-Governmental Liaison Service.)

Working with Africa

AFRICA is facing a series of major interrelated crises. Of that there is no doubt. A continent with a rich past and a precarious future, a vast range of peoples, cultures and topographies, it is fast becoming united by common and tragically deep-rooted problems.

For almost two decades, per capita food production in Sub-Saharan Africa has declined annually leaving widespread chronic malnutrition in its wake.

The infant mortality rate of over 100 out of every 1000 children dying before their first birthday is still unacceptably high.

Soil erosion, deforestation and increasing desertification are creating the conditions in which drought and famine can exact a fearsome toll. And conflict remains the root cause of crisis and destruction in too many African countries...

Radical change is needed to reverse this grim situation. And this is exactly why UNA will continue its 'Working With Africa' Campaign throughout 1989 as the major part of its work. UNA will seek the maximum support of all its Branches, Affiliates and individual members.

(source: *New World*, Jan/Feb 1989.)

The UN at work

UNA has pressed the British Government to increase its official aid to the minimum UN recommended target of 0.7% of Gross National Product. It is currently a miserable 0.28%.

THE destruction of the environment is now one of the most critical issues on Africa's agenda. Encroaching deserts and diminishing woodlands have been brought on partly by the needs of the poorest to farm marginal land and to cut wood for fuel.

The unplanned cutting of trees – estimated by the UN Environmental Programme at 3.2 million acres annually in Africa alone – drastically reduces the amount of water that can be retained by soil, leading to erosion, overflowing rivers and flooding.

THE UN has made significant progress in the search for an end to the **WESTERN SAHARA** conflict. On 30 August 1988 Morocco and the Polisario movement agreed in principle to the Secretary-General's peace plan. This provides for a ceasefire and UN-supervised referendum through which the people of the region may determine their future.

THE war between the **ETHIOPIAN** Government and **ERITREAN** secessionists continues. Here too, development is crippled by high government military expenditure. UNA is campaigning for a UN mediated settlement. The civil war is having not just national but international repercussions. The UN could play a valuable role in drawing up peace proposals if the international community is prepared to show the will to use it.

UNA is giving practical support to African self-sufficiency and development. One initiative involves a UNA International Service women's project in Cape Verde. It assesses the potential and advises on the establishment of cooperative schemes – for example in poultry keeping and pig farming, making preserves and processing sisal – so that women can be used as fully as possible in development. Before it began in 1981 unemployed women of working age represented 38% of the population. Each pound raised for this project is matched by the EEC.

UNA has taken up with the UK Treasury, the World Bank and the International Monetary Fund the particular terms and conditions of lending and finance for Africa.

MOZAMBIQUE has been devastated by continuing war, in which the South African backed Mozambique National Resistance has waged a brutal campaign against the Government. The result has been the death of thousands and the displacement within the country and abroad of many millions.

UNA, as well as supporting the international emergency relief programme organised by the UN, has been urging the British Government to do everything possible to secure peace and stability in Mozambique.

THE WORK OF UN AGENCIES: A SUMMARY

Name of the agency	Main function
Food and Agricultural Organisation (FAO)	To raise levels of nutrition throughout the world and prevent world hunger by improving the efficiency of the production and supply of food
World Health Organisation (WHO)	To help promote the highest possible level of health throughout the world
United Nations Educational Scientific and Cultural Organisation (UNESCO)	To promote the progress of education throughout the world and to develop science and the arts
United Nations International Children's Emergency Fund (UNICEF)	To help children who are in need, especially the poorest children in the poorest areas of the world
International Labour Organisation (ILO)	To improve working conditions throughout the world

*Q*UESTIONS

1. Explain why 1986 was important in the UN's involvement in Africa.
2. What did the UN discover in 1988?
3. Describe the UN Secretary General's view about helping African countries.
4. Read the extract: 'Working with Africa'. What problems has the UN identified in Africa?

*A*CTIVITIES

1. Choose any two of the UN Specialised Agencies. Find out more about their work either from classroom or library sources, or by writing to them.

2. Study newspapers and magazines to find more snippets of information about the UN's work in Africa.

KEYWORDS

The following Keywords are used in this Unit. Make sure you have understood what they mean.

specialised agency   **World Bank**

AFRICA – THE FUTURE?

Where does Africa go from here? The aid programmes of the last twenty-five years have not realised their great expectations. The optimism that the need for aid would fall away has been shattered. Many countries in Sub-Saharan Africa are poorer now than they were in 1980. The countries of the developing world now divide quite clearly into three groups. These are:

- countries with enough resources to become newly industrialised in the years ahead, which will need less aid;
- countries with some resources in agriculture or mineral wealth which need specific aid to develop their economies;
- countries which lack resources and whose people face severe problems in maintaining even their present low level of existence – for these countries aid has become a permanent need.

Many of the countries of Sub-Saharan Africa fall into this third group. For them, the future is bleak.

Giraffe steak
Wildlife conservation

A FEW years ago conservationists would have been horrified at the idea of finding a giraffe steak served at a restaurant. But today some seriously consider that eating wildlife is the best way to save it. Wildlife ranching is increasing in Africa because it is proving a better way of maintaining animal stocks than keeping them in game parks...

Diane Brady/Gemini
(source: *New Internationalist*, July 1989.)

The future: the world in the year 2000?

TWO THIRD WORLDS

The term 'Third World' came to seem rather outmoded as developing countries divided into many different characters and degrees of prosperity. More of them got in on the industrial act – Sri Lanka was the latest brave new industrializing country, while India finally took off as a major supplier of iron and steel on the global stage. And those countries already in on the act surged ahead – notably South Korea, which moved into the top ten richest countries in the world. Meanwhile the poorest nations of all were left even further behind as an effective 'fourth world'.

AFRICA'S LAST CHANCE

It is up to Africans themselves to avert the human and ecological catastrophe that threatens to engulf their continent in the 1990s. Help will be needed from the international community on a substantial scale. But political renewal and the fostering of popular and genuinely accountable institutions – which have to go hand-in-hand with economic reform if 30 years of decline are to be reversed – must come from within each country.

This is the message of the ground-breaking report on the future of Africa just published by the World Bank. The implication of the report is that those countries where political recession, corruption and extreme inequality go unchecked can expect to see international support withdrawn.

(source: *South* Magazine, December 1989.)

Endangered species: an African elephant with her calf, Amboselli Game Reserve, Kenya

The holiday money boomerang

Tourism earns foreign exchange for developing countries. But how much of it can they keep?

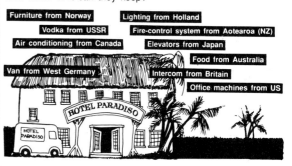

Furniture from Norway
Lighting from Holland
Vodka from USSR
Fire-control system from Aotearoa (NZ)
Air conditioning from Canada
Elevators from Japan
Food from Australia
Van from West Germany
Intercom from Britain
Office machines from US

HOTEL PARADISO

QUESTIONS

1. What does Africa have to do if it is to accept its 'last chance'?

2. Why might increased income from tourism not be a solution to some countries' problems?

3. Explain why in future we might have to describe the poorest countries as '**The Fourth World**'.

KEYWORDS

The following Keywords are used in this Unit. Make sure you have understood what they mean.

Fourth World